The Tsar's Lieutenant
The Soviet Marshal

THOS. G. BUTSON

PRAEGER

PRAEGER SPECIAL STUDIES • PRAEGER SCIENTIFIC

New York • Philadelphia • Eastbourne, UK
Toronto • Hong Kong • Tokyo • Sydney

Library of Congress Cataloging in Publication Data

Butson, Thomas G.
　　The tsar's lieutenant.

　　Bibliography: p.
　　Includes index.
　　1. Tukhachevskiĭ, M. N. (Mikhail Nikolaevich), 1893–
1937.　2. Soviet Union—History—Revolution, 1917–1921.
3. Generals—Soviet Union—Biography.　4. Soviet Union.
Armiia—Biography.　I. Title.
DK254.T8B87　1984　　　947.084'1'0924　　　84-4741
ISBN 0-03-070683-1 (alk. paper)

Quotations: Shostakovich, Dmitri. As related to and edited by Solomon Volkov, translated by Antonia W. Bouis. *Testimony.* Harper & Row, New York, 1979. Hamish Hamilton Ltd., London, 1979. Reprinted with permission.

Published in 1984 by Praeger Publishers
CBS Educational and Professional Publishing,
a Division of CBS Inc.
521 Fifth Avenue, New York, NY 10175 USA

© 1984 by Thos. G. Butson

All rights reserved

456789　052　987654321

Printed in the United States of America
on acid-free paper

ACKNOWLEDGMENTS

WRITING A BOOK like this is much like putting together a jigsaw puzzle with many of the parts missing. Some of the elements have been obscured by time and some by the deliberate efforts of Tukhachevsky's enemies. Some of the distortions have been repeated so frequently that they have been accepted as fact. This volume represents an attempt to portray as accurately as possible, despite these handicaps, the life of one of the most remarkable men of the twentieth century. If there are errors, responsibility for them rests with me.

The idea for the book arose from a graduate course at Long Island University taught by Dr. Sydney Horowitz. As the writing progressed, Dr. Horowitz read the manuscript, and many of his suggestions are incorporated in the final version.

Other invaluable help was given by colleagues at the *New York Times*. Raymond H. Anderson encouraged me to complete the book at times when it seemed impossible, and directed me to material in Moscow. John F. Burns, out of Canadian comradeship, and in return for help in his Moscow kitchen, introduced me to surviving relatives of Tukhachevsky's colleagues. The indefatigable Theodore Shabad made available his encyclopedic knowledge of the Russian language and geography, as well as items from his reading of the Russian press. The staff of the *Times* library hunted up obscure books and didn't complain too loudly when I kept them too long. Andrew Sabbatini provided the maps.

The staff of the Slavonic Division of the New York Public Library and the 43rd Street annex of the Central Library provided an overwhelming array of material, without which it would have been impossible even to commence this project. They were unfailingly courteous and helpful.

In Paris courteous librarians at the Bibliothèque Russe Tourguenev and the Université de Paris at Nanterre opened up a wealth of material that was of great assistance.

The Rare Book and Manuscript Library at Columbia University made available its priceless collection of émigré Russian manuscripts.

My own imperfect knowledge of Russian made translation of colloquial or technical material difficult. For assistance I usually turned to Anthony Mango or his son Nicholas. Their contributions to this book are enormous.

My friend Dr. Nancy Flowers often interrupted her own studies to borrow long-out-of-print volumes from libraries across the country. She took as much interest in Tukhachevsky as she did in the anthropology of the Amazon, her own field of expertise. I am deeply in her debt.

My wife, Elizabeth, filled many roles in the preparation of this book. She was sometimes translator, sometimes editor, sometimes critic—and always helpful. To her and my children, Jennifer, Miles, Tom, and Alexander—who generally didn't invade my chaotic files and desk unduly—I give grateful thanks.

CONTENTS

1. FROM TRIUMPH TO TRAGEDY   1
2. PRELUDE TO THE REVOLUTION   7
3. CIVIL WAR: THE DEFEAT OF KOLCHAK   25
4. MORE CIVIL WAR:
   THE DEFEAT OF DENIKIN   59
5. DEFEAT AT THE GATES OF WARSAW   79
6. COUNTERREVOLUTIONS IN KRONSTADT
   AND TAMBOV   111
7. A PARTNERSHIP WITH FRUNZE   147
8. INTERVAL IN LENINGRAD   165
9. AT THE PINNACLE OF POWER   185
10. BEHEADING THE MILITARY   221
11. POST MORTEM   233
    NOTES   241
    BIBLIOGRAPHY   257
    MAPS   267
    INDEX   275

1
FROM TRIUMPH TO TRAGEDY

THE FIRST TWO DECADES of the Russian Revolution were of course dominated by the personalities of Lenin, Trotsky, and Stalin. But on another level—a less obviously political level—no one played a more influential role than Mikhail Nikolaevich Tukhachevsky.

A former junior officer in one of the most celebrated regiments of the Tsarist Guards, Tukhachevsky, perhaps more than any other Red commander, was responsible for the defeat of the White armies that sought to overthrow Lenin's regime. The 26-year-old commander provided the Bolsheviks with their first notable military successes by repelling, and then routing, the forces of Admiral Kolchak in Siberia. Until Tukhachevsky's victory it had seemed that nothing could prevent Kolchak and his Czech allies from capturing Moscow. After Kolchak's downfall, when a new threat arose from General Denikin in the south, again it was Tukhachevsky who directed the successful counterattack. For a second time he had saved the regime. Then, when Marshal Pilsudski's Polish armies threatened in the east, again it was Tukhachevsky who was called upon to repel them. In the Russo-Polish War of 1920, like the Moor Abd ar-Rahman at Tours so many centuries before, in his moments of greatest triumph and greatest disappointment, Tukhachevsky came within a hair of leading his army into the heart of a very frightened Europe.

Lenin also called on Tukhachevsky when internal dissent threatened to turn into dangerous counterrevolution. Thus, when a mutiny broke out in 1921 at the naval fortress of Kronstadt and seemed likely to infect the whole Baltic region with the perilous germs of revolt, Tukhachevsky was summoned to direct the crushing of the rebellion. He did so with a severity that made his name a synonym for callousness among leftist opponents of the Bolsheviks. Similarly, when the time came to subdue a long-standing rebellion among the peasantry of Tambov Province, Lenin turned once more to Tukhachevsky, this time making full use of the young general's reputation for rigorous repression in announcing his choice.

From these beginnings as a brilliant field commander, Tukhachevsky developed into a military theoretician of international stature. He was unusual among the senior military figures of his time for the emphasis he placed on developing new weapons and new methods of waging war. Thus, when many of his fellow Red generals and those in Western Europe were still wedded to the cavalry as a potent section of the military, Tukhachevsky was joining Basil Liddell Hart, J. F. C. Fuller, and Charles de Gaulle in urging development of the tank as the premier battlefield weapon. Similarly, he is generally credited with being the first senior officer to recognize and develop the use of paratroops for offensive purposes. And it was through his support that the Soviet scientists pursued their primitive experiments with rockets that led to the development of the highly successful Katyusha weapons of World War II and eventually to the Sputnik and Cosmos space programs.

Indeed, it was under Tukhachevsky's leadership and through his energetic guidance that the modern Red Army came into being. His ideas on mobility and defense are still basic to its makeup. For example, the development of air transport, to which he devoted so much attention, enabled the Soviets to stage the massive airlifts that supplied the Syrians in the 1973 Middle East war and that supported Russia's Ethiopian allies later in the 1970s. Likewise, Tukhachevsky's willingness to use the Red Army as an instrument of political subjugation has found echoes in Hungary, Czechoslovakia, and Poland long after his death.

But military affairs were not Tukhachevsky's only preoccupation. To an exceptional degree, he was a leading figure in the artistic and cultural life of the young Soviet state. From his boyhood, he had been an enthusiastic if mediocre musician. And as one of the prominent members of the Soviet hierarchy, he lent his patronage to help the careers of several Russian artists who later gained fame in their own right. The most notable of these was Dmitri Shostakovich. They first met as young men, and their friendship developed and lasted until Tukhachevsky's death. Indeed, in his old age Shostakovich credited Tukhachevsky with helping save him from one of Stalin's purges, and lamented that the marshal had not been able to save himself from the executioner.

The "ifs" of history are fascinating and by no means unimportant. No figure in twentieth-century history is surrounded by more fascinating "ifs" than is Tukhachevsky. If he had survived to lead Soviet soldiers into World War II, with his intimate knowledge of German strategic theory and its practitioners, with whom he had been trained, would the war have developed differently? The benefit of hindsight suggests that under Tukhachevsky—a military gambler in the mold of George Patton—and the military intellectual elite that perished with him, the Soviet Union would have been better prepared and the initial debacle that followed the launching of Hitler's Operation Barbarossa would have been avoided. Indeed, the war might have been shortened by years. Tukhachevsky was one of the few prominent European figures who, in the mid-1930s, was able to foresee where Hitler's ultimate aims would take him, and in speech after speech and article after article warned not only the Soviet Union but also the nations of Western Europe of the need to prepare for war. If Tukhachevsky had survived into the postwar period, like his junior and less sophisticated subordinate Georgi K. Zhukov, what difference would his internationalist outlook and his personal acquaintance with such personalities as his one-time prison mate Charles de Gaulle have made? Given Tukhachevsky's admiration for France and his fascination with Napoleonic history — some say that was the cause of his downfall — the possibilities are certainly intriguing.

In recent years in the Soviet Union, a new emphasis has been placed on Tukhachevsky's role as a political figure. During his lifetime, by virtue of his leadership of the military establishment, he was seen as being involved in politics mainly in those areas that concerned the army. But now a different aspect is seen. Tukhachevsky was associated for many years with veteran Bolshevik politicians, including Sergei Kirov, Sergei Ordzhonikidze, and Valerian Kuibyshev. Particularly after 1934 these men, it is now believed, formed a loose opposition to Stalin's policies, if not to his continued leadership. The result, of course, was a sequence of bloody events that removed them from the scene. First Kirov was murdered — perhaps, as Nikita Khrushchev has suggested, with Stalin's connivance. Then Ordzhonikidze committed suicide after a violent quarrel with Stalin, and Kuibyshev died in mysterious circumstances. The one to survive longest was Tukhachevsky. But when he was hurriedly executed in the late spring of 1937, the last possible challenger to Stalin as supreme ruler was liquidated. If Tukhachevsky had indeed tried to overthrow Stalin at that time, would he have been able to succeed? Tukhachevsky did have an extensive and loyal following among the highest ranks of the military and in certain other segments of the Soviet apparatus, but whether that following was powerful enough to combat Stalin's political clout must remain an unanswered question.

Throughout his later life, Tukhachevsky was an odd man out in the Soviet leadership. His military renown, his cultural sophistication and his associations with musicians and other artistic figures, and his aristocratic lineage set him apart from Stalin's immediate circle, where the earthy peasant backgrounds of Klementi Voroshilov and Semyon Budenny were less prone to suspicion, and therefore more easily welcomed. By inclination, too, Tukhachevsky was a loner. Shostakovich observed: "Tukhachevsky was alone. He had no friends, only fawners and companions for amorous expeditions."[1] And his sister-in-law said: "Mikhail Nikolaevich had not the faintest notion of friendship. According to his view, he could have friendship when and where he pleased."² Tukhachevsky was a proud man, almost to the point of being overbearing. He was certain of his own abilities and views, and not inclined to suffer gladly those he regarded as either fools or less gifted. As his treatment of the Kronstadt and Tambov rebels starkly illustrated, he had a ruthless streak that on occasion verged on cruelty. But his obvious concern for his soldiers, illustrated even in the darkest hours of the Civil War, won him lasting popularity. And yet he was also a stern disciplinarian, fully capable of inflicting the harshest punishments on miscreants. Toward his mother, his brothers and sisters, and his daughter he displayed the deepest family affection. Yet his first wife committed suicide when she felt she had angered and betrayed him. And although his second wife remained loyal to him to the grave, his treatment of her was not notable for fidelity.

Tukhachevsky burst on the Soviet landscape like a young Napoleon, a swift sword at Lenin's right hand. He, more than any other man, built the Red Army into a potent striking force. By the time he was 40, he was one of the most powerful men in the Soviet Union. Perhaps even powerful enough to challenge Stalin.

Had Tukhachevsky lived, it seems certain that Hitler's invasion of Russia would have met much more robust opposition. But the hard reality of life decreed otherwise. Tukhachevsky was executed, along with most of his sympathizers in the army, almost on the eve of World War II. He died as he lived, flamboyantly and not a little mysteriously. Officially, he died accused of having been willing to betray his country to the very forces against which he had warned so often. It was not until nearly a quarter of a century later that his name was cleared posthumously, after Nikita Khrushchev's "secret speech." Since then, by starts and spurts, the Soviet authorities have gradually rehabilitated his reputation until the true measure of his life has been brought into perspective.

2
PRELUDE TO THE REVOLUTION

TUKHACHEVSKY WAS BORN on February 16, 1893, on the heavily mortgaged, 500-acre estate of an aristocratic family near the village of Vishegor in Smolensk Province. By one tradition, the Tukhachevskys shared a common ancestor with the famous Tolstoy family. He was Indris, a semi-legendary Lithuanian or Teutonic warrior of the fourteenth century. Like Indris, many of the Tukhachevsky men had been celebrated soldiers, having led battles against Sigismond of Poland, having served with Suvorov and even having gone abroad to serve other monarchs, such as the King of Wurttemberg. By another tradition, the Tukhachevskys were descended from Baudouin VIII, the crusading count of Flanders. In one version of Tukhachevsky's life, this seemingly unlikely ancestry came about when one of Baudouin's sons was wandering homeward after a disastrous crusade. For whatever reason, the young Belgian appeared in Odessa, then a Byzantine city, with a Turkish wife and not much more than his sword. Like many of his fellows in similar situations, he took service with a local nobleman who gave him, in return, the lands around the village of Tukhachev. At some time later, the family moved to the Smolensk area.[1]

But that was only part of Tukhachevsky's lineage. On his mother's side, his ancestry was much more plebeian—and Russian. As a young man, Tukhachevsky's father, Nikolai, had taken a fancy to Mavra Petrovna Milehov, the daughter of a peasant from the neighboring village. Therefore, eyebrows among the gentry were doubtless raised when Nikolai's mother, Sophia Alevtinovna, the grande dame of the family, gave her approval to a marriage between the young couple. Although much about his later life was open to question, the fact that young Nikolai Tukhachevsky was willing to sacrifice his opportunities for advancement either as a military man or as an administrator—for in the class-bound system of tsarist Russia, that was what he was doing—spoke volumes for the depth of his affection.[2]

The Nikolai Tukhachevskys had four sons and five daughters.[3] From what little can be learned about Nikolai Tukhachevsky, it seems that he was much dominated by his mother—as was the whole family—and he lived a relatively obscure, genteel life despite the family's lack of wealth. His daughter Olga later remembered her father as a cultured man, fond of music, and, perhaps more important, a convinced atheist. He brought up his children in the same belief, a relatively risky thing to do in church-ridden tsarist Russia.[4]

Mavra Petrovna was apparently of sterner character, and her readiness to face adversity, to undertake manual labor, had a great effect on her children, Mikhail not the least. The influence of these two strong-willed women, his mother and his grandmother, was to affect Mikhail Tukhachevsky throughout his career, and his continued association with his mother's family was to give him the common touch that made him a favorite with the soldiers he commanded. From his grandmother, Tukhachevsky inherited a passion for music. Sophia had been a pupil of Nikolai Rubinstein, who, like his more famous brother Anton, had been one of the most celebrated European pianists of the late nineteenth century. Sophia was a skilled pianist, and musical figures from Moscow and St. Petersburg were frequent visitors to the Tukhachevsky estate. It is said that Nikolai Rubinstein was among them.[5]

Also among the musical guests was Nikolai S. Zhilayev, later described by Shostakovich as "one of my teachers." Zhilayev was an authority on Aleksandr N. Scriabin, a composer who greatly influenced Shostakovich and other modern Russian composers. Zhilayev remained friends with Tukhachevsky throughout the years, and he too became a victim of Stalin's purges.[6]

By the time of the latest of these visits, the Tukhachevskys had been forced to sell their estate in the Smolensk area; the weight of the mortgages had finally gotten too heavy. They were living outside the city of Penza, where Sophia Alevtinovna had property of her own. It was there, in 1904, that Tukhachevsky's formal education began at the Penza Boys' Gymnasium. He was big for his age, tall and thick-chested, so much so that his classmates called him "the Monster." He was an able student but also something of a rebel. By the time he enrolled, he had learned French from the governess who had supervised the children's early lessons because their mother was practically illiterate. At the gymnasium he learned German and Latin, the latter well enough to plow through Caesar's *Gallic Wars*.[7]

Some idea of how the youngster behaved is given by remarks on his reports: "Despite his ability, he studies badly." "Three out of five for application; two for attention." "Was reprimanded three times for talking in class." "M. T. does not study the Bible."[8]

When Tukhachevsky was in his second year at Penza, the Russo-Japanese War broke out. It was a revolutionary time in all of Russia, a time of national shame, a time when the very basis of Russian institutions and the role of the Romanovs in particular were being questioned. Penza, formerly a haven for political exiles and a center of literary liberals, caught the mood; and in 1905 the local reservists refused to go to the front when they were called to the colors.[9]

Tukhachevsky staged a rebellion of his own. As in every Russian school of the time, religious teaching was emphasized at Penza. Young Mikhail endured the homilies and stories about the saints, but on at least one occasion could not resist taunting the priest about them. When the lesson for that day was over, Mikhail asked with mock humility: "Tell me, Father, at the next lesson will you tell us fairy tales again?" He was sent out of the room.

A worse scrape was to come. As part of the school record,

a careful tally was kept of the number of times each pupil went to confession and took Communion. When he was in the fifth form, it was discovered that Tukhachevsky had done neither, and his father was summoned. Such defiance could have ended in the boy's expulsion, but Nikolai, ignoring his own scruples, persuaded his son to bow to the authorities. Since it was the father's influence that had led him to his present embarrassment, it must have been a humiliating experience for young Mikhail.[10]

After such a scandal, it became clear that Penza was no place for the iconoclastic Tukhachevskys. They moved to Moscow, where young Mikhail in 1909 entered the sixth form at the Tenth Moscow Gymnasium. Nikolai Tukhachevsky wanted to give his children a sound liberal education, but Mikhail had other ideas. Much against his father's wishes, for Nikolai knew the social and class obstacles involved for a young man of partly peasant origin, Mikhail had decided on a military career. After much argument, however, the boy had his way. He was transferred from the gymnasium to Moscow's First Catherinian Cadet Corps. At first, as his father had predicted, the snobbery of the cadets made Mikhail an outsider. But soon his athletic ability and his intelligence made such an impression that he was appointed sergeant major of the corps.[11]

In the cadet corps and at the Alexandrovsky Military Academy in Moscow, which he entered in 1911, a great change came over Tukhachevsky. The devil-may-care prankster was replaced by a serious student displaying, for the first time, signs of the driving ambition that was to be maintained almost until the day of his death.

During his childhood at Penza, Mikhail had been fond of reading an old book about Suvorov, the great eighteenth-century Russian general, with whom his ancestors had served. And the boy had listened eagerly to debates about the failures of General Aleksei N. Kuropatkin and his subordinates in the Russo-Japanese War. Now Mikhail was immersed in military life. He devoted himself to studying the writings of Clausewitz and the histories of Napoleon, Blucher, Suvorov, and Helmuth K. von Moltke. On the parade ground he was an impressive figure: taller than average, his barrel chest filling his uniform, and his rather prominent gray eyes capable of a chilling dominance. A cool, ambitious, and almost domineering young man. By the time he graduated, he was at the top of his class.

But the more playful past was not entirely forgotten. On summer vacations and whenever else he could, Tukhachevsky paid diligent and—in the manner of the time and his upbringing—discreet court to pretty Marucia Ignatiev, a friend of his sister Marie, a student at the Chor-Manserevska High School.[12]

The year 1914 was epochal for Europe, and it was no less so for Mikhail Tukhachevsky. He experienced personal tragedy: his father and his sister Nadia, an artist who had graduated from the Strogonov Art College, died. And Russia was plunged into World war I.[13] Also in 1914, Tukhachevsky began his formal march toward military fame. After completing his studies at the Aleksandrovsky Academy, he was gazetted a junior lieutenant in the elite Semyenovsky Guards, one of the regiments founded by Peter the Great and honored over the centuries for the bravery of its men and its devotion to tradition starting from the time of Poltava.

Thus the time came for the young man to leave Moscow. His departure was a scene being duplicated all over wartime Europe. The nervous young soldiers and their relatives gathered at the train station for tearful good-byes. In Tukhachevsky's case, his mother and the rest of the family clustered round him. His mother was especially sad, recently widowed and now certain she was seeing the last of her son. Tukhachevsky tried to console her, even joked, but a family friend recalled later that he seemed distracted and kept looking up and down the platform as if seeking something or someone. Finally the train started to move. Tukhachevsky jumped aboard, but stayed on the step. At that moment, a young girl—perhaps it was Marucia—materialized from the crowd. Tukhachevsky leaped from the train, ran to the girl, hugged her, gallantly kissed her hand, and then raced back to the train. Everyone, including Mavra Petrovna and the girl, began to wail.[14]

From Moscow, Tukhachevsky traveled to St. Petersburg, where he joined a detachment in reserve. At that time, although a commission in the Semyenovsky Guards was a coveted thing, his future prospects did not seem great to anyone but himself. For promotion in the elite regiments depended to a great extent on wealth and social position, and the Tukhachevskys, having squandered their patrimony over the recent decades, had little of either.

The outbreak of the war against Germany and Austria was

to change that, as it was to change almost everything else in Russia. From the opening salvos of the war, the apparently divided loyalties of the imperial family caused uncertainty—even anger—among the Russians. The German-born empress was the subject of many vicious stories. A deep and barely submerged current of popular opinion would have sent her back to Germany. Robert Bruce Lockhart wrote in his diary early in the war: "Today an officer telephoned to ask when England was going to rid Russia of this German woman?"[15]

Not only Tsarina Alexandra's origins had made her unpopular. The citizenry, particularly bourgeois and aristocratic circles, were appalled by her relationship with the shifty Siberian mystic Gregory Rasputin. After the setbacks suffered by the Russian Army in Galicia in May 1915, the tsar dismissed General Vladimir Suklominov as commander. The first 10 months of the war had cost Russia 3.8 million men.[16] And after further defeats, the new commander, the tsar's cousin, Grand Duke Nicholas, was fired as well. The empress had been influential in that decision, and she also had a say in naming the grand duke's successor. Against the wishes of his advisers, Tsar Nicholas II named himself commander. In her husband's absence at the front, the vulnerable empress came further under the influence of Rasputin. Even Rasputin's assassination on December 30, 1916, by Prince Felix Yusupov and his associates did not lessen the Russian people's distaste for the unfortunate tsarina. Changing the name of the capital from the German-sounding St. Petersburg to Petrograd did little to help.

Tukhachevsky did not have time to dwell on such matters. Assigned to the Sixth Company of the Second Semyenovsky Battalion, he quickly found himself in action against the Austro-Hungarian Army near Cracow. They were heady times for the young officer, and in a letter home after two months at the front, he displayed the chauvinism and tendency to brag that impressed many but antagonized others later in his career. "I am convinced," he wrote, "that all that is needed for me to achieve what I want is bravery and self-confidence. . . . I told myself that I shall either be a general by thirty, or that I shall not be alive by then."[17]

It did not take Tukhachevsky long to display the bravery and capacity for quick military decision that were the hallmarks of his future. On September 2, 1914, Tukhachevsky's company was ordered to take part in a flanking movement against the Austrians, an exercise achieved with a success rare among Russian maneuvers. The Austrians, startled by the sudden appearance of the Russians where they were not expected, fell back in disarray across the San River, destroying the bridges as they retreated. It so happened that the bridge in the Sixth Company's sector was of wood and the retreating enemy had set fire to it. Undeterred, Tukhachevsky charged across the flaming span, safely leading his men to the other bank. The Austrians fled in panic, but not before many had been killed or taken prisoner. For their bravery, the company's commander was awarded the coveted Cross of St. George, but Tukhachevsky—apparently somewhat to his chagrin, since he believed that it was his initiative that had produced success—had to content himself with the lesser Cross of St. Vladimir with crossed swords.[18]

The first news Tukhachevsky's family got of this exploit came almost by chance. Mikhail's brother Nikolai brought home a copy of the newspaper *Russkoye Slovo*, which had a garbled version of the incident and ended with the ominous sentence "The fate of the heroes is unknown."[19]

Not until much later did they hear of other escapades. One old soldier who was with Tukhachevsky in those early days of the war recalled that in the autumn of 1914, the Semyenovsky Guards occupied positions near Cracow, on the Vistula. The Germans were dug in on higher ground across the river, making scouting of their placement difficult. Tukhachevsky took it upon himself to remedy the situation. He had noticed a low, sandy island in the middle of the river from which he could get a closer look at the enemy. Somewhere he acquired a small fisherman's boat. After nightfall, he lay prone in the dinghy and, using his hands for paddles, made his way cautiously to the island. After spending the night reconnoitering the position, he returned at dawn with much valuable information.[20]

From the beginning of the war, the Russian High Command's strategy was to go immediately on the offensive. This was because the Russian leadership had reached an agreement with the French whereby Russia had pledged to have 800,000 men mobilized within two weeks of declaring war. The War Ministry pressed the army commanders to achieve this figure, even though it meant committing men to the front who were not properly trained or equipped. Further, the ministry had promised not only to get the men into uniform but also to launch an attack to relieve the pressure on the Western Front. The Russians therefore assembled two main armies, one commanded by General P. K. Rennenkampf in the vicinity of Vilna, the other under General A. V. Samsonov farther south, near Warsaw. It was typical of the Russian Army that Rennenkampf and Samsonov despised each other and had once come to blows on a Manchurian railroad siding during the Russo-Japanese War. The idea now was that Rennenkampf would make an initial thrust in the north, drawing German reserves to that area. Soon after, Samsonov would drive northward along the Vistula to cut the German rear.

The strategy was fine; the execution, dismal. Almost unbelievably, Russian radio signals were transmitted uncoded. At first the Germans could not believe what they were hearing, deciding that this was the height of Russian duplicity, a clever trap. But not so one of the rising stars of the German command, Lieutenant Colonel Max Hoffman. He recognized Russian stupidity for what it was. The result was utter disaster for the Russians, ending in personal tragedy for Samsonov. In moving closer to the scene of the battle, his headquarters got lost in the forest. After a tumultuous scene with his junior officers, Samsonov walked out into the night of August 28, 1914, and blew his brains out.

Worse was to come. In yet another foolhardy offensive, the Russian command launched a thrust through the Carpathian Mountains, aiming at Hungary. It was a misguided venture, made in the depth of winter. From the start, despite early successes, it was doomed. An accompanying pincer movement toward southeastern Germany fizzled when the commander was captured by the Germans. For Tukhachevsky personally the campaign ended in disaster. On February 19, 1915, the Germans attacked the sector of the front held by the Semyenovsky Guards. During the day, the German heavy artillery had pounded the Russians, but at nightfall there came a lull. Tukhachevsky was trying to catch some sleep when a surprise sortie by a German detachment caught his company unawares. During fierce hand-to-hand fighting, the German artillery returned to action. A shell landed in Tukhachevsky's trench, knocking him unconscious.

When he came to, he was a prisoner. The remainder of the army, 100,000 strong, was wiped out.[21] Along with the other Russian officers captured in the ill-fated campaign, Tukhachevsky was placed on a train bound for a prison camp on Rugen Island, in the icy Baltic Sea.

Tukhachevsky's family got word of his misfortune when the news was printed in the newspaper *Russkii Invalid*. Some time later, through the International Red Cross, they began to receive postcards, which always began: "I am alive and in good health and everything is fine." The postcards contained other brief comments, such as "Today they issued us . . . honey that has the color and taste of shoe polish." Sometimes he would write that he hoped to see them soon. Then there would be an interruption in the mail; Tukhachevsky had made another attempt to escape. Sometimes there were even more direct hints about his intentions; for example, on one occasion Tukhachevsky told his mother to read the *Lay of the Host of Igor*, in part the legend of an escape by the tenth-century duke of Kiev.[22]

Life in the prison camps was rigorous, especially for the Russians. British and French prisoners got some relief from the monotonous diet through Red Cross parcels from home. But the Russian Red Cross, like so much else in tsarist Russia, was notoriously inefficient. Not many parcels got through from Moscow, so those that did reach the camps were especially valuable, not only for the food they contained but also for the news in the papers in which they were often wrapped.[23]

At that early stage of the war, it was almost a matter of noblesse oblige for a young officer on either side to try to escape. In the Strahlsund Camp, where Tukhachevsky was confined, it was certainly a constant preoccupation, even in the harshness of a Baltic winter. Tukhachevsky was just as eager as any of his colleagues to get back into action, but he was more deliberate than most of the others. He would wait for warmer weather, slip away during the daily exercise march, and, under cover of night, get to the sea, where he would steal a boat and sail to Sweden.

On a warm June Sunday, he made his break. He succeeded in evading the guards and hid himself in the grainfields. For two weeks he escaped recapture, hiding in the grain by day and going out at night to search along the coast for a boat. Unhappily for him, no boat was to be found. Finally, on a stormy summer night, a German patrol stumbled upon him. Half dead from hunger and badly bitten by mosquitoes, he was dragged back to the prison camp. Placed in solitary confinement for the attempt to escape, Tukhachevsky lost none of his defiance of German authority, for which he already had won a reputation in the camp. In an attempt to reduce the martial spirit of the officer-prisoners, the German commandant issued an order that they be relieved of their badges of rank and regiment. Tukhachevsky stubbornly refused to comply. When the Germans tried to get their way by force, he replied with a ferocious attack on the guards. The upshot was that he lost his badges and was shipped to Beskov, a camp that held a hundred or so other "incorrigibles."[24]

The commandant of Beskov minced no words. Any infraction of his orders and regulations would lead straight to the solitary cells. But Tukhachevsky had all the insouciance of a youth of 21. He had barely arrived in Beskov when he sent a note to the commandant announcing his desire to escape to rejoin the Russian Army. The commandant saw no humor in the message, and within half an hour Tukhachevsky was in "the hole." The commandant apparently thought that Tukhachevsky was not quite right in the head and, eager to be rid of a prisoner who seemed to promise trouble, quickly had the young lieutenant transferred. That was just what Tukhachevsky had wanted.

In short order he found himself at Badstauer, a camp Mecklenberg, where confinement was less rigorous. All the while Tukhachevsky's desire to escape was intensifying. It was not long before he had hatched a new plot. Accompanied by a young ensign, he set to work to carry it out. To understand the scheme, it is necessary to understand the nature of the war, especially as it was waged by the officer class, in the relatively early days of World War I. At that time, to be an officer was to be very much a gentleman, and even one's enemy would see to it that, by comparison with the humbler prisoners, the officers had at least some semblance of the appurtenances of their station. Thus officer-prisoners could not be expected to perform such menial chores as laundering clothes or cleaning latrines. That was done by lesser ranks among the prisoners of war. British orderlies looked after British officers; Russian orderlies, after Russian officers. So it was at Badstauer.

Tukhachevsky's plan bore this in mind. When the orderlies came to clean the officers' cells, he and the ensign would simply switch uniforms with them and march out of the camp at night. After all, to the Germans, all the Russians looked alike. Along the way it would be relatively easy to slip out of the loosely guarded column, and so to freedom.

The plan worked perfectly. One July night, Tukhachevsky and his comrade made the switch and joined the other orderlies on the wagon that was to take them back to their barracks. As the wagon crossed a ditch, they slipped off and hid until it was dark enough to move safely. Then they began a circuitous, 26-day, 500-mile journey they hoped would take them to the Dutch frontier. By day, they hid wherever they could—in forests, in wheat fields, in ditches. By night they continued their march. Aided by a rough map and a compass probably smuggled in as part of a French food parcel, and allowing for detours, they were able to make about 15 miles a night. The escape had been well planned. They had not only the map and the compass but also, in their pockets, some rations and matches. Their food quickly ran out, but they managed to steal some potatoes from a field and found some duck eggs in a riverside nest. The potatoes and the eggs were cooked in fires lit in secure places, usually in ravines during daylight, when they were less likely to be noticed. Finally they reached the frontier. But at the apparent moment of success, Tukhachevsky's audacity proved to be his undoing.

Freedom lay across just one more river, but instead of swimming, the youthful pair decided to get over by walking boldly across the bridge. Just as they reached it, a German sentry spotted them. Tukhachevsky and his companion fled; Tukhachevsky to the left, his companion to the right. Unfortunately, the sentry went left. After a long chase, he caught the Russian, whom he took for a spy. Tukhachevsky would admit only that he was a prisoner of war and Russian. The Germans, thinking that he had escaped from a nearby prison camp, took him there. The camp authorities did not recognize him and refused to take custody. Finally, he was lodged in the town jail, which was loosely guarded. During the night Tukhachevsky was able to escape, and this time he managed to get within 30 yards of the frontier before he was recaptured. Discouraged by the obvious risks of remaining in so heavily patrolled an area, the disconsolate lieutenant revealed his name and where he had come from. The local Germans quickly sent him back to Badstauer, but the commandant there had had enough of him. He sent Tukhachevsky to a camp for recidivist escapers at Zorndorf, the ancient fortress in Brandenberg where, in 1758, Frederick the Great had defeated the Russians.[25]

There was only one way out of Zorndorf, by tunneling. In company with a French and a British officer, Tukhachevsky was soon digging furiously. Once again, however, he was doomed to failure. The tunnel was complete and the time for escape was set. But half an hour before the planned departure, the trio was betrayed—according to more than one source, by another Russian.[26]

So Tukhachevsky once more moved up the scale of escape-proof prisons, this time to the forbidding Bavarian fortress of Ingolstadt IX, Germany's ultimate repository for troublesome escapers. At various times it held from 150 to 200 British, French, and Russian officers. British Flight Lieutenant A. J. Evans, who was there in 1917, estimated that of about 130 prisoners at that time, almost all had tried to escape more than once and about half of them were still actively trying to do so.

The fortress was indeed forbidding. Situated on the rolling downs of Bavaria, it had to the north a high wall broken only by a well-guarded gate. About 100 feet inside the exterior wall was a five-foot-deep moat surrounding the fort. Across the moat was a single drawbridge, giving access through the 60-foot-high walls of the fort. Inside the walls were two courtyards, one inhabited by the officer-prisoners and the other by servants and orderlies. Prisoners were confined, six to a cell, under the ramparts. There were also solitary confinement cells, and it was a measure of the obstreperousness of the inmates that there was a two-month lag between sentencing and incarceration in the punishment cells.

"There were only two possible ways of getting out," Evans wrote later. "One was to go by the main gate past three sentries, three gates and a guardhouse; and the other was to go through the moat. It was impossible to tunnel under the moat. It had been tried, and water came into the tunnel as soon as it got below water level."[27]

Language was a problem, not only for negotiations between the prisoners and their jailers, but also among the prisoners themselves. The British, despite steady efforts to learn French and Russian, dealt mainly with the French, whose language most understood at least rudimentarily. The Russians, particularly the aristocrats like Tukhachevsky, usually spoke French and some German, but little or no English. They also dealt mainly with the French.

Life was monotonous, if not exactly grim. A typical day's rations consisted of one potato, one small plate of soup made with leftover bones, one cup of acorn coffee, one lump of sugar, two mouthfuls of fish, one mouthful of meat, four or five beans, and a small loaf of bread. The bread was so hard that one British group used a loaf for a rugger ball. The Red Cross parcels again provided welcome breaks—and occasionally, in those days before X-rays, a compass or a map.

The day's routine was centered on, at first, three and later—as the escape attempts became more frequent—four roll calls. The first was a bed check at 7 A.M. Then there was a muster at 11:30 A.M. and another between 4 and 7 P.M. The fourth came at 9 P.M. The prisoners usually took lessons in foreign languages or military affairs from noon to 2 P.M. From 2 to 4 P.M. they played games, usually tennis or field hockey, in the courtyard. At 4 P.M. the British had their traditional tea, while the other prisoners resumed their lessons, read, or played bridge. There was plenty of time for political discussion, in which Tukhachevsky eagerly took part and surprised his French cellmates, most of them ultraconservative, with his radical opinions. Partly because of a shortage of oil for lamps, lights out came with the 9 P.M. bed check.

But everything was not quite so cut and dried. The atmosphere in the camp was one of sullen wariness on the part of the Germans. The guards were mostly elderly reservists, lightly armed. They knew that in an all-out attack, they could not hope to control the young prisoners, who not only were much fitter but also outnumbered them three to one. On the part of the prisoners, there was a sustained effort to outwit their captors and to humiliate them whenever possible. Sometimes this conflict was almost like that between schoolboys and masters at a boarding school. On one occasion, the French and Russian prisoners decided that they wanted to get hold of a strongbox in the commandant's office that held maps, compasses, and other gear taken from captured escapees. A group of Russian and French officers, on some pretext or other, charged into the commandant's office. Pushing, shoving, and yelling, they confronted the startled Germans. While the guards and German officers were distracted, trying to discover what the fuss was all about and to restore order, the wooden strongbox was hustled to a nearby cell. There it was ripped apart and burned, the pieces being sent to several cells for quicker destruction. The contents were spirited back to their original owners before the Germans realized what was going on.

Among these unruly young men was a towering French captain, as ambitious as young Tukhachevsky and equally sure of his own importance: Charles de Gaulle. The first meeting between the two was scarcely auspicious. One day Tukhachevsky approached de Gaulle, who had been nicknamed "the Constable" partly because of his height and partly because of his taciturn nature.

Said Tukhachevsky, "Are you sad because the war is lost?"

"It is not lost. It is almost won," growled the Frenchman, who, like the Russian, had been sent to Ingolstadt because of his attempts to escape from other camps.

"No, no! I meant that you are sad because you are out of it, that it is lost to you," said Tukhachevsky.

De Gaulle, who even then did not suffer banter gladly, turned away.

Tukhachevsky shouted after him: "What's the use of being sad? The present may not be ours, but perhaps the future will be."

That broke the ice, and de Gaulle smiled. Thereafter, they had many political and military discussions, during which they advanced remarkably similar views on military tactics and the future of warfare.[28]

It was in Ingolstadt, too, that Tukhachevsky's path crossed that of another young man destined to be important in the history of the twentieth century: Monsignor Eugenio Pacelli, papal nuncio in Munich, who was to become Pope Pius XII. On a visit to the camp to meet some Polish officers soon after arriving in Bavaria in 1917, he got into conversation with some of the Russians. The fate of Catholic Poland was obviously of concern to the Vatican, and Pacelli expressed the hope that Poland would be liberated from the rule of the Orthodox Romanovs. Tukhachevsky, however, displayed his chauvinism by telling the future pope in no uncertain terms that he would do all in his power to keep Poland a Russian dominion. Neither of those stubborn men knew how important the argument would prove for later events.[29]

The compulsion to escape continued to affect the lives of the inmates. A few attempts were successful, others were not, sometimes with tragic results. But life in the camp was never given over to despondency.

Tukhachevsky remained fond of classical music, especially of Beethoven's Ninth Symphony. Somewhere he had bought an old violin, and tried to master the instrument. According to a cellmate, who later wrote under the name of Pierre Fervacque: "Mikhail would scrape his fiddle. For pretense only, since he was incapable of the least piece. . . . Very often he would ask Captain T. to play a Beethoven sonata.

"One day, impatient and desperate at not being able to evoke the soul of Beethoven, he threw his violin under his bed and left it to gather dust with his old boots."[30]

Later in life, Tukhachevsky was to return to this fascination with violins, although from a different aspect. As a hobby, even during the rigors of the Civil War, he took up violinmaking and became expert at it. So much so that his creations were much prized, and a gadget he invented for measuring a violin bow came to be called the Tukhachevsky device.[31]

While Tukhachevsky was fretting in Ingolstadt, tumultuous events were in progress in Russia. Beginning on March 7, 1917, large-scale demonstrations broke out in Petrograd to protest Nicholas II's handling of the war. By March 15, Nicholas had abdicated the throne and a provisional, tentatively democratic government had been established. Further turmoil followed Vladimer Ilych Lenin's return to Russia, after the famous journey across Germany in the sealed train. No one seemed to be in charge until a new government was formed in July, with Alexander Kerensky as prime minister. But Kerensky's hold on power was brief. General L. G. Kornilov, named commander in chief of the armed forces in August, tried to stage a coup from the right. He advanced on Petrograd, only to be thrown back, largely because of Trotsky's hastily organized militia. The Kornilov scare greatly enhanced the standing of the Bolsheviks. The common troops deserted Kornilov's cause because, as the American diplomat Raymond Robins said: "The war is dead in the heart of the Russian soldier."[32]

Then came the blow from the left. On November 7, the Bolsheviks seized power in Petrograd. A week later they controlled Moscow. There followed the unevenly matched peace negotiations with the Germans at Brest-Litovsk. When the tide of the discussions turned against the Russians, Trotsky coined his enigmatic "no war and no peace" formula, only to have it blow up in his face. When a new German offensive seemed about to overwhelm the fledgling Soviet state, Lenin ordered that his delegates sign the now very uneven peace treaty. Indirectly, the cessation of hostilities brought freedom to Tukhachevsky, far away in Bavaria.

With Russia out of the war, the prison authorities began to treat the Russian inmates more leniently. As one concession, the Russian officers were permitted to leave the fortress for an hour each day, after giving their word that they would return. On departing, each prisoner had to sign the register opposite his name. Tukhachevsky and another Russian, Chernovietsky, cooked up a ruse by which they signed, not beside their own names, but beside each other's. This, they reasoned with convenient logic, released them from their parole. The British officers were aghast at such perfidy. The French believed it wouldn't work. Fervacque said that he tried to persuade Tukhachevsky not to try a plan that was "too Oriental." The events in Russia were even used to try to dissuade the would-be escapers.

"You're from a noble family," the French officers told Tukhachevsky. "If you go back to Russia now, you'll be shot."

"Shot?" retorted the young lieutenant. "I'll be a general by the time I'm 25."

He was 24, and there was little time left to fulfill the old dream.[33]

Finally the appointed day arrived, a Saturday. Fervacque had somewhere obtained a suit of civilian clothes. Tukhachevsky put them on under his uniform, not the most comfortable outfit on a warm autumn day. The prisoners strolled out, guarded by a sergeant and some territorials. As they walked past some woods, Tukhachevsky and Chernovietsky slipped away, across the roadside and into the trees. The sergeant and the territorials gave chase. A shot rang out. But quickly the Germans had to give up and return the other, British, prisoners to the fort. A quarter of an hour later, tracking dogs were brought into the chase. They were taken to Tukhachevsky's cell to familiarize themselves with his scent, but finely ground tobacco had been sprinkled over all the fugitive's belongings. The dogs, sneezing violently, were useless. Some time later the Germans found Tukhachevsky's discarded uniform. Three days later, the Germans caught Chernovietsky and brought him back to Ingolstadt, hungry, battered, and unhappy. But of Tukhachevsky there was no further trace.

A report in a German newspaper some weeks afterward of an unidentified corpse discovered near the Swiss border, apparently the victim of hunger and cold, led some of the prisoners to believe that Tukhachevsky had perished.[34] But they were wrong. After some trying moments, including one occasion when he was hiding in a haystack and a farmer plunged his fork into the hay, Tukhachevsky stumbled toward freedom. Somehow he managed to cover the 700 miles, apparently mostly on foot. At last he managed to reach Russia and was reunited with his family. It was a joyful time, although some of the gaiety was diminished by the news that Mikhail's younger brother Igor, a promising pianist, had died. After a brief stay at the Penza estate, Mikhail returned to Petrograd, where he rejoined the remnants of the Semyenovsky Regiment. Soon afterward, Mikhail Nikolaevich Tukhachevsky, the former Tsarist Guard, became a committed soldier of the Bolshevik Revolution.[35]

3
CIVIL WAR: THE DEFEAT OF KOLCHAK

IT WAS ONE THING for the Bolsheviks to seize power in Petrograd and Moscow. It was quite a different matter for them to hold on to what they had seized and to extend their control over the sprawling and often hostile mass of the country. The dimensions of the challenge to their authority—and of their audacity in asserting their claim to power—are difficult to envisage some seven decades later. Their biggest weapons were their own ideological fervor—the positive conviction that they alone were right—and the anarchy and venality among their opponents.

To the outside world, caught up in the debate over Woodrow Wilson's fourteen-point proposal for peace with Germany that had been issued in January 1918, the Bolsheviks' chances for success seemed remote. The Treaty of Brest-Litovsk, as Lenin himself recognized, had dismembered prewar Russia. Germany annexed eastern Poland, the Baltic states, and the entire Ukraine. Finland was hived off to be an independent state. Turkey, Germany's ally, got the districts of Kars and Batum. Territory was not the only loss. The annexations deprived the Bolsheviks of a quarter of prewar Russia's population, half of its industry, and three-quarters of its iron and steel production.

Moreover, although they had apparent control of the internal political machinery, the Bolsheviks' Russia was surrounded by hostility. At first this centered in the Kuban and the Volunteer Army commanded by Kornilov and other former tsarist officers infuriated by the humiliation of Brest-Litovsk. But eventually it came to be dominated by General Anton Ivanovich Denikin, who had defied the caste system to rise above his far from aristocratic origins to reach the highest ranks of the imperial army. To the north, another White army was forming under General Nicholas Nikolaevich Yudenich and was posing a threat to Petrograd.

But initially the greatest menace lay in the east. At the heart of that threat was the so-called Czech Legion, recruited by Allied agents from among Czechoslovakian prisoners of war. In the beginning the Czechoslovaks wanted only to get out of Russia and to get back to fighting the Germans and the Austrians for the independence of their country. But, as Tukhachevsky wrote later, bribed and cajoled by the British and the French and importuned by the Russian Whites, they became the spearhead of the anti-Bolshevik campaign in the east.[1] In the waning days of 1917, this 45,000-man force had been placed under titular French command by the Allies, eager to use it as an eastern diversion against the Germans. But increasingly it had it own dynamics and ambitions. Eventually, toward the end of 1918, the Czechs and Russian Whites who had joined them came under the command of Admiral Alexander Vasilyevich Kolchak, the one-time commander of the tsar's Black Sea fleet, now aspiring to be dictator of all the Russians.

Kolchak had been one of the few senior officers to emerge from the Russo-Japanese War with a distinguished record, and he had won further renown for his daring Arctic explorations in subsequent years. He was 45 years old in 1918 and was regarded as being Britain's protégé in the kaleidoscopic political scene in Russia.[2]

For Russia, with one foot in the bloody past and one foot in what was to be an even bloodier future, it was a time of tumultuous change. It was no less so for Tukhachevsky. The Red

Army had been born on February 23, 1918, and Tukhachevsky was soon numbered in its ranks. Whether he was really inspired by political inclination—he had joined the Communist Party in April—is doubtful despite the radical opinions he had expressed to his fellow prisoners of war in Germany. And although Tukhachevsky later enunciated the doctrine of revolutionary war and the catch phrases of Leninism permeated his speeches and writing, it seems more likely that in 1918 chauvinism and personal ambition were his main motivations.

Valerian Kuibyshev and his younger brother Nikolai, who like Tukhachevsky had studied at the Aleksandrovsky Academy, apparently played an important part in persuading Tukhachevsky to join the Bolsheviks.[3] The elder Kuibyshev had been destined by his father, a captain in the tsarist army, to follow a military career, but had been diverted into political activities. In 1918 he was one of the most prominent among Lenin's younger disciples, and it was probably because of his sponsorship that Tukhachevsky was given such important tasks so soon after joining the Bolsheviks. Later, Valerian Kuibyshev would be associated with Stalin in the internal party struggles against Trotsky and Zinoviev. But his death in 1938, ostensibly from a heart attack brought on by heavy drinking, has since become something of a mystery. At one time it was "revealed" that Kuibyshev had supposedly been poisoned by Stalin's enemies, but in recent years suspicion has been cast on Stalin or some of his associates as the real instruments of Kuibyshev's death.[4]

It was apparently about this time that Tukhachevsky met Lenin. Shostakovich says that when the young soldier was introduced to the Soviet leader, Lenin's first question was about how Tukhachevsky had managed to get out of Germany. It seemed that Lenin suspected that the Germans had helped Tukhachevsky back to Russia, just as they had assisted the Bolshevik leader on his famous train ride to Petrograd.[5] The meeting was apparently amicable, for, as Shostakovich says: "Lenin sensed that Tukhachevsky was a kindred spirit. He delegated the most responsible jobs to the obscure lieutenant."

Tukhachevsky spent the spring of 1918 training units of the ragtag new army in the Moscow region. But that interlude was soon interrupted. The Czech Legion had staged an uprising at Chelyabinsk on May 29, and before long the Civil War was in full roar. The Bolsheviks had achieved some successes—Kornilov had been killed when a shell landed near his headquarters at Ekaterinodar on April 13—but for the most part they were on the defensive, hanging on in the face of near-insurrection among the citizenry they nominally governed and in the face of growing external threats as well.

In June, Tukhachevsky was given command of the First Army on the Eastern Front against the Czechs. His dream had come true; if not in name, since the Red Army then had no such rank, in actual fact he was a general at 25.

The situation was desperate. At the end of June, the British intervention force landed at Murmansk. On July 6 the Social Revolutionaries, seeking to provoke German reprisals against the Bolshevik regime, assassinated Count Wilhelm von Mirbach, the kaiser's ambassador to Russia. Simultaneously they attempted to provoke a counterrevolution in Moscow. It was put down ferociously. But such was the mood of fear that 12 days later, the Bolshevik commander at Ekaterinburg ordered the execution of Tsar Nicholas and his family, an action that removed the Romanov dynasty at one blow but also lent a holy fervor to the White cause.

The Socialist Revolutionaries' plans misfired badly. There were no reprisals from a Germany preoccupied with the more serious threat on the Western Front. The Germans satisfied themselves by moving their embassy to the dubious safety of Pskov.

While the Bolshevik politicians were solidifying their control of the government organs in Moscow, Tukhachevsky was traveling east to take up his command. Arriving on the Volga Front, he found the army he was to command little better than a rabble. They were more used to the ways of the freebooting front commander, Mikhail Aztemevich Muraviev, a former tsarist colonel, than to the practices of the stern young newcomer from Moscow. Muraviev had served the Bolsheviks well in defending Petrograd from the Kornilov threat, but he had won a greater reputation for butchery, looting, and rapine in the Ukraine and in a campaign against the Rumanians. After chasing the Ukrainian nationalists out of Kiev, he had turned his troops loose on the city for four days. By one account they massacred 2,000 former tsarist officers who had been captured. But Muraviev ignored the depredations, preferring to celebrate his victory by getting publicly drunk on captured champagne.[6]

In contrast, Tukhachevsky intended to maintain strict discipline and to concentrate all his efforts on repelling the Czechoslovaks. Typical of his somewhat pompous approach was a proclamation he issued to his new command:

> Comrades:
>
> Our goal? To strike as soon as possible at the Czechs and counterrevolutionaries toward the fertile plains of Siberia. To do this, it is necessary without further delay to advance. It is necessary to take the offensive. The least setback is a step toward death.
>
> Strict obedience and attention to orders coming from responsible commanders, without debate and muttering. Such is, in wartime, the first and essential condition for victory.
>
> Have no doubt, comrades: The Workers and Peasants authorities have an eye on everything. The smallest action of your commanders will not escape their notice. Any divergence will draw from them severe reprisals.
>
> Commander of the First Army
Tukhachevsky[7]

Tukhachevsky was accompanied by his sponsor among the Bolsheviks, Valerian Kuibyshev, who had been named commissar to the First Army. In those days of uncertain political loyalties—and even in later days of still uncertain politics—a reliable party functionary was assigned to keep watch on all Red commanders, and Kuibyshev was to keep Tukhachevsky on the straight Leninist way. Their first task was to stabilize the front. That was accomplished on June 9, in two attacks. The offensive was successful, resulting in the capture of the towns of Syzran and Bugulma.

That done, Tukhachevsky boarded his command train to move to Simbirsk, where he planned to meet the front commander, Muraviev, to plan the continuation of the campaign against the Czechs. What Tukhachevsky did not know was that Muraviev had decided to switch his allegiance.

Muraviev, whose prewar behavior had scandalized St. Petersburg society, was sailing toward Simbirsk with a bizarre retinue of hangers-on, male and female. He traveled in the former imperial yacht, *Mezhen*, guarded by a picked band of sailors and entertained by girl singers brought specially for the purpose. Along the way he had arrested some Bolshevik political workers and thrown them into the hold of the vessel. At the same time he announced that he had renounced allegiance to the Bolsheviks and now would align himself against the Bolsheviks. Surrounded by his Tatar, Bashkir, and Chuvash soldiers, he finally reached Simbirsk.[8]

The response of the Soviet leaders in the area—those still out of Muraviev's clutches—was to issue an order saying "In view of these treacheries, anyone coming in contact with him will be considered duty-bound to shoot him like a mad dog, an enemy of Soviet Russia."[9]

Tukhachevsky waited in his train at the Simbirsk station. Soon after Muraviev reached Simbirsk, Tukhachevsky went to the landing stage to report, and was immediately arrested. Muraviev had not taken long to realize that Tukhachevsky, even though he was an aristocrat and a former Imperial Guardsman, was now fully committed to the Leninist cause.

Tukhachevsky later recalled: "In the first moments, after all this, as Muraviev left to besiege the Soviet headquarters, the Red Army men wanted immediately to shoot me, but they were extremely surprised when, to a question from some of them about why I had been arrested, I replied: 'Because I am a Bolshevik.' It was the start of a friendly chat. Hearing about the Left S. R. uprising in Moscow and receiving an explanation of Muraviev's treachery, the Red Army men immediately chose delegates and spokesmen for themselves from the armored division to discuss the questions."[10] The soldiers were still not sure of Tukhachevsky, however. They carried him off to prison, where he was lodged in a solitary cell. Similarly detained were the Bolsheviks from the yacht and some other Red Army officers.

Muraviev, meanwhile, had called a public meeting in the town's largest hotel, the Trinity, where he formally proposed an end to the war against the Czechoslovaks and joining their fight against the Bolsheviks and the Germans. Muraviev's troops then proceeded to get drunk again. In his cell, where random shooting by the celebrants could easily be heard, Tukhachevsky must have thought that his end was near.

But Muraviev and his men had not managed to apprehend all the Bolsheviks. In the evening a young Latvian officer, Iosif

M. Vareikis, and others who remained loyal to Lenin stormed the prison and freed Tukhachevsky and the other Bolsheviks. A thankful Tukhachevsky later said: "Comrade Vareikis showed colossal energy and leadership."[11]

Under a pretext of negotiations, the group summoned Muraviev to a midnight meeting. Thinking that he was going to a conference with the town fathers about the authority of his newly proclaimed Republic of Povolzhe, Muraviev hastened to the appointed place. At the entrance to the military school where the meeting was to be held, Muraviev was told about Tukhachevsky's release, but he did not stop. Gaudily uniformed in scarlet breeches, with his saber-bearing Circassians and his coterie of sailors, he climbed to the third-floor meeting room. Entering the hall, he saw Tukhachevsky, Boris M. Feldman, and his other erstwhile prisoners. Defying them, he strode to the center of the room and gave them an ultimatum:

"Enemies or friends? Time is vital. The word is: To arms! I have the army with me. The whole front. I am master of Simbirsk. Tomorrow I will be in Kazan. It is useless to waste time with speeches. Come . . . ."

"You are full of shit, Muraviev!" someone shouted.

At that point Muraviev banged his fist angrily on the table and strode toward the door. As he pushed forward, a melee broke out but subsided as the angry Muraviev strode to the exit, brandishing his revolver. He threw open the door, only to find his way blocked by Red Latvian soldiers who had been hidden in the next room. Muraviev hurled himself on the Latvians. Shots rang out. Muraviev fell, still clutching his pistol, his blood oozing onto the floor.[12]

Tukhachevsky had survived, but the chaos surrounding the Muraviev affair was a body blow to the incipient Red offensive. Not a few of the Red commanders had sided with the rebellion, and their treachery left the command structure in a shambles. Instead of advancing beyond Simbirsk, the Red troops fell back in disarray. Such was the dislocation of the Red Army that on July 22, the White general Vladimir Oskarovich Kappel was able to capture Simbirsk with a force that numbered just 283 men.[13]

In the Kremlin, desperate measures were decided upon. Ioakhim Ioakhimovich Vatsetis, a former Tsarist colonel and among Trotsky's closest associates, was dispatched to replace Muraviev as commander of the Eastern Front.

Capitalizing on this situation, the Czechs resumed their advance, plunging toward the heart of Russia. On July 26, they captured Ekaterinburg. The Red Army was forced out of Kazan four days later. Behind them the Reds left a treasure, monetary and military. The Whites captured great quantities of medical supplies and even a copy of Trotsky's codes. With those the Whites were able to decipher telegrams from Lenin that gave them a valid and encouraging picture of the desperation of the Bolshevik side. In addition, the victors captured the main gold reserves of the former imperial government, which had been moved from Petrograd to Samara to avoid their falling into the hands of the Germans, and then had been moved back to Kazan. By one French account, the treasure consisted of 1.7 million francs in gold, 500,000 in platinum, and 900 million in silver.[14] Town after town had fallen to the Czechs and their White Russian allies: Stavropol on July 14, Simbirsk on July 22, and soon afterward the important railroad town of Buzuluk was in their hands.

Not that there wasn't some fight left on the Bolshevik side. Trotsky, in fact, seemed to be a one-man army. After ordering the conscription of all tsarist officers and NCOs, he set out in his armored train for the Volga. His destination was the town of Sviyazhsk, on the west bank of the Volga opposite Kazan. It was the extreme eastern position held by the Reds, directly connected to the heartland of Russia. The scene that greeted Trotsky would have daunted a less fervid man. In the face of the enemy advances, desertions were decimating the Red forces. The officers, most of them tsarist leftovers, were hopelessly confused. Bolshevik commissars trying to rally them were inexperienced and equally confused. It was a situation made for the hero of the 1905 revolution. He descended from his train and exhorted the Red forces with all the considerable rhetoric he could muster.

On occasion Trotsky commanded by example, personally leading his troops to the firing line. He was at the head of a group of sailors from Kronstadt, commanded by Lieutenant F. F. Raskolnikov, on a daring night raid against Kazan. The losses among the Kronstadt men were heavy, but the White artillery on the Volga's banks was silenced.

All the while, Trotsky was sending a volley of demands back to Moscow. He wanted Lenin to send him devoted Communists "ready to die" to reinforce his wavering troops. He demanded a supply of pistols, even a military band. Morale and propaganda were much on his mind. To that end, he kept urging Lenin and his colleagues to authorize the issuance of medals, banned in the new Russia, to those who showed bravery on the Volga Front. He requested that the popular poet Demian Bedni be sent to the war zone.

There was another side to Trotsky. Cowardice and desertion were ruthlessly punished. "I issue this warning," he said, "if any detachment retreats without orders, the first to be shot will be the commissar, the next the commander." In some cases the threat was carried out. Nor could humanitarianism move him. On August 17, Lenin advised him that the Red Cross wanted to ship food from Nizhni Novgorod, held by the Bolsheviks, to White-held Samara. Lenin thought that it was permissible. Trotsky did not. He did not want any outside meddlers to witness his planned "burning and scorching" of the "bourgeois sections" of Kazan. Trotsky got his way.[15]

The reinvigorated Red soldiers—reinvigorated not least by Trotsky's threats of what would befall them if they failed—went on the attack. On September 10, the Reds' Fifth Army, at that time commanded by P. A. Slaven, stormed and seized Kazan, the ancient Tatar capital. In disorder the Whites fell back toward the Kama River.[16]

While his colleagues had been preparing for the attack on Kazan, Tukhachevsky had been preoccupied with his own preparations for the assault on Simbirsk, from which the Reds had retreated in the debacle following the Muraviev affair. The young commander had spent the preceding weeks trying to build up his badly disheartened units. As an untried commander he was closely watched by the Bolshevik authorities. In particular, the newly appointed commander of the front, Vatsetis, on July 18 summoned Tukhachevsky to a meeting at Ruzayevka, where they went over Tukhachevsky's plans for a new assault to recapture Simbirsk. At that stage the outlook seemed dismal for the shattered First Army, but Tukhachevsky's plans were approved by Vatsetis and P. A. Kobozev, a veteran Bolshevik who was head of the political apparatus on the front.[17]

But the main intention of the Reds was to recapture Kazan, and Tukhachevsky was importuned to divert some of his forces to help. As politely as he could, but with typical stubbornness, Tukhachevsky declined, maintaining that his units had already been stripped to the minimum. He prevailed.[18]

During the conversation Tukhachevsky had been asked to assess his chances for success. With all the self-confidence of youth, he answered that within three days he would retake Simbirsk. Knowing all too well the state of his army and its previous record, Vatsetis and Kobozev wondered if he was talking nonsense.

The battle began on the night of September 9, and it was not long before the Red forces, particularly those commanded by the dashing Armenian Gai Dmitriyevich Gai, started to advance. They quickly captured the villages of Prislonka and Ignatovka on the outskirts of Simbirsk. During the next day more villages fell, but the battle seemed to hang in the balance. Adopting Trotsky's methods, Tukhachevsky displayed a ruthlessness that quickly ended any thoughts of retreat among the Red soldiers. Under threat of summary execution for showing the least sign of hesitation, the First Army pressed on. Despite heavy losses, the Reds continued to advance until, on September 12, they reached the outskirts of Simbirsk. By 10 that evening, Tukhachevsky's forces had the town surrounded on three sides.

The only way out for the Whites was across the Volga. By noon of September 12, they had started to flee across the river. As the Whites left, the Reds entered the deserted city. Then it was time to send Trotsky a telegram that became famous for its terse understatement: "After an operation of exactly three days Simbirsk has been taken. Army Commander Tukhachevsky."[19]

Trotsky was seldom one to be laconic, however. In passing on the news to Lenin, who had barely survived an attempt on his life, Trotsky embellished the report. "The capture of your birthplace [Simbirsk] will avenge your first wound. That of Samara will avenge the second," he told the wounded leader. Years later Trotsky was to say: "That day [the day Simbirsk was recaptured] was a noteworthy date in the history of the Red Army. At once we felt firm ground under our feet. The time of our first helpless efforts was over: thenceforth we were able to fight and win."[20]

Tukhachevsky's victorious troops were briefly allowed to celebrate their success, but as soon as matters seemed to threaten to get out of hand, the young commander and his subordinates, Gai and Vitovt K. Putna, cracked down. Tukhachevsky ordered that looters be shot without trial, and more than 100 of his men were said to have been executed for ignoring the command. Needless to say, the pillaging quickly stopped.[21]

Suddenly the Bolshevik cause had been transported from the edge of despair to the edge of hope. Behind the lines and on other fronts, however, grave events had been occurring, as had been suggested in Trotsky's message to Lenin. On August 30 a Socialist Revolutionary extremist, Dora (Fanny) Kaplan, had tried to assassinate Lenin, seriously wounding him. And in Petrograd one of Kaplan's associates had murdered the head of the local Cheka, Moses Solomonovich Uritsky. In the south the White Army, now led by General Anton I. Denikin, had captured Odessa on August 18 and was marching into the heart of the Ukraine. Kiev fell to the Whites on September 2 and Denikin was hailed as a savior by the citizens. Ringing church bells greeted the arrival of his troops. The cossacks flocked to his colors. Even the Ukrainian nationalist Semyon Petlura volunteered to join his forces to Denikin's.[22]

But there was a basic weakness in the White campaign, above and beyond the rival ambitions of the leaders of the three White fronts, which, as Baron Peter Wrangel wrote in his memoirs, were always a factor. These divisions were aggravated by the White soldiers' proclivity for brigandage. Again Wrangel saw the danger in this: "Initially, having suffered so much from the Bolsheviks and desiring only to live in peace, the population welcomed our troops with raptures of enthusiasm when we arrived. Soon, however, it had to undergo once more the horrors of pillage, violence and tyranny. Result: confusion at the front and rebellion at the rear."[23]

Apart from the viciousness of their troops and the rivalries among their leaders, the Whites' real problem was that while the Bolsheviks were united in what they conceived as a righteous cause, the Whites had no clear political motive beyond the defeat and humiliation of the Reds. The Reds might differ on immediate tactics—Stalin was particularly obstreperous and often counterproductive, as the histories of the 1918 battle for Tsaritsyn and the 1920 battle for Lvov would show—but for all of them the only final goal was a Communist Russia. On the Eastern Front, the Whites made an attempt to remedy this situation with the formation of the Political Directory of Ufa. But it was a makeshift construction, mainly the work of the French officers who had arrived in the region, and in view of the shifting tide of battle, it had little relation to reality. Eventually it was to give way to the dictatorship of Kolchak. Tukhachevsky's victory at Simbirsk and Slaven's at Kazan were heralds of what was ahead.

At the time, however, things seemed much different. Denikin's advance into the heartland of Russia seemed to be unstoppable. The final collapse of the Central Powers in November 1918 and the removal of Austrian and German units from the south would have seemed to benefit the Whites, since it should have meant that the anti-Communist Allied regimes could have diverted troops and munitions to help Denikin, Kolchak, and Yudenich. But the almost unbelievable confusion and incompetence among the French officers and bureaucrats who were sent to the region, and the opposition of the politicians of France to getting further involved in Russia, proved to be a serious obstacle to Denikin's success.

As the threat mounted in the south and the Reds hurriedly sought to reinforce the front, a rapid change of priorities occurred. The Czech Legion and their allies in the Ufa Directory were in retreat. At first Tukhachevsky proceeded cautiously against them. On the night after the capture of Simbirsk, he moved to force a way across the Volga. The way across lay over an iron railroad bridge, which was still under enemy fire. Tukhachevsky sent a driverless locomotive across the kilometer-long span. When it had crossed safely, an armored train followed. Then came an infantry brigade. For a while heavy artillery fire covered the area, but in the face of the daring frontal assault, the Whites wavered. More than anything, this assault displayed the new spirit of the First Army, which, when Tukhachevsky had joined it at the end of June, had been in chaos. There had been no organized command structure, and no one knew exactly how many troops were left in the command. And the troops who remained got their food by holding up supply trains passing through their area.[24]

From the beginning, Tukhachevsky pressed relentlessly forward. Between September 19 and October 7, most of the towns on the Volga and the Kama, including Ufa, fell to the Reds. To the southeast, Samara was again under Red control. Thus, to Moscow it seemed prudent to switch some units from the east to the struggle in the south against Denikin. Tukhachevsky was among those transferred, being sent in January 1919 to command the Eighth Army on the Southern Front.

On December 19, 1918, French troops under General Franchet d'Esperey had arrived in Odessa to support the White armies. In Paris, Wilson, Clemenceau, Lloyd George, and the other Allied leaders were negotiating the shape of the new Europe but vacillating on what to do about Russia. What was to have been the spearhead of France's decisive intervention in southern Russia was left uncertain. The situation was not helped by conflict between the French and Denikin, who operated in what the Allies considered the British zone of influence but tried to extend his authority over Odessa, which was in the French zone.[25]

By March the confusion among the Whites was turning to panic as the opportunisitc Ukrainian cossack Ataman Grigoriev joined the Red side and began to advance on Odessa. Before his assault, the French African troops and some Greek support units fled, leaving behind most of their heavy equipment. Included in the spoils were two tanks, the Red Army's first. In an intriguing throwback to pre-revolutionary practice, the victorious Ukrainians offered one of the tanks to Lenin. He declined the gift, however, and the tanks stayed at the front.[26]

The disarray of the Whites in the south was not matched on the Eastern Front. The Civil War was a conflict of great swings and upheavals, being fought over vast distances and uncertain lines of battle. Today's victory was all too often followed by tomorrow's reverse. The plugging of one loophole seemed only to lead to penetration somewhere else. The ferocity of the warfare was intense. A sense of lurking betrayal permeated both sides. Just as Tukhachevsky threatened to send deserters before the firing squad, so the Whites exterminated any of their former tsarist comrades who fell into their hands. The Red commanders Singhelyev and Melnikov were summarily shot after being captured. A son of the Red general Brusilov was lynched on a convenient tree. And worse was to come.[27]

Just when things seemed to be under control for Lenin and

his associates, there came a renewed threat on the Eastern Front. The setbacks there had begun in December 1918, when, in a move that caught the Bolsheviks by surprise, the armies of Kolchak—who had declared himself dictator on November 18—had overrun the key city of Perm. The Perm debacle was of great concern to Lenin and the Central Committee, and Stalin and Felix Dzerzhinsky were sent to find out what had happened. Stalin's conclusion, seconded by Dzerzhinsky, was that Trotsky's policy of conscripting any ablebodied male, regardless of political sympathies, lay at the root of the setback. The report was later to be a central issue in the polemics between Stalin and Trotsky.[28]

During the winter, Kolchak enlarged his salient, moving as far west as Ufa. It was a bitter time for the fledgling Soviet state. Fighting a war on three fronts and facing an increasingly hostile domestic population, the last straw for the men in Moscow was the onslaught of the Spanish influenza pandemic. One of Bolshevism's brightest young leaders, Yakov Mikhailovich Sverdlov, fell to the disease at the age of 34. Even Bela Kun's proclamation of the Hungarian Soviet Republic seemed to promise more trouble than succor.

Thus the Eighth Congress of the Russian Communist Party that opened in Moscow on March 18, 1919, was the scene of much angry debate. The peasant question, especially collectivization, threatened to split the party. But even angrier polemics flowed on the question of using tsarist officers and NCOs in the Red Army. Finally, Lenin sided with Trotsky, who favored continued use of the military specialists, as they were called. Said Lenin: "We have had recourse to the help of bourgeois specialists who are soaked through and through with the bourgeois attitude of mind, who have betrayed us and who will go on betraying us for years. Nevertheless, if it is a question of whether we are going to build communism with the hands of pure Communists and nobody else and without the help of the bourgeois specialists, it is a childish idea . . . ." The Tukhachevskys and Vatsetises of the Red Army were to stay.[29]

At about the time the Communist Party Congress opened in Moscow, Kolchak launched an attack toward the Volga, the intent of which was all too clear. The Whites were aiming first to take Kazan, and then Nizhni Novgorod, before plunging headlong toward Moscow. In a second prong of the offensive, the southern wing of Kolchack's armies would be aimed at Samara and Simbirsk. From there they would join the remainder of Denikin's forces in the south, while the northern wing would meet the White group led by General Eugene Miller.

On March 4, 52,000 Czechoslovak and White soldiers, led by General Rudolf Gajda, moved against the Second and Third Red Armies on the northern sector of the Eastern Front. Gadja was one of the more unusual characters who rose to brief prominence in the Civil War. A former Austrian hospital orderly, he went over to the Serbs in 1915, made his way to Salonika and Odessa, and subsequently joined the Czech Legion in Russia. Like Tukhachevsky, he was not yet 30, and he was intent on making the most of the opportunities that came his way. When his tactics succeeded, he was a hero among the White leadership, but later his scorn for their vacillation and corruption brought upon him the full fury of Admiral Kolchak. Along with Kappel and Wrangel, he was to be among the minority of White commanders who realized how the war could be won. And like them, in the end he was to suffer for his beliefs.[30]

As Gajda's offensive got under way, town after town fell to the Czech Legion, until they reached the banks of the Kama. Then, on March 6, the southern group of White armies, led by General Khanzhin, 48,000 strong, swept toward the town of Birsk, threatening the rear of the Red Armies, including the First Army in front of Samara.

The Czechoslovak offensive was soon to reopen and intensify the division in the Bolshevik leadership on tactics to counter the attack. At the center of the dispute were two former tsarist officers, Vatsetis and Sergei Sergeyevich Kamenev. Vatsetis was Trotsky's man and, nominally, at least, he was the superior officer, being the commander in chief. Stalin supported Kamenev and wanted Vatsetis replaced. Questions were raised about Vatsetis' loyalty to the Red cause; the Muraviev affair had not been quickly forgotten. Cautiously stepping into the dispute, the Politburo decided that Vatsetis would take charge of the Eastern Front, while Kamenev would devote himself exclusively to the war in the south. It was a papered-over solution that could not last. Vatsetis was sent east, where the previous commander, Mikhail V. Frunze, would now be directly under the eyes of the commander in chief.[31]

Frunze was a veteran Bolshevik, and what was in effect a demotion must have irritated him. He had been born in Pishpek, Central Asia, in 1885, and had studied economics at the St. Petersburg Technical School until he was expelled for political activities in 1904. After participating in the 1905 Revolution, he worked underground until 1917, after which his undoubted military ability came to the fore. He was one of the Red military figures who crushed the remnants of the Kerensky regime in Moscow in 1917. Although he was practically deified in Soviet military and political circles after his early and controversial death in 1925, he lacked the background and military ingenuity of Tukhachevsky, who had been brought back from the fighting against Denikin early in March and given command of the Fifth Red Army. With the spring nearing, there was a lull on the front, with Kolchak's northern thrust stationary about 80 miles east of Kazan.

On both sides it was a time for gathering strength and tidying up loose ends. Kolchak was preoccupied with suppressing Red agitation behind his lines. Strikes in Omsk, Tomsk, Irkutsk, and elsewhere were put down ferociously. All the members of the Siberian Communist Party Central Committee were shot early in April. There were also Red partisan uprisings against the Whites, and the butchery involved in their suppression was almost unbelievable. One such uprising at Atbassar, on the Ishim River, ended with 1,000 partisans being shot and then, according to one account, being mutilated by having their noses, hands, and ears cut off.[32]

Kolchak's position had also been weakened by open dissatisfaction among the Czechoslovaks with their Russian allies. Only the division commanded by Gajda remained loyal to Kolchak; the rest, with French assistance, began to withdraw from Russia, heading east toward Vladivostok. As a stopgap measure, Kolchak appointed General P. Janin, head of the French military mission, as commander in chief of his forces. A thoroughly discouraged Janin tried to pull together the antagonistic White elements and the remaining Czechoslovaks, but his efforts were doomed from the outset. Gajda, for his loyalty, was named to head the White Siberian Army. Kolchak, however, was becoming increasingly unhappy with Janin's advice, and was leaning more and more on the suggestions of Colonel John Ward, a British political officer attached to his staff.[33]

As matters stood, however, the initiative seemed to stand with the Whites, since Kolchak was poised in a good position to join the White forces in the north, now led by General N. N. Yudenich and the British intervention force commander, Major General William E. Ironside, and with Denikin to the south. Kolchak's aim was to hold the center, if not to move it forward. At first the plan seemed to be working. The Reds in the northern sector of the Eastern Front gave way, evacuating the basin of the Kama River. On the southern part of the front, the Whites were threatening Samara.

The snow that still remained made fighting difficult except for a few ski-equipped troops. The conditions also increased the possibility of encirclement, and that had been one reason for the quick retreat of the Red units in the Kama area. Much of the fighting, as the ground conditions deteriorated, was near the railroads, which provided some mobility.

In addition to the weather, another factor played a crucial part in deciding the battles. The conflict was not perceived by the great mass of the Russian people as a civil war with the same clear-cut lines of allegiance as the American war between the North and the South in the 1860s. As one writer put it, soon after, the "ordinary troops were apt to consider the result of a battle before engaging in it."[34] This was borne out in the center of the front, where Khanzhin was the White commander. One of his better units, the Ufa Rifle Division, was attacking along a rail line in the direction of Birsk. His advance was greatly speeded up when two Red battalions switched to his side. Ufa fell on March 13, and Sterlatimak on April 4.[35]

Their successes, however, had exposed basic weaknesses of the Whites. Not the least of these were corruption and sheer brutality on the part of some of the adherents of the Kolchak regime.

Some idea of the dimensions of the graft involved can be gained from the operations of General Gajda's Siberian Army. At the end of May 1919, that army had an official strength of 120,000 men. A month later it had shrunk to 100,000. Even so, the White headquarters at Omsk was supplying it with rations and munitions for 275,000. The difference was siphoned off and sold to the highest bidder by venal commanders along the supply route. At about this time, the British, now Kolchak's main provisioners, supplied him with uniforms for 100,000 men; most of the clothing eventually was worn by Red soldiers.[36]

As the Whites waited, the Reds moved quickly onto the offensive. Mobilizing the disheartened troops was no easy task. When Tukhachevsky arrived in Krotovka on April 5, 1919, to take command of the Fifth Army, he found it worn down from fighting almost nonstop since the previous summer. For most of that time, it had been engaged in rearguard actions, it was desperately short of ammunition, and the command structure had become demoralized. Putna, who since December had commanded the Fifth Army's 27th Omsk Division, later recounted the way things were: "The end of March and the beginning of April were spent in difficult, unequal fighting. We were retreating, fighting back as much as we could but we did not have enough strength. At the end of April, it looked as if we would be thrown into the Volga. The Whites were two or three days' march from the Volga. The party then proclaimed: 'Everyone to the east!'"[37] Putna was referring to the April 11 decision of the Central Committe that mobilized workers and placed a priority on reinforcing the collapsing Eastern Front.

Putna was telling only part of the story, however. On March 20, the Revolutionary Military Soviet of the Eastern Front, then consisting of S. S. Kamenev and S. E. Gusev, reported to Vatsetis: "The situation on the Fifth Army front is highly unfavorable. The enemy penetrated deep behind the left flank of the 27th Division. All the measures taken by the commander of the Fifth Army to liquidate this pincer movement have not had the desired results."[38]

The magnitude of the task confronting the Red commanders perhaps can best be understood by considering the dimensions of the front. It stretched north from the Caspian Sea to the North Ural tundra, 1,100 miles distant. Dispersed over the terrain, arid in the south but marshy and wooded in the north, were about 100,000 Red infantry and cavalry. Matched against them, early in March, Kolchak mustered about 145,000 troops. In spots the balance of forces was even more in the Whites' favor. For example, Khanzhin commanded a 50,000-man group in the center, threatening the Red Fifth Army, which was down to about 10,000 men.

The disposition of the Red armies was as follows. In the south were the Fourth and Turkestan armies, which were soon to be reorganized into the southern group commanded by Frunze.

The First Army, fighting east of Orenburg, was commanded by Gai. In the center, near Ufa, was the Fifth Army. At the extreme left flank were the Second Army, commanded by V. I. Shorin, and the Third Army, led by S. A. Mezheninov.[39] In the reorganization carried out on April 10, Frunze's southern group was expanded to take in the Fourth and Fifth armies. The two armies in the north were grouped under the command of Shorin, another former tsarist colonel.

It was about this time that Tukhachevsky met Frunze, and immediately developed a close rapport with the older man. On April 19, the two held a conversation by direct wire, discussing an attack that the Whites had launched on the railroad center of Buguruslan. Frunze, knowing the weakness of Tukhachevsky's position, nevertheless urged him to try to withstand the assault. Tukhachevsky was not optimistic. "I do not think it will be possible to hold on to Buguruslan," he said. Frunze responded: "If we manage to hang on to the Buguruslan lines, further [White] operations will have to be suspended because the roads will be impassable. Your opinion will be taken into account when general directives are worked out."

There was a similar conversation the following day. Tukhachevsky reported: "The rivers are already free of ice and there is hardly any snow left in the fields. I go out on horseback in order to watch the roads, and even though I am not acquainted with these parts, I do not think [White] operations will be impossible for two weeks. I think that in a few days the roads will be passable, even though difficult. And in a week's time I am expecting major operations." Then he added: "The Whites are very much stronger than we are. They have regrouped and I believe they are ready. So I believe that next week decisive operations will resume."[40]

Tukhachevsky faced a formidable opponent. The White Western Army was commanded by Khanzhin, a 50-year-old former tsarist general who had served in the Russo-Japanese war and in World War I. He was a cossack who had graduated from the Artillery Academy and had served as a teacher at an artillery school for officers.

Then began a hasty regrouping of the Red forces, particularly the assimilation of the reinforcements that were arriving from Moscow. The situation was so crucial that the Moscow reinforcements, especially the political workers whose job it was to reinvigorate the wavering troops, headed straight from the trains to the battlefield. Because of its beleaguered position, the Fifth Army got special attention.[41]

Because of Stalin-era political considerations, credit for the tactics adopted is generally given to Frunze, but from material released later during Khrushchev's de-Stalinization period, it seems that Tukhachevsky played the most important role in the development of the plan of attack. The nature of the plan certainly bears his characteristics, his personal adaptation of the Suvorov dictum: "A quick appraisal, speed, shock."

Tukhachevsky and Frunze concentrated 36,000 troops in front of the town of Buzuluk on the Samara River, some miles south of Buguruslan. This meant that the remainder of the Red troops were strung out in a dangerously thin line over several hundred miles. But worsening ground conditions lessened the hazard. And the concentration of forces gave Tukhachevsky tactical superiority at the point he had chosen to try to pierce the White lines.[41]

On May 4, the offensive began. Wheeling to the right, the Fifth Army was launched against Khanzhin's forces. The strength of the blow was such that the Whites reeled back before it and Tukhachevsky was able to halt briefly to solidify his salient while occupying a strategic site on the Ik River. Threatened with encirclement if they tried to defend Buzuluk, Khanzhin's Whites retreated rapidly.[42] But on May 9, the Whites, who still outnumbered Tukhachevsky's army, launched a counterattack south of Bugulma. By May 12, the Whites had been soundly defeated. More than 2,000 were taken prisoner, and on May 13 Tukhachevsky's troops recaptured Bugulma. The Whites had been driven back ore than 100 miles and, from disarray, the Reds had gone to an ebullient mood, eager to continue the attack.[43]

The capture of Buzuluk on the main rail line showed the inherent flaw in the earlier strategy of Kolchak's commanders. The two pincer arms of his forces were vulnerable to being outflanked. But what began as a tactical retreat quickly developed into a rout. By June 6, the Reds had forced their way across the Belaya River on the northern part of the front. The Whites fell back behind the Ufimka River, and it was apparent that the heart had gone out of Khanzhin's men. The fact that they were now destroying vital rail bridges as they went, including one at Dimoa, signified all too clearly that the threat to Moscow from the east was past. Moreover, now that the Reds had cut into the center of Kolchak's line and were threatening to push northeast toward Ekaterinburg, the White's right flank was dangerously overextended and vulnerable. General Gajda, once eager to thrust northward to effect the link with Yudenich and Ironside, because of the disasters that had occurred on his left flank, now had to get back to safety as fast as he could.[44]

The commanders on the Eastern Front, Frunze and Tukhachevsky, believed that their plans were going swimmingly. But their enthusiasm apparently was not shared by Trotsky and his associates. After the capture of Buguruslan, which opened the way to Belebey and Ufa, Tukhachevsky and Frunze were eager to press their advantage. Sergei Kamenev supported them. But Vatsetis was more cautious, and Trotsky supported him. True, there was some reason for the high command's caution: Past experience had shown, in the case of both White and Red offensives, that rapid advances poorly supported from the rear had often left armies in dangerously exposed positions and had resulted in setbacks. However, Tukhachevsky and Frunze had a better feel for the reality of the situation, and Kamenev apparently shared their optimism. Striking while they had the advantage was the intention of the two young generals, already displaying a unity of spirit that was later to have great influence on the development of the Red Army. Frunze must have been somewhat overwhelmed by his young associate. "He is a cold man, a stranger to all the joys of youth, and his sole passion is war," the veteran Bolshevik was later quoted as saying. "He is a great gambler, intrepid, but almost too daring."[45]

However, Kamenev was recalled, and he was replaced by General Aleksandr A. Samoylo, a veteran tsarist officer who previously had served the Bolsheviks on the Northern Front. Almost twice Tukhachevsky's age, he was inclined to look with disdain on the obstreperous young commander. Tukhachevsky returned the disdain. It was immediately apparent that Samoylo was the complete opposite of the vigorous young men who led key parts of his command. He vacillated where they would have rushed in. He changed his mind where they were decisive. They were certain of victory where he was doubtful. They were better tacticians. Tukhachevsky, for one, was openly scornful of the new front commander. "Instead of pursuing the enemy," Tukhachevsky wrote later, "we were marking time."

In those frenetic days on the Eastern Front, Tukhachevsky's response was even more direct. With unbridled superciliousness he sent a telegram to Samoylo, under whose direct orders he had been chafing:

> As of May 10, presumably for reasons which are unknown to me, you have given five tasks to the Fifth Army, which on each occasion repealed the previous order. To begin with, we were required to advance to the north into the rear of the enemy, operating along the Vyatka River. Then, the direction of the advance was changed 130 degrees toward Belebey. The next directive asked us to advance partly to the north and partly to the east. Then we were told to cross the Kama River near the mouth of the Vyatka. After that I was asked myself to choose where to cross the Kama. And finally we were ordered to cross, not the Kama, but the Belaya River. These mutually conflicting orders have completely tired out the divisions, the units have become all mixed up, communications have broken down and so on. In conclusion, the army commander [Tukhachevsky] requests the commander of the Eastern Front to comply with Article 19 of the Field Regulations issued in 1918.[46]

The impertinent young Fifth Army commander did not have to explain that directive to Samoylo; it said that before issuing an order, a commander was required to think.[47]

Understandably, Samoylo was furious, and insisted the young offender be called to account for discrediting a superior officer. However, the Revolutionary Military Council of the front did not support him, ruling that Tukhachevsky had not refused to carry out the orders but had merely demanded that they be more precise.[48]

What Tukhachevsky and Frunze had perceived from the outset soon became apparent to the authorities in Moscow. The Revolutionary Military Soviet of the Eastern Front—Gusev, Mikhail Lashevich, and K. K. Yurenev—added their own strenuous protests about the removal of Kamenev and the ineptitude of Samoylo. Their importunings did not go unheeded, and on May

29, Lenin sent them the following telegram, a typical mixture of military orders and political propaganda:

> On your insistence, Kamenev has been reappointed. If we do not capture the Urals before the winter, I consider that the revolution will inevitably perish. Exert all efforts. Any friction between Kamenev and the staff should be reported to me in good time, in code. Pay particular attention to the reinforcements, mobilize all the population near the front. Take care of political work. Send me ciphered telegrams every week about results. Read this telegram to all prominent Communists and workers from Petersburg. Report receipt. Pay particular attention to the mobilization of the Orenberg cossacks. You are responsible to ensure that there is no decomposition and that morale should not collapse.
>
> Lenin[49]

Kamenev was back on the job after a three-week hiatus. Headquarters interference did not, however, cease with the change in command in the east. Trotsky and Vatsetis were still preoccupied with the need to build a defensive position before launching the Urals campaign. On June 6, they sent a new directive to the Eastern Front.

> As a result of the overall situation on the other fronts of the Republic, the immediate task of the armies on the Eastern Front will be as follows:
>
> 1: To seize the course of the Belaya River as soon as possible, from Buguruslan to the mouth and to solidify this line by creating strong, defensive points in the areas of Uralsk, Orenburg, Starlatimak, Ufa and Birsk.
>
> 2: To defeat Kolchak's troops operating on the right bank of the Kama in the direction of Kazanburg and Perm and to seize the course of the Kama from the mouth of the Belaya to Perm, inclusive, and to fortify this line by creating strong defensive points around Sarapul, Ossa and Perm.
>
> 3: Without delay, in the next few days, to crush the uprising in the oblasts of the Urals and Orenburg.

4: To secure control over the Kama and Belaya Rivers, not only by means of the aforesaid fortified areas but by also ensuring that our flotillas have the upper hand.[50]

Needless to say, the new orders created great resentment among the commanders in the east, who had hoped that with the removal of Samoylo, the interference from the high command would cease. But Trotsky and Vatsetis were not acting out of orneriness.

In his biography of Stalin, a not-unbiased Trotsky put the situation this way:

> The advance against Kolchak, after two periods of retreat, was now proceeding with complete success. Vatsetis considered the chief danger was now in the south and proposed to keep the Army of the Eastern Front in the Urals during the winter, until the danger should subside sufficiently, in order to transfer a number of divisions to the Southern Front.... I was in favor of assuring an uninterrupted offensive against Kolchak. However, the concrete question was determined by the relation of forces and general strategic situation. If Kolchak had serious reserves beyond the Urals, then to engage in battles beyond the Urals would have constituted a danger, for it would have required new replacements of fresh Communists and commanders, while all of that was at the present necessary for the Southern Front. [After saying that he had given Vatsetis a free hand in dealing with the situation, Trotsky goes on:] Under these conditions, a conflict developed between Vatsetis and Kamenev. Objecting to a number of evasive replies by the Eastern Front, which tried to conduct its own policy, Vatsetis demanded the replacement of Kamenev.[51]

Trotsky continues:

> Stalin pounced upon the conflict between the Eastern Front and the Commander-in-Chief. He treated Vatsetis, who had officially condemned his interference in strategic matters, with hostility and lay in wait for an opportunity to wreak vengeance on him. Now, such an opportunity presented itself. Smilga, Lashevich and Gusev proposed, obviously with the co-operation of Stalin, to appoint Kamenev Commander-

in-Chief. The success on the Eastern Front bribed Lenin and broke down my resistance.[52]

The matter did not end there, but the dispute was soon overshadowed by events in the east. Despite Trotsky's and Vatsetis' inhibitions, the commanders on the Eastern Front were eager to get through the Urals and to crush Kolchak. The question was how to do so. Patrols and thrusts against the White lines revealed that the Kolchak forces, taking advantage of the terrain, were apparently getting ready to stand their ground. There were two main routes for a possible advance, about 80 miles apart. One was along the main railroad toward Zlatoust, which lay among the Karatan Mountains. The other was by the Siberian Highway, through Baiki, Duvan, and Satku. To choose either would mean a prolonged siege and undoubtedly heavy casualties. Success was by no means assured, despite insurrections and other chaos in the White rear.

But Tukhachevsky had discovered a third route, overlooked previously because of its extreme difficulty. He would send his army through the narrow gorge of the torrential Yuruzan River, following it until he could emerge in the rear of the Whites at Zlatoust.

The idea of surprise was attractive, but it was also very dangerous. If the Red troops were caught in the narrow valley, they would be sitting targets for the White armies on the heights above. Further, while the main Red thrust was traversing the treacherous valley, what would prevent the Whites from resuming the offensive against the reduced Red forces that would not be directly involved and would be spread out over more than 125 miles of the front? Tukhachevsky was obviously aware of the perils of being outflanked in this manner, but he had an answer, a diversionary lunge to the north that would occupy the Whites.[53]

The plan was approved by the Revolutionary Military Soviet of the front, a not surprising outcome since, like Tukhachevsky, they were eager to strike a death blow at Kolchak's army. But there were preliminaries to be taken care of before the Fifth Army began its tricky maneuver. Frunze's Southern Group was ordered to advance toward Uralsk and Orenburg. The Second and Third armies would synchronize their own attempts to break through the mountains with Tukhachevsky's. However, at the outset, the

Second Army ran into trouble in trying to cross the Kama River. By that time the Fifth Army had already moved much farther to the east and now faced the danger of having its left flank perilously exposed. To compensate for this, the Fifth Army had to undertake a precautionary action. Tukhachevsky sent his 26th, 27th, and 45th divisions into an attack toward Krasnoyufimsk, into the rear of the Whites who were behind the Kama. The Kolchak forces were forced to retreat. The Second Army was then able to cross the Kama and resume its advance. On the night of June 24, the Fifth Army began the crossing of the Ufa River, preparatory to entering the valley of the Yuruzan and attacking the rear of the Whites' Western Third Army, which was guarding the approaches to Zlatoust.[54]

Late the same day, Tukhachevsky's men began the ascent of the Yuruzan. In the vanguard was the 228th Regiment from Petrograd, followed by the 26th and 27th divisions. The going was extremely rough. The road was narrow and steep; the least misstep could send a soldier to his death in the rushing river. With great difficulty artillery pieces were dragged inch by inch over the rugged terrain. It was slow going, but on July 5, the 27th Division, commanded by Aleksandr V. Pavlov, climbed out on the high plateau above Zlatoust, catching Khanzhin's 12th White Division at exercises. The Reds attacked at once; their success was total.

But for a week the remainder of the White army put up a furious resistance. Finally on July 13, the 26th and 27th divisions, after encircling the city, forced their way into Zlatoust. By that time the Whites were in full retreat. For the Reds, Tukhachevsky's daring strategy had succeeded to the fullest degree; for the Whites the day of disaster had arrived.[55]

The jubilant Revolutionary Military Soviet of the front reported to Moscow: "The valiant troops of the Fifth Army under the inspired command of Tukhachevsky, after heavy fighting, destroyed the troops of the enemy and crossed the Urals."[56]

There was some apprehension in the Red command staff as Tukhachevsky raced on toward the Siberian plain. The next objective was the city of Chelyabinsk. On July 23, the Red forces approached the city, moving to surround it in a wide circle. The Whites were not going to surrender without a fierce struggle the key city where the Czech Legion's revolt had begun in May 1918.

And like their Red counterparts, Kappel and the other White commanders felt that Tukhachevsky was racing ahead too fast, that he was overreaching himself and might be induced to set his own trap.

Thus, at the end of July, in the White view, Tukhachevsky's Fifth Army was trapped between two White armies, one to the north and the other to the south, near Chelyabinsk. But Tukhachevsky pressed ahead relentlessly. Helped by Communists from Chelyabinsk, the 242nd and 243rd Red regiments fought their way into the city on July 24. At the same time, the Whites launched their pincer attack. Bloody fighting continued for four days, but by July 29, the outcome was clear. Tukhachevsky had gambled and won. The Whites again were in retreat.[57]

Writing about the battle more than a decade later, Tukhachevsky seemed to indicate that all his problems were not caused by the Whites. According to him, at the height of the battle on July 27, the Soviet High Command had rearranged the front, transferring units of the Second Army to the Southeastern Front and directing that the Third Army take over the Second Army's sector around Tumen and Tobolsk. Given the wide dispersal of the Red armies—the First Army was near Orenburg and the Third Army near Ekaterinburg—it was natural that the Whites would try to dislodge the Red force nearest their main concentration, the Fifth Army. But at this crucial stage the Bolshevik leadership instituted another of its sweeping, frequent changes in the army command structure. As usual, this change had been preceded by rancorous debate. At one stage Trotsky had resigned as war commissar, but Lenin talked him into resuming the post. Vatsetis, however, was replaced as commander in chief by Sergei Kamenev, which caused a new shuffle of command on the Eastern Front. A new sector, the Turkestan Front, was created in the south, with Frunze named commander. The new commander in the east was a Latvian named Vladimir A. Ol'derroge.

The noble-born Ol'derroge had served in the Russo-Japanese War, had commanded a division in World War I, and had occupied various staff positions in the tsarist army, all with notably undistinguished results. Such was his record that Lenin described him as "scum."[58] "It is hard to imagine where Trotsky found such people," snapped Tukhachevsky later. "Ol'derroge was a man whom nobody knew and who at best was a mediocrity. He did everything possible to frustrate our pursuit of Kolchak."[59] Years later, the events at Chelyabinsk still angered him.

According to Tukhachevsky, on August 20, 1919, the Fifth Army, having crossed the Tobol River, was advancing on Petropavlovsk. The cossack areas, on the right flank of the army as it was pushing ahead, made it necessary to take special steps to protect that flank. As rapidly as possible, a fortified area—the Red nomenclature for a strong defensive zone—was set up in the Troitsky-Kustanaisky area, and steps were taken to establish another fortified area around Kokchatev. Tukhachevsky says that the main forces of the Fifth Army were to advance along the Zverynogolovskaya-Petropavlovsk road, thereby ensuring that the main body of the Whites, in their retreat, were firmly anchored to the railroad line. Such moves would make it possible to deal with any trouble the cossacks on the right flank might have created. Ol'derroge, however, ordered a complete regrouping. The main forces of the Fifth Army were to be concentrated near the railway line and were to attack the Whites frontally. The Zverynogolovskaya road was to be secured with minimal forces. There was a fierce exchange of telegrams, but Ol'derroge insisted on the regrouping as ordered.

"The Whites made use of that mistake," wrote Tukhachevsky. "They nailed down units of the Fifth Army from the front. And they moved two infantry divisions and the newly formed cavalry group of General Domozhirov against the Fifth Army's right flank and its rear, from the south."

The Whites, however, were unable to close the pincer.

Tukhachevsky goes on: "By concentrating some troops in a salient to the right of the Fifth Army, it became possible to weaken the enemy counterattack, but nonetheless, the Fifth Army, while fighting stubbornly, had to retreat during the month of September and finally to withdraw behind the Tobol River."[60]

Tukhachevsky's squabbles were not only with Ol'derroge. His flamboyant manner and dress stood out among the prim conservatism of the former tsarist officers and the gray Communist functionaries. Genrikh K. Eykhe, a hero of the October Revolution and now commander of Tukhachevsky's 26th Division, later recalled meeting Tukhachevsky at Chelyabinsk as the battle was about to start. "As always," he wrote, "he was in his parade dress—yellow high boots, raspberry-colored riding breeches, a red field shirt and green helmet." Over the years, Tukhachevsky and Eykhe were never close friends, and there is no mistaking the scorn in the description.[61]

Even while the retreat from the Tobol was in progress, the Reds had begun building up for the next attack. Every ablebodied male in the Chelyabinsk area was conscripted. The new troops were given battle training and a cavalry division was formed. Winter uniforms were laid in. Ammunition was stockpiled. New and more complete means of communication were arranged. Engineers got ready for a second crossing of the Tobol.

Elsewhere on the front, the Reds had made some spectacular advances. On July 3, Perm once again came under the Red flag. At that stage, the Whites were dealt a stunning blow; the Immortals Regiment of General Gajda defected en masse to the Reds. Ekaterinburg, which the Immortals had been defending, lay open to the Reds. It fell on July 17.[62]

All along the front, the fighting had been ferocious. In the battle for Ufa, which had fallen to the Reds on June 11, the Communist army lost 6,000 killed and wounded. That was more than made up for, however, by the 25,000 White prisoners taken. Feelings were bitter; treason, suspected or real, brought instant death, often by hanging, with a telegraph pole for a gallows.[63]

The Reds were weary, but their state was nothing compared with Kolchak's. As if his enemies were not giving him enough trouble, he was also at the mercy of his friends, especially of Ataman Grigor Mikhailovich Semyonov, the leader of the Don cossacks and a sort of front for the Japanese interventionist forces.[64]

Semyonov was only three years older than Tukhachevsky, but was as unlike the Red commander in appearance and manner as it was possible to be. Stocky, dark, and with piercing black eyes, he favored a fearsome mustache. At his peak he mustered an army of 60,000 men that included Buryats, Yakuts, cossacks, and other assorted Mongols. His depredations took him from western Siberia to the Far East, and no other unit in the Civil War matched the ataman's troops or those of his nominal subordinate, Kalmykov, in the horrors of their debauchery and villainy. In June 1920, Sayres, secretary of the American Railway Corps, described him this way:

General Semyonov is a Buriat, a half Tatar and a robber. He was financed by the Japanese and the Allies. His train lay alongside mine for 90 days and I knew the gentleman quite well, and when you hear stories about the nationalization of Russian women—all of which have been disproved—I want to tell you this—and I do not think you are going to see it reported in the newspapers—General Semyonov had 30 of the most beautiful women that I ever saw held in his train. He ran back and forth over the Trans-Siberian Railroad, robbing and pillaging. He robbed the Chinese banks and customs houses. In three days' time in Chita, he took 60 million rubles and stripped every man, woman and child, taking every bit of valuables that they had about them. I was there at the time.[65]

More than sixty years later, even with the knowledge of Hitler's Germany, it is not easy to understand the barbarity of a wild man like Semyonov. To the bloodthirsty cossack leader, anyone who was not wholeheartedly for him was against him and deserved to die. At Chita, he set up wholesale execution camps. On August 19, 1919, at one of those citadels of horror, 1,500 Red prisoners of war who had been jammed into 52 boxcars for the journey from the west, were unloaded and massacred, apparently for a kind of macabre sport.[66]

As the conditions behind the White lines deteriorated, the Semyonovs and Kalmykovs grew bolder. Any pretense of orderliness and civilization had disappeared. Refugees crowded the little towns. The roads were axle-deep in mud. Soldiers and their families begged door-to-door for food. Officers' and soldiers' wives alike turned to prostitution to get bread. Children were often abandoned by their parents, the younger ones left to perish of exposure and hunger by the roadside.

Throughout the summer, the dimensions of Kolchak's disaster grew. By the end of September, the Czech Legion, the one segment of the anti-Bolshevik army that still held some semblance of order, announced that it was leaving Siberia and would evacuate through Vladivostok. Kolchak's fury was immense and useless. His subordinates, including General Gajda, were plotting mutiny. In a stormy confrontation, Kolchak finally dismissed Gajda. According to one account of the encounter, during this meeting Kolchak broke an inkwell and several pencils in his frustration. Gajda's dismissal, coming so soon after he had been named commander of the Western and Siberian White armies, was the final blow to White morale.[67]

In contrast, the Reds were quickly building up their strength in the east, although there had been crises in other places, especially when Yudenich penetrated to the outskirts of Petrograd and when Denikin once more threatened to break through to Moscow in the south.

On October 14, Tukhachevsky's Fifth Army, aligned with the Third Army, was ready to return to the offensive from Chelyabinsk. Tukhachevsky tells how the attack developed:

> On this occasion, the forces were grouped in a manner consistent with the circumstances. The Fifth Army's main attack group was on the right flank. Its task was to defeat the left flank of the Whites and to secure the retreat of their main forces north of the railway line. The advance developed very successfully. The Whites were defeated and disorganized. Petropavlovsk was captured on October 27. Constant pursuit was organized but here Ol'derroge again messed things up. The newly formed cavalry division of the First Army had been sent into Kolchak's rear between Omsk and Tatarsk. Ol'derroge countermanded that maneuver and sent the division into the Kokchetav fortified area, even though the Fifth Army sent an entire rifle division in that direction and despite the fact that, at that time, the Kokchetav area presented no special danger. If we had had cavalry in the fighting near Omsk, it is quite likely that Kolchak could not have left and in any event we would have captured much sooner his trains with military stores.[68]

Despite Ol'derroge's timidity, Kolchak's days were numbered. On November 14, Tukhachevsky led his victorious Fifth Army into the former White capital of Omsk, having advanced 375 miles in the previous month. Kolchak's army began to disintegrate further under the frontal assault of the Fifth Army and the nibbling of partisans on its flanks. By December 4, Ivan Smirnov, the commissar with the army, could report to Trotsky: "Kolchak has lost his army. There will be no more battles. The tempo of the pursuit is such that by the 20th of December, Barnaul and Novonikolayevsky will be in our hands."[69]

Smirnov had underestimated the pace. By December 22, the Fifth Army, now joined by the Third Army, was in Tomsk, and by the end of the first week in January 1920, the Reds were in Krasnoyarsk. For 247 days, despite setbacks, Tukhachevsky's men had been on the march, averaging an advance of ten miles a day in horrendous conditions over a distance roughly equal to that between New York and San Francisco—or between Moscow and Paris.

It was all over for Kolchak, the haughty despot who had aspired to replace the Romanovs as ruler of all Russia. Early in February, he was arrested by what passed for civil authorities in Irkutsk. Within days, real control of the city passed to the local Soviet of Workers and Peasants. Control of Kolchak and his paramour, Anna Timareva, who had abandoned her naval officer husband to follow Kolchak from the Crimea to Siberia, passed too. After a brief trial, Kolchak was executed by firing squad on February 7, 1920, and his corpse was slipped under the ice of the frozen Angara River. He made one last request to the commander of the firing squad. "Would you be so good," he asked, "as to get a message to my wife in Paris, to say that I bless my son?" The Red officer was noncommittal. "If I remember," he said.[70]

The exact cost of Kolchak's misbegotten campaign to conquer Russia will never be known. But more than a million people had perished, either as members of the opposing armies or as victims of atrocities or other effects of the war. The manner of death was almost always violent. Groups trying to flee by sled were marooned when their horses collapsed, leaving the passengers to perish in the cold that frequently went to 40 degrees below zero. Women caught by marauding soldiers become brigands were stripped, raped, and left to die. Typhus killed thousands. Prisoners were shot out of hand. Starving men ate dead horses when they could find them; snow or bark when they couldn't. Corruption, the vast distances and incoherent communications of Siberia, insubordination, jealousy, and confusion and incompetence among his own generals and those of his French, British, and Japanese allies all played a part in Kolchak's downfall. But his own intransigence and folly did not help. He really was a martial fish out of water. As Semyonov later said: "For us, an admiral is a kind of civilian."[71]

Some of the White officers, it is true, had been involved purely out of a sense of duty. The most notable of these was the heroic Kappel. But fate was no less kind to him. During the retreat from Omsk to Irkutsk, he fell through the ice of a river, caught a severe chill, and suffered frostbitten legs. Some weeks later he died; his distraught soldiers carried his body back to Harbin, where he was buried.

But that did not diminish the achievements of Tukhachevsky and his men. Their army too had to conquer disease, cold, hunger, distance, and incompetence in command. But the Reds were sustained by other, more potent factors. They believed in their cause, that it was just; and in the end, because of that, they triumphed.

They were perhaps surprised by the feats of their troops and their young commander. But the Whites were even more stunned. After the fall of Omsk, Kolchak's elderly subordinate Rimsky-Korsakov was brought before the commander of the Fifth Red Army. He stared at the boyish general. "You—the army commander, you are . . . Tukhachevsky!"

"That's right," responded Tukhachevsky. "Nearly all the generals ran away from us. We had to be content with lieutenants and captains. I am Army Commander Tukhachevsky."[72]

Tukhachevsky was not in at the end of the campaign. Soon after the capture of Omsk, he had been transferred to new duties on the Southern Front, his command being taken over by Eykhe. Eykhe was to survive a bout with typhus later in the campaign and go on to great political prominence in Stalinist Russia. But he, too, eventually fell to the firing squad.

The effects of the campaign against Kolchak were to be felt widely in the future Red Army. The young men who served under Tukhachevsky and Frunze were among the most brilliant military leaders modern Russia developed. Men like the Armenian Gai— his real name was Gaik Bzhiskian; the Latvian-born Robert P. Eideman, who had first led partisan units in Siberia and then headed regular Red Army units; the Jew Boris Feldman, who had met Tukhachevsky in the Muraviev affair; the Lithuanian Vitovt Putna, a trained artist turned soldier; and others eventually formed a group around the dominant figure of Tukhachevsky. And in the lesser ranks involved in the campaign was the future marshal Rodion Malinovsky, who fought Kolchak as a sergeant.

They were generally former tsarist underofficers, well trained in military affairs but also educated and cultured men interested in the arts and the world outside Soviet Russia. They were to become professional soldiers, dedicated to molding a professional Red Army. They would eventually come into conflict with the rough-and-ready, up-from-the-ranks group that was later associated with Klementi Voroshilov and Semyon Budenny. Like their hero and leader Tukhachevsky, most of them would fall victim to the executioner before they were 50.

4

MORE CIVIL WAR: THE DEFEAT OF DENIKIN

AS TUKHACHEVSKY'S ARMY had been plunging into the vastness of Siberia, other Red armies had not been achieving such successes. The most dangerous situation was in the south, where the food supplies of the Ukraine and the coal of the Donbas were in peril. Denikin had launched a determined offensive in May 1919, just as the Vatsetis-Kamenev dispute was at its height and just as Tukhachevsky's drive to finish off Kolchak was beginning in the Urals.

Anton Ivanovich Denikin was born in the little Polish town of Wloclawek, near Warsaw, in 1872. His father had been pensioned off from the tsar's army in 1869 and two years later, at the age of 64, had married for the second time. The elder Denikin's pension was small, and given his background, it was certain almost from his son's birth that finances would dictate that he would follow his father into the military. The death of the father in 1885 worsened the family's situation, but in 1890, young Denikin entered the Kiev officer candidate school. It was a far cry from the Alexandrovsky Academy where young Tukhachevsky and the other sons of the aristocracy were trained. Students at the school existed on the same rations as ordinary soldiers and received the paltry pay of the lowest-level privates. But it was from such schools that the bulk of the new Russian officer class came: men like Denikin, Kornilov, and Alekseyev, who would later become the leaders of the White cause. After completing the two-year course, Denikin received his commission as a second lieutenant and was stationed in the Polish city of Biala, 100 miles from Warsaw.[1]

After entering the boring life of garrison duty in the Polish provinces, broken only by a brief spell in St. Petersburg, during which he won a reputation as something of a troublemaker, Denikin served in the Far East during the Russo-Japanese War. The young captain became known for his bravery and for his astuteness as a staff officer. During the 1905 Revolution, Denikin's sympathies were with the monarchy, but he sided with the reformist policies of Count Sergei I. Witte, rather than with the far leftists such as Trotsky. After further garrison duty, Denikin returned to front-line service at the outbreak of World War I. He was posted to the staff of General A. A. Brusilov's Eighth Army on the Southwestern Front, to fight against the Austro-Hungarians. During the war, Denikin increased his reputation for personal bravery and strategic acumen in an army that otherwise was best known for its failures and ineptitude. Then came the revolution. The upheaval in Russia was tumultuous, but it was even worse in the army. The chaos catapulted Denikin to new heights. Sixteen days after the tsar abdicated, Denikin was named chief of staff to the new supreme commander, General Alekseyev. But that did not last long. On May 22, 1917, General Alekseyev was dismissed and his place taken by Brusilov, who was more amenable to the policies of the Kerensky regime.

Denikin returned to combat as the commander of the Western Front. But the revolutionary fervor had caught the army, disrupting the authority of the command. The government's decision to stage an offensive for which the soldiers had no heart merely worsened the chaos. Brusilov was dismissed and his place was taken by Kornilov. The soldiers mutinied and arrested their officers, Denikin among them. Further upheavals followed in quick order. Kornilov and Kerensky became antagonists, the dispute culminating in the general's abortive attempt at a putsch.

Then came the October Revolution, and it was clear to Denikin and the other generals that if they were to preserve anything of the old Russia, the time had come to act. Denikin and his close associates broke out—or were freed—from their prison, and by various routes assembled in the Don region to organize what became the anti-Bolshevik Volunteer Army.[2]

The events of the preceding years did not promise well for the new army. But, at least in the beginning, it was a much more cohesive force than that commanded by Admiral Kolchak. For example, the chain of command was more easily established, with Kornilov at its head. As a result, the army quickly went on the offensive. But there was soon a setback. A Red artillery shell landed on Kornilov's headquarters outside Ekaterinodar in April 1918, mortally wounding the White commander.

His successor was Anton Denikin. The new commander was a peppery little man, adept in military matters and, despite his belief that Russia's political system needed a drastic overhaul, a stern opponent of what he saw as the anarchistic policies of Lenin and Trotsky. Personally he was honest but, like Kolchak, he was to be frustrated by the freebooting ways of some of his subordinates and by the anti-Jewish views of many of them. Denikin was a reformer, but eventually he was defeated by much the same round of jealousy, insubordination, vacillation, corruption, and brutality on the part of his colleagues and allies that doomed all the White armies. While the depredations of Semyonov and Kalmakov terrorized Siberia, in the south the Ukrainian cossack chief, Semyon V. Petlura, and others like him rampaged across the country, shifting allegiance as the tide of success ebbed and flowed. There was a vicious anti-Jewish aspect to Petlura's campaigns; in the town of Proskurov, for example, two of his subordinates were said to have robbed 6,500 Jews, massacred them, and dumped them into a common grave.[3]

Denikin was also beset by uncertainty, contradiction, and eventually desertion by the British and the French who had originally encouraged him. He was certainly more politically aware than the leaden Kolchak, and his slogan "Russia, One and Indivisible" was attractive to the Russians among his followers. But understandably it raised suspicions among the country's other ethnic groups, not least among Ukrainians, with whom he was constantly involved, and the Poles, who stayed neutral but on the side of the Bolsheviks as long as it suited them.

The better terrain of the south provided much more mobility and flexibility for the armies. And the Whites, at least in the beginning, were fighting a popular war; patriotism—some of it Ukrainian rather than Russian, oddly enough—brought Denikin many allies. For though the southerners were divided in patriotic loyalties, they were certainly united in their hatred for atheistic Bolshevism.

Red mistakes also helped Denikin. The kulaks of the south had no sympathy for the Bolsheviks' plans concerning the land. They and their town cousins had even less liking for the terror campaigns of Dzerzhinsky and the Cheka. (They didn't like the policy of Denikin's regime much either; the Whites returned many confiscated estates to their prewar owners.)

But, for one brief season, triumph seemed to be within Denikin's grasp. The offensive began in May 1919. With British and French assistance, Denikin had built up his army to 180,000 troops, relatively well supplied with rifles, about 30 artillery pieces, and even a handful of British tanks and armored cars. His strategy was to thrust into the Red front from two directions. The main part of the army, led by Denikin, was to take the direct route, first to Kharkov and then across the plains to Moscow. The second wing, commanded by Baron Wrangel, was to circle east toward Tsaritsyn, hoping to link up with Kolchak in the east. In the center, a body of Don cossacks led by General E. M. Mamontov was assigned to harass and harry any weaknesses in the Red front.

Wrangel and Mamontov were as unlike each other as they were both unlike Denikin, and while their activities would bring initial success to the Whites, they would also help to sow the seeds of the eventual White disintegration. Whereas Wrangel tended to look with all due deliberation at the whole front, Mamontov and his cavalry dashed in lightning raids all over the place. One such raid, into Tambov Province, resulted in an unlikely link with Social Revolutionary insurgents who were to play an important part in Tukhachevsky's future career as a Red commander.

Wrangel was 40 years old in 1919. He came from an aristocratic family, and like Tukhachevsky had begun his career in the Imperial Guards. In physical appearance he was an imposing man, well over six feet tall and ramrod straight. He was fiercely anti-Bolshevik, yet he had little enthusiasm for the reformist tendencies and what he saw as vacillation on the part of Denikin and the commander's immediate aides. Wrangel, almost alone among the White leaders, saw the advantages that could come from closer coordination of all the White fronts. The failure to achieve that coordination would enable the Reds, with their interior lines of communication, to move forces from trouble spot to trouble spot, and finally to achieve victory.

The initial White operations in the south went exceedingly well. On May 24, 1919, Denikin's men burst through the Red screen south of Kharkov. On June 25, the White troops led by General A. P. Kutepov entered the city of Kharkov. The White cavalry led by General Skhuro had seized Ekaterinoslav. And almost simultaneously Wrangel had captured Tsaritsyn. Then Denikin set out to widen his base. On August 2, his forces took Odessa, and eight days later his men marched into Kiev.

Denikin was greatly helped by far distant events. At this time, General Yudenich was preparing an offensive aimed at Petrograd. The Red leadership was close to panic. Their fear was heightened on September 25, when White sympathizers set off a bomb at Bolshevik Party headquarters in Moscow. But, as so often in the past, the peripatetic Trotsky came to the rescue. He hastened to Petrograd and led the routing of Yudenich from the outskirts of Peter the Great's capital. Yudenich was interned in Estonia.

The removal of the threat in the north, however, did not end the recriminations among the Red leadership, particularly in the south. That was where the greatest danger now seemed to lie as the Whites plunged forward. By October 14, the vanguard of Denikin's army had reached the city of Orel, just 150 miles south of Moscow. Because of this rapid advance and because the Red counterattacks continued to fail, the search for scapegoats on the Red side intensified. Vatsetis was the most prominent target. As Trotsky goes to inordinate lengths to point out, Vatsetis had been sniped at almost continuously. Trotsky blames most of the backbiting on Stalin, and there is good reason to believe that even at that stage, when he was a relative second ranker among the Bolshevik hierarchy, Stalin was indeed the instigator. But he was not alone; the younger military leaders, Tukhachevsky among them, thought Vatsetis was too timid, too unimaginative, too slow.

On July 3, Trotsky gave in. In his biography of Stalin, the Soviet war commissar described how Vatsetis was dismissed. The description provides a concise, albeit biased, picture of the conflicting power centers that were already beginning to form in the Red apparatus.

> In the middle of May our advancing and in large measure exhausted army clashed with the fresh troops of Denikin and began to fall back. We lost everything we had gained and over and above that all of the Ukraine, which recently had been liberated. Meantime, on the Eastern Front, where the former colonel, Kamenev, was in command, with Smilga and Lashevich as members of the Revolutionary Council of War, the situation had improved to such an extent and matters were proceeding so well that I gave up going there altogether and almost forgot what Kamenev looked like. Intoxicated with their success, Smilga, Lashevich and Gusev carried their commander on their shoulders, drank *Bruderschaft* with him and wrote the most enthusiastic reports about him to Moscow.[4]

After describing the opposition of Vatsetis (and himself) to a continued offensive in the Urals, which Kamenev, Tukhachevsky, and the other Eastern Front commanders ignored successfully, Trotsky goes to describe how he finally agreed to the replacement of Vatsetis as commander in chief. But, as Trotsky takes great pleasure in pointing out, the appointment of Sergei Kamenev did not end the Red miseries in the south. New disasters were soon to follow.

The enduring weaknesses of the Red Southern Front continued to be exposed. Some of the factors that bedeviled the Bolsheviks, it is true, also affected the Whites. The nationalistic, if not anarchistic, activities of the Ukrainian leader Petlura and the peasant chieftain Nestor Makhno were of particular significance. Their shifting loyalties—fighting whichever Russians, Red or White, seemed to be threatening their narrow interests at the time—caused inherent instability to both the major disputants. But the chief Red weakness was the lack of a strong cavalry group to oppose the cossack army led by General Mamontov. Between August 10 and 20, 1919, Mamontov's horde—in their behavior the Don cossacks were as much brigands as soldiers—had pierced the Red lines to occupy Kozlov and Tambov, causing considerable apprehension in the Red command. Although the arms they left in Tambov were to bolster the Antonov uprising there two years later, elsewhere Mamontov's incursions backfired on the White cause; the looting and rapine that was loosed on what was essentially a neutral population helped convince the peasants that life under the Reds was preferable to that under the Whites.

But at that stage, the tide seemed to have turned in favor of Denikin. So much so that the Poles, who had been confined mostly to the sidelines, sent a delegation to Denikin's headquarters at Taganrog. The consultation was inconclusive, but its very occurrence was psychologically upsetting to the Bolshevik leadership. A combined Polish-White offensive could well have doomed the Soviet republic. Even Bela Kun's proclamation of a Hungarian Soviet state on March 21, 1919, and Communist successes in Bavaria offered less hope of being a counterpoint to the threat posed by Denikin than they did of becoming distracting nuisances.

By the end of September 1919, the Reds were forced to face the realities of the situation. They therefore undertook a complete change of command on the Southern Front. One of the first tasks was to remove the Polish threat. This was done in a series of secret consultations between the Kremlin and the Pilsudski government. The net result was that the Reds were able to move troops from the sector facing the Poles to the area facing Denikin.[5]

But once again a division of opinion in the Red command upset the execution of a counteroffensive against Denikin. The new commander in chief, Kamenev, had developed a plan to attack Denikin's apparent principal source of strength, Mamontov's Don cossack army. But by the time, in early August, when the attack was to be launched, the main thrust of Denikin's advance had shifted from the Don to the Kuban. As Trotsky pointed out, to concentrate the fighting in the Don would only antagonize the Don population without stopping Denikin's advances elsewhere.[6] The quarrel in the Red leadership over the correct strategy for the Southern Front was bitter in the extreme. Aleksandr I. Yegorov, the actual front commander, was openly insubordinate, refusing to carry out Kamenev's plan. Trotsky once again offered his resignation as war commissar to try to get the plan changed. The bitterness among the Red leaders at this time can be judged from the fact that in July, Vatsetis, the former commander in chief, was accused of treason and was arrested. He was later freed but relegated to an inconsequential position.

It was in this period that Tukhachevsky handed over command of the Fifth Army on the Eastern Front to Eykhe and returned to Moscow to collect his honors; for his victorious campaign he was awarded the Order of the Red Banner.

A bizarre tragedy then befell the young hero. From time to time, he had been visited at the front by his sisters and his young wife, Marucia. On the most recent occasion, despite the rigorous penalties for infringement of smuggling laws, she was returning to her parents carrying some sacks of flour, rice, and other hard-to-come-by foods. In normal circumstances, the wife of such a high commander of the Red Army would not have been subjected to police searches, but for some reason her baggage was inspected and the contraband discovered. As scandal broke over her unfortunate head—a scandal that was apparently beyond her endurance—Marucia committed suicide. In their private car on his special train, she shot herself with her husband's pistol.[7]

Following this unhappy incident, Tukhachevsky was left to cool his heels in Moscow. The brilliant success against Kolchak seemed to count for nothing. Despite his frequent pleas for return to an active command, he remained on the sidelines in the capital. And when he eventually did go south, he was very much an outsider. Trotsky reports receiving a plaintive message from Tukhachevsky.

> Kursk, January 19, 1920
>
> To the Chairman of the Revolutionary Council of War of the Republic, Chairman Trotsky, Moscow.
>
> I appeal to you with the urgent plea to free me from unemployment. For almost three weeks I have been for no good reason at the headquarters of the Southwestern Front and have done nothing for almost two months. I can find out neither the cause of the delay nor can I secure a further appointment. If during the almost two years that I have commanded various armies I have demonstrated any merit at all, I beg you to give me the opportunity to apply my talents to actual work, and if none such can be found at the front, then

let me have something to do in transportation or in the Commissariat of War.

Army Commander Tukhachevsky[8]

Trotsky implies that Stalin, who was de facto in charge of the front, was to blame for Tukhachevsky's inactivity, but offers no concrete evidence. However, the clique centered on Voroshilov was already forming at Stalin's back. This group had little in common with an aristocrat—who was little more than a boy—fond of Beethoven and modern poetry. Tukhachevsky was an outsider. And Stalin had little use for outsiders.

On October 15, 1919, the Central Committee, acting on Trotsky's suggestions, adopted 13 decrees for the conduct of the war in the south. But there was considerable delay in implementing them. One reason was that matters were going badly for the Reds on the Caucasian Front, where Budenny's cavalry was tied down. Typhus was also taking its toll of the Red troops. In view of the serious situation in the Caucasus, the Central Committee decided to move Stalin there. But Stalin dodged the command, preferring to stay in the Southwest.

The Red offensive finally got under way, and on October 20, 1919, the Red troops led by another young commander, Yeronim P. Uborevich, managed to recapture Orel. Four days later, Budenny and part of the Red Eighth Army forced their way into Voronezh. The Red cause was given a fillip in November when the Ukrainian Petlura—ever the weathervane—shifted his allegiance to the Bolsheviks. The time for decisive action against Denikin seemed to have come. On November 14, the Politburo issued one of its periodic fiats that had little relation to the actual events. It was necessary, said the eminences of the Kremlin, to press on to capture Kursk. By November 18, the task had been completed.[9]

Voroshilov and Budenny played a major part in the Red successes achieved at this time. Whatever might be said about Voroshilov later—either as a military strategist of doubtful capacity, or as a political toady to Stalin in the worst days of the dictator's purges—in the campaign against Denikin his ideas were undoubtedly correct. He saw that the Red Army, composed mostly of infantry units, lacked the mobility of the enemy.[10] That doesn't mean his initial proposed response was entirely correct.

But it was tried. Voroshilov suggested the formulation in which every infantry unit had a small squad of mounted troops to conduct reconnaissance. The idea proved inadequate, and eventually the Reds decided to form their own cavalry army.

The result was the First Cavalry Corps, led by Budenny. One of his brigade commanders was a former barrelmaker from Bessarabia, Semyon K. Timoshenko; and attached to Timoshenko's group was a former tsarist NCO, 22-year-old Georgi K. Zhukov. And in a very junior role, a low-ranking commissar, was a former Donbas coal miner, Nikita S. Khrushchev.[11]

At the time of the Denikin campaign, Budenny was in his late thirties. He had been born in 1883 to a peasant family that had moved from Voronezh Province to Platovskaya, near the Manich River, so he knew the area well. He had been recruited into the army in 1903 and had taken part in the Russo-Japanese War. After that war, he served in the Primorsky Dragoon Regiment, and in 1907 he was sent to the Cavalry School in St. Petersburg. There he received training in breaking riding horses. Budenny graduated first in his class and seemed on the way to achieving his ambition—to become a civilian riding instructor at the end of his military career. However, he returned to his regiment as a noncommissioned officer. With the outbreak of World War I in 1914, he was transferred to the Seversky Dragoons. Ironically, in one of those twists so frequent in the Civil War, his platoon commander was a Tatar, Lieutenant Kuchuk Ulagai, later to be one of Denikin's most trusted generals. During the early stages of the war, Budenny's regiment was moved from the Western Front to the Caucasus and the fighting against the Turks. Budenny received all the awards of the Order of St. George available to a common soldier for the bravery he showed in that campaign. With the rise of the Bolsheviks, the opportunistic Budenny soon switched his allegiance and quickly rose to prominence in the Red Army.[12]

He was the army's most famous cavalry commander, head initially of the First Cavalry Division and later of the First Cavalry Corps. Formed for the most part from tsarist troopers, the First Cavalry Division was a fearsome group. And among them, Budenny was the fiercest. It was said that he did not so much command his troops as impress his personality on them by being able to outride, outshoot, and outdrink them. To Budenny's commissar, the steady, plodding Voroshilov, the cavalryman's indifference to the canons of Bolshevism was a matter of some concern.

Budenny's troopers overran Taganrog, Denikin's former headquarters, on January 6, 1920, and Rostov on January 8. Harking back to the cossack traditions, the Red cavalry engaged in a fury of plunder and pillaging in Rostov. Denikin was able to get clear and regroup. The Whites took up a position near the town of Bataisk, about six miles south of Rostov. The terrain— Bataisk was on the heights above the Don River—and Denikin's artillery made a frontal assault most difficult. Marshy lowlands along the river also hampered cavalry mobility.

Denikin made a desperate effort to rally his forces. He had suffered a setback but, given the confusion in the opposing command, he was far from defeated. In a speech to the Don cossack *krug*, or legislature, on January 16, he quoted Trotsky's assessment of the situation:

> Lack of supplies, disrupted communications, hunger, cold, the secret and open discontent of the masses with ourselves— all threaten with consequences which our power, already strained to the limit, will not be able to overcome. Our enemy, too, is completely exhausted, and the whole question is now which of us will be able to survive the winter. We are in no condition to fight and neither are they. For this reason, we must take the offensive at all costs.[13]

Denikin said, with the benefit of hindsight, "As matters stood, the material conditions on either side were identical. Victory depended on the spirit."[14]

Even as Denikin was finally wooing the cossacks with promises of land reform, Trotsky and his colleagues were rearranging the Southern Front to begin the offensive they, too, felt was essential. To formalize what was already the case, the front was divided into two sections. The Southwestern Front, from the Polish border to around Kursk, was placed under Yegorov's command. The Caucasus Front, from the Kursk area in an arc to the Caspian Sea, was led by V. I. Shorin. In the center of the eastern half of the arc was Budenny's cavalry. And facing Budenny was the White bastion that became known as the Bataisk Cork. Tukhachevsky, no longer on the sidelines, was named to command the 13th Army on Budenny's right flank, although it is doubtful that he actually assumed the post.

Vasily Ivanovich Shorin had joined the tsar's army the year before Tukhachevsky was born. He was a military man of the old school who, after relatively distinguished service in World War I, had joined the Bolshevik side in September 1918. As commander of the Second Army in the summer of 1919, he had proved competent but far from brilliant. His cautious, unimaginative tactics were soon to cause a collision with the fiery Budenny.

During the reorganization of the Red command, the Don River, which had been a major obstacle to the advance, froze solid. Shorin wasted no time in trying to take advantage of this change. His first objective was to remove the Bataisk Cork, which posed a persistent threat of a White breakthrough.

On January 17, 1920—while Tukhachevsky was apparently lingering morosely at Kursk—Shorin launched Budenny's troopers in a frontal assault on Bataisk. It was unsuccessful. A second attempt was made on January 19, again without dislodging the Whites. Further attacks were mounted on January 20 and 21, all ending in failure. In retrospect, Shorin's plan was extremely ill-conceived. The terrain was highly unsuitable for cavalry maneuvers. Even though the river was frozen, Bataisk was surrounded by swamps that were still treacherous for large bodies of horsemen. Budenny and Voroshilov were appalled at what seemed an obvious waste of the Red Army's precious cavalry. They wanted no more of Shorin's plan. Shorin replied angrily that the debacle was their fault; they had dissipated the strength of their army in the sacking of Rostov. Budenny and Voroshilov persisted in their demand for a different maneuver, an attack that would circle around Bataisk. But Shorin was insistent. And on January 28, the cavalry again charged Bataisk. This time there was some success, but the weakened horsemen could not follow up their advantage.[15]

Thus, when Mamontov counterattacked on January 29, the Reds once again had to give ground. The White cavalry leader followed up this initial success, and on February 1 and 2 drove the Reds back across the Don and the Manich.

Budenny and Voroshilov were furious, and sent an angry message to the Revolutionary Military Council of the Republic:

Since January 12, in accordance with the last directives of the Caucasian Front command, the cavalry has been thrown into battle alone, without the general offensive of all the armies. In the fierce battles between January 12 and February 2, the cavalry lost 3,000 men. . . . Urgent measures are needed to strengthen the infantry in the Manich area as is the urgent change to an offensive on the entire front. The Red Cavalry is losing blood in unequal battles. The cavalry has been reduced to half its normal size and is worthless. Only urgent and extreme measures can save the situation. All my appeals to the front command have remained unanswered. I am awaiting urgent orders.

Budenny
Voroshilov[16]

On January 26, the Revolutionary Military Council of the Republic took urgent and extreme action. Shorin was unceremoniously dumped as the front commander and sent to a minor post in Siberia. His replacement was Mikhail Nikolaevich Tukhachevsky.[17] The choice must have been somewhat of a surprise to Tukhachevsky. Earlier in January, during discussions of the troubled Caucasus Front, he had suggested that Frunze be recalled from Turkestan and placed in charge of the fighting in the south.[18]

Tukhachevsky's new command was not in good shape. The quarrels between Budenny and Shorin were but one instance of the divided nature of the front. Another major incident threatened the stability of the cavalry. On February 3, a commissar recently sent from Moscow, V. I. Mikeledze, was murdered in mysterious circumstances. The subsequent inquiry implicated the cavalry commander, B. M. Dumenko, and some of his associates in a plot that would have betrayed the cavalry to the Whites. After a quick trial, they were shot.[19]

Denikin, having repulsed several Red attacks during January, was preparing to go onto the offensive about the middle of February. His main objective was to break through the Red line and sweep in the direction of Novocherkassk. With Nestor Makhno causing trouble for the Red Southwestern Front, particularly for the 14th Army, and with the Ukrainians likely to swing allegiance again, a breakthrough into the middle Don might well have been a terminal blow for the Bolsheviks.[20]

This threat from Denikin, which was obvious to the Reds, and the other factors on the Caucasus Front were causing deep concern in Moscow. With unaccustomed asperity, Lenin ordered the reluctant Stalin, who was in the southwest, to expedite the sending of reinforcements to the Southwestern Front to help Tukhachevsky. Stalin answered:

> It is not clear to me why the concern about the Caucasian Front is imposed first of all on me. In the order of things the responsibility for strengthening the Caucasian Front rests entirely with the Revolutionary Council of War of the Republic, whose members, according to my information, are in excellent health, and not with Stalin, who is overloaded with work anyway.
>
> February 20, 1920[21]

But Lenin insisted, although whether the reinforcements were sent is unknown. Coming as it did in the middle of what everyone but Stalin seemed to understand was the pivotal battle against Denikin, it was an enlightening preview of a similar and more costly episode a few months later, in the climactic days of the Russo-Polish War.

By Febuary 7, Tukhachevsky had formalized a new plan of attack, more in line with Budenny's and Voroshilov's suggestions. But he needed time to implement it, and the Whites were still threatening. On that day, therefore, Tukhachevsky telegraphed Grigory Y. Sokolnikov, commander of the Red Eighth Army, to warn him that there were indications that the Whites were regrouping and concentrating their cavalry around Bataisk and further south, near Novocherkassk.[22]

Tukhachevsky ordered his army commanders to try to hold their ground as much as possible. He instructed the obstreperous Budenny not to fight his own war by staging an independent raid into the White rear. He did suggest, however, that a diversionary raid might be launched on Homystovsk to relieve some of the pressure around Bataisk.

On February 12, Tukhachevsky telegraphed his commanders the details of a new general offensive against Denikin. It would begin at dawn on February 14.

Tukhachevsky had five armies, including Budenny's cavalry,

under his command. It was his first opportunity to plan an offensive of such scope, and while he had the advantage of being able to learn from his predecessor's mistakes, the exercise was strictly of his own making, although it was checked with Ordzhonikidze, the ranking political commissar on the front. Therefore, it is interesting to note that whereas in later years, particularly in connection with the Russo-Polish War that was soon to break out, Tukhachevsky was accused of strategic rashness, his offensive against Denikin was marked by deliberation, precision, and stern discipline.

On Tukhachevsky's right flank, in an arc along the south bank of the Don, was the Eighth Army. It was ordered to attack southward, toward Kagalnitskaya and away from Bataisk, and to occupy the banks of the Kagalnik River in the first few days of the offensive.

To the east of the Eighth Army, just north of the Manich River, was the Red Ninth Army. It was to launch its main attack southward, toward the village of Novogorovsky, and to reach the line running from Novoprotopovskaya to Novogorovsky by February 19.

Budenny's cavalry, stationed between and slightly behind the Ninth and the Tenth armies, was assigned to slash into the area where the White Don cossack and Caucasus armies met. By February 21, it was to aim for Tikhoretskaya.

The Tenth Army was ordered to cut behind the White Caucasus Army and prevent its retreat. To do that, Tukhachevsky ordered it to advance to a line running from Belayev to Belaya Glina-Uspenskaya by February 19. It was also ordered to send a planning detachment to Novo Aleksandrovskaya and Novotroistkaya to facilitate liaison with the 11th Army.

The right-flank detachments of the 11th Army—the left flank reached almost to the shore of the Caspian Sea—was to occupy the strategic cities of Stavropol and Aramvir within a few days after the offensive was launched.

Tukhachevsky's battle orders clearly defined the limits within which each army would operate. The tone of his instructions seemed designed to prevent free-lance activities on the part of any subordinate commander. He also insisted that the attack should begin simultaneously in all the affected areas and that, in accord with Suvorov's shock maxim, it should be carried out with all the available forces engaged from the outset. There was to be no excessive caution, such as keeping overlarge reserves out of action, a tendency that bedeviled Russian commands in both World War I and the Civil War.[23]

Tukhachevsky's strategy was simple. He would pin down the left flank of the White Army while thrusting through the center and preventing retreat by circling behind the Whites' right flank.

Conditions favored the sweeping maneuvers that Tukhachevsky anticipated. The rivers were frozen solid in the depth of the Russian winter. The bulk of the White forces was concentrated on the extreme left flank, lengthening and complicating their always fragile lines of communication. And, as had been the case with Kolchak, Denikin's armies had embittered a large section of the indigenous population with their forced seizures, their looting, and their cruelty. In the wake of their recent setbacks, quarrels had broken out openly among the White leaders, and there was a spreading movement to replace Denikin as supreme commander with the more vigorous Wrangel. And, finally, that old nemesis corruption had undermined the morale of the White forces. British munitions and matériel never reached the troops for which they were intended. One visitor to Denikin's soldiers at this time reported that the British had sent nurses' uniforms for the hospital staffs tending the White wounded. None of the nurses on duty, he said, had any such uniforms, although pretty girls in the White-held cities could be seen wearing what looked suspiciously like made-over nurses' outfits. As on the Eastern Front, the British had sent 300,000 army uniforms for Denikin's men, but this observer estimated that fewer than 50,000 of Denikin's 150,000 soldiers ever got their clothing. The same writer noted another weakness afflicting the Whites: poor communications and inaccurate—usually overly boastful—reports. He said that despite the frequently poor reception, the most accurate advice on the state of the fighting came from Red radio broadcasts.[24]

The battle was joined. In the initial fighting, the White Cossack Army broke through the right flank of the Ninth Red Army, threatening to doom Tukhachevsky's main thrust. But he reacted coolly, ordering the Eighth Army to close up and fill the gap. He also instructed the Tenth Army, commanded by Gai, to shift closer to the Ninth and to help bolster the troubled Red force. This apparently caused some delay in the Eighth Army's push toward Kagalnitskaya, which in turn delayed the Budenny breakthrough. Then, on February 17, the cavalry section of Gai's Tenth Army took a severe mauling at the hands of the White cossack general P. K. Popov. But the Reds counterattacked and dealt heavy losses to the White corps led by General Pavlov near Ataman-Yegorlyskaya.

Nevertheless, Tukhachevsky pressed forward with his attack. The Eighth Army, after heavy fighting, managed to get control of Rostov but was not able to hold the city for long. To distract what they had perceived as the principal Red threat to the Tikhoretskaya area, the Whites mounted a full-scale counter-offensive against Rostov, and on February 21, the Eighth Army was forced to evacuate the city. The Whites' hopes were further raised when their forces overran the towns of Aksaiskaya, Hopry, Gnilovskaya, and Temernak. But Tukhachevsky had anticipated a thrust in that direction and held to his original goal of assaulting Tikhoretskaya.

The White successes proved to be short-lived. Despite their advances, the essential part of their front was crumbling. On March 2, the Red Army finally occupied Bataisk, that stubborn symbol of their previous failures. On the same day, Tukhachevsky's men reached their main objective, the town of Tikhoretskaya. Budenny's cavalry proved the validity of Tukhachevsky's moving them from the constricting swamps and limited maneuvering room of the lower Don to the open spaces of the Manich by reaching Tikhoretskaya at the head of the Red advance.

Denikin, too, realized the importance of the loss of Tikhoretskaya. "From that time onwards," he wrote later, "our massed cavalry, sometimes doubly superior in numbers to the enemy, hovered round their flank but avoided an encounter. A prey to demoralization, it was finally merged in the common human avalanche of military detachments, unarmed crowds and huge multitudes of refugees uncontrollably rolling westward."[25]

By March 19, parts of the Red Army were transferred across the Kuban for the assault on Ekaterinodar. The White Army was now in headlong retreat toward Novorossisk. Their misfortunes were worsened by the news from the east: on January 25, Admiral Kolchak had been executed.

At the end of February, with the campaign having clearly swung in their favor, Tukhachevsky and Budenny met for the first time, at Bataisk. It was not an auspicious encounter. Budenny and Voroshilov, with the typical insouciance of the cossacks, were roving about the front, seeking provisions and forage for their unit. Almost by chance, as they were passing through Bataisk, they learned that their commander was there in his special train. They promptly decided to call on him. On entering his private car, they ran slap into him in the narrow passage leading to the main room of the car. Understandably, Tukhachevsky was taken aback. Budenny and Voroshilov hurriedly introduced themselves and received a gruff response. Tukhachevsky wanted to know why they had disregarded some aspect of his orders for the offensive. Budenny replied that circumstances, particularly the need for fodder, had not been propitious. Tukhachevsky left without saying a further word.

Budenny was surprised by the encounter. "We were astonished at the youth of the front commander," he wrote. "To my eyes he was not more than 25. He held himself stiffly, even in an intimidating way, in a way that was not natural to him." The ebullient Budenny put it down to youth, regarding Tukhachevsky merely as "a young fellow, good looking, in glowing health, but not yet accustomed to his high position."

Later Budenny and Voroshilov sought out Ordzhonikidze to seek his opinion of Tukhachevsky. He could not enlighten them much beyond saying that Tukhachevsky obviously knew how to control armies and that, unlike so many of their other former tsarist officers, he was committed to the Bolshevik cause.[26]

As his men were driven back, Denikin had moved his headquarters from Taganrog to Tikhoretskaya, and then to Ekaterinodar, and finally to Novorossisk. That was the last hope, because it was the only port in that area of the Black Sea from which an embarkation of any sizable White force could be achieved. Denikin was in a hopeless position. His subordinates were mutinous. His troops were thoroughly demoralized, wanting only to get away from the war and the disease and disaster that surrounded them. The White front was now, for all intents, cut in two. Denikin was hemmed into the Kuban, while the other half, led by General N. N. Shilling, was being beaten back into the Crimea by Petlura's Ukrainian cossacks and the Soviet Southwestern Army. As this happened, there was new pressure for the appointment of Wrangel as the White commander in chief. Wrangel added fuel to the controversy by accusing Denikin of all sorts of malfeasance but mostly accusing him and his aides of sheer incompetence. Wrangel was particularly bitter at Denikin for failing to achieve a link with Kolchak in the east. Said Wrangel: "The troops of Admiral Kolchak, treacherously abandoned by us, were defeated." Denikin was thoroughly pessimistic, as well he might have been. Writing to his wife, he said: "I am sick at heart. Surrounded by strife. What strange people to fight for power. A power which has oppressed me like a heavy yoke and tied me like a slave to a cart too heavy to pull."[27]

By the middle of March, as the southern thaw was beginning, the White Army had dissolved into complete anarchy. Tukhachevsky continued to press forward, moving across the Kuban River on March 19 to the vicinity of Ust'Labinsky and Ekaterinodar. Denikin had hoped to make a stand on the Kuban, but pell-mell the Whites—volunteers and cossacks alike—crowded into the final safety valve, the port of Novorossisk.

A colonel in the White Army described the tumult. He saw incredible confusion, with army trains crowded into the depot and innumerable carts blocking the streets so that pedestrian traffic was extremely difficult. But one of the things that most struck him was the hopelessness of the people "standing and sitting on, under and between the carts, in the midst of the abandoned guns and riderless horses." He describes the frustrating attempts to find means of evacuating his men and their equipment, only to be told that there would barely be room for the men and their small arms. Everything else would have to be destroyed. First the horses were unsaddled. Then all of the other equipment was thrown into the sea. Finally the guns were rolled slowly off the pier. Shooting could be heard nearby, followed by the heavy thud of horses falling, killed rather than be left to the Bolsheviks. He sat on the pier watching a huge fire in a warehouse nearby. Looters were running from it, carrying chocolate, rice, cans of corned beef, "everything that we lacked and is now being left to the Bolsheviks." Fires began to spread everywhere. Through field glasses he could see columns of troops moving wearily into the port. Out to sea sat British and French warships. "Nearest to us is the huge and dirty French *Waldeck Rousseau*." Suddenly one of its cannons was fired. A British destroyer nearby followed suit.[28]

In describing his own departure from the doomed city, Denikin spoke in much the same way. At sea, he wrote:

> The outlines of Novorossisk were still clearly visible. A destroyer turned and sailed full speed back into the bay. A gun boomed, machine guns started barking; the destroyer which had gone to pick up the rear-guard was engaged in a skirmish with the advance guard of the Reds who had entered the town. Then silence fell. The outlines of the coast, the Caucasian Range, became shrouded in mist and receded into the distance—into the past. A past full of suffering and humiliation.[29]

Tukhachevsky's final advance was conducted with deliberate speed. Straggling remnants of the White Army were swept up, one by one, until, on March 27, the victorious Reds marched into the shambles that was all that was left of Novorossisk. Scattered skirmishing continued until, on May 2, the final holdouts of Denikin's army surrendered in Sochi.

With its entry into Novorossisk on March 27, the command of the Caucasus Front had reported to Lenin the full facts of Denikin's debacle. The southern counterrevolution had been effectively destroyed, and in addition the Reds had captured 12,000 White officers, 100,000 soldiers, 300 artillery pieces, 500 machine guns, 200,000 rifles, a great quantity of ammunition and transportation supplies, 240 locomotives in working order, 6 armored trains, and a great quantity of oil, gasoline, and other supplies[30]

The skillful execution of the final offensive against Denikin had placed Tukhachevsky on a new level among the Bolshevik military commanders. Where the impetuous pursuit of Kolchak through Siberia and the Urals had seemed to be the deed of a reckless but lucky youth, the cool deliberation of the mass assault against the Whites in the south seemed to promise a genuinely great military talent. It was Tukhachevsky's first exposure to real fame. But it was also a prelude to disaster.

5
DEFEAT AT THE GATES OF WARSAW

WHILE THE BOLSHEVIKS had been occupied with eliminating Kolchak and Denikin, they had been careful not to unduly antagonize another potential enemy to the west, the resurgent nationalists of a new Poland, created by the victorious Western allies at the end of World War I.

But eventually, for various reasons, the de facto truce was no longer convenient for both parties. And in what was known as the Russo-Polish War of 1920, Poland became a bulwark for the apprehensive states of Western Europe against what they saw as the oriental hordes of Bolshevism. By comparison with the carnage of the Somme and Passchendale and the holocaust that was to engulf Europe less than two decades later, the campaigns of 1920 were small stuff. But at the time, they were seen as a pivotal struggle and, indeed, there is a strong argument to be made for the assertion that the outcome helped to change the course of Russian and European history. For, against all odds, the upstart Poles were victorious. Lenin's dream of exporting his revolution to the rest of Europe was abandoned for a generation. And conversely, there arose a myth of Polish military prowess that helped lull Britain and France into their policy of appeasement that merely encouraged Hitler and brought on the tragedy of World War II, in which Poland was an early and principal victim.

The 1920 war can be divided into four periods. The first was a period of Polish opportunism, an imperialistic drive to re-create a Polish-dominated federation stretching from the Baltic to the Black Sea. The second was a period of uncertainty in which the Red Army, with Tukhachevsky as the leading commander in the field, groped for means to repel the Polish advances into the Ukraine and the Baltic littoral. The third was a smashing Russian campaign, engineered principally by Tukhachevsky, that seemed likely to overwhelm Poland and perhaps even to spark revolution in Germany that might in turn sweep into France and even to Britain. The fourth period was Tukhachevsky's downfall, the rout of his armies, and the consolidation of the Polish state as a temporary buffer between East and West. This final phase, especially the climactic battle of Warsaw, involved enormous stakes. So much so that one not totally unbiased observer called it "the 18th Decisive Battle of the World," on a level with Marathon and Waterloo.[1]

The Poles took the early initiative by striking in April 1919, just as Denikin was about to launch his offensive from the south toward Moscow. With little opposition, they were quickly able to occupy Russian-held Vilna, the ancient Lithuanian capital. Leading the drive was a former anti-tsarist revolutionary, Joseph Pilsudski, who had been born in the area on December 5, 1867.

Although his family had come from Lithuania, from the beginning Pilsudski had identified with the cause of Polish nationalism. He seems to have inherited from his father a distaste for Russian suzerainty and to have added to it a veneer of socialist politics. The young Pilsudski's anti-Russianism had apparently been reinforced by his education in a Vilna school staffed by Russians who were contemptuous of all things Polish.[2]

From Vilna, Pilsudski went to the University of Kharkov to study medicine. But after about a year, he was back in his native city, involved in trying to overthrow the Romanov dynasty. He was soon arrested, along with his brother, and charged with plotting to kill Tsar Alexander II.

Pilsudski would later claim that his involvement was "accidental," but he was convicted and sentenced to five years' exile in Siberia.[3] When he returned from Siberia in 1892, he had been further radicalized in his politics, and easily fell in with others of like mind who were forming the Polish Socialist Party. But even at that stage of his career, politics seems to have been less important to him than using the Socialist movement to further insurrection against the Russians. However, on the face of it, Pilsudski was an ardent member of the movement, and in 1893 — the year of Tukhachevsky's birth — he joined in plans to publish an underground Socialist newspaper. The first issue of *Robotnik* appeared about a year later, with Pilsudski as chief editor, printer, and distributor. About this time, Pilsudski married, and his wife joined him in producing the paper. Its circulation was small — about 2,000 copies of each 12-page issue — but it was influential enough to irritate the Russian authorities. In 1896 Pilsudski found himself again in jail in Warsaw.[4]

The citadel where he was incarcerated was believed to be escapeproof, but Pilsudski was resourceful. By feigning insanity he managed to get transferred to a military hospital in St. Petersburg, where, with the aid of a fellow Polish Socialist on the staff, he escaped. First he went to Kiev, where *Robotnik* was then being published. But eventually he and his wife, who had joined him, moved to Cracow. It was there that they put out the little paper — it published only 36 issues in all — for the next few years.[5]

Pilsudski might have remained one more obscure dissident had it not been for the events of 1905. The revolution of that year seemed to provide a heaven-sent opportunity for his nationalist agitation, and the group around him took advantage of the Russian authorities' preoccupation with more pressing events. For example, at that time Pilsudski turned to robbery to help finance his group. He was apparently no amateur; in one robbery he rifled a train of three million rubles belonging to the Russian government treasury.[6]

Despite that boost for the revolution, Poland remained part of the Russian empire, and it was not until the outbreak of World War I that Pilsudski was given a chance to operate on a grander scale. In the belief that Russia's enemy was Poland's friend, and within two weeks of the outbreak of hostilities, he and his men were in action on the Austro-German side against the tsar.

As Tukhachevsky had quickly discovered, the Russian armies were no match for the Germans, but the Austro-German success proved unfortunate for Pilsudski. As they drove their offensive through Poland, the Germans showed no sign of giving the country the independence Poles had dreamed of regaining for more than a century. "Today," Pilsudski was quoted as having said in 1915, "the Germans have taken the place of the Russians in Poland. We must resist the Germans."[7] By July 1917, Pilsudski had become such a nuisance that the Germans arrested him and tossed him into the fortress at Magdeburg.[8]

Then, again, the fortunes of war turned. As the difficulties on the Western Front began to increase, the Germans tried to mend their fences in the east by granting the restless Poles a measure of independence, and they tried to enlist Pilsudski in this effort. But it was not until the guns finally fell silent on November 11, 1918, that he was released from jail.

In the fractious community of politicians, revolutionaries, and pretenders to authority who gravitated to Warsaw, Pilsudski quickly established himself as the dominant figure in the new Poland that the Western allies agreed should be re-created between defeated Germany and chaotic Russia, where Lenin's revolution had not yet established itself beyond dispute.

As the tides of the Russian Civil War ebbed and flowed, Pulsudski was a cautious spectator. At various times he seemed to side with the Whites, but then he would suddenly make an accommodation with the Reds. In actuality, he was concerned only with furthering Polish dominion. Thus, when Denikin seemed likely to break through from Orel to Moscow, the Poles did not come to his aid, as the White commander urged, but instead held back, allowing the Reds to move troops from the Polish frontier to be used in defense of the revolution.

The reason for this was simple; Pilsudski was convinced that neither Denikin nor Kolchak would countenance the fulfillment of his dreams for Poland. They might have acquiesced, under pressure from London and Paris, to an independent Poland, but they certainly would never have agreed to Pilsudski's plans for a Baltic-to-Black Sea federation including Lithuania, Latvia,

Estonia, and the Ukraine. The Reds might be more amenable to such a plan, Pilsudski believed, convinced in part through the representations of a boyhood friend, Julian Markhlevsky. Markhlevsky before the war had been a prominent Polish Communist, and had returned to his homeland at the end of 1918. At first without the knowledge of Moscow, he had worked in Warsaw to convince Pilsudski that the best policy was to side with the Bolsheviks. Later, after a secret journey to Russia, he acted with the approval of Georgi V. Chicherin, the commissar for foreign affairs, and the Moscow regime. By October 1919 he was conducting furtive negotiations with the Poles and planning a formal meeting with Pilsudski. According to Louis Fischer, these discussions were kept secret to avoid compromising Pilsudski with the French and the British, who were trying to cordon off the Bolsheviks. Fischer says that both Pilsudski and Markhlevsky were avid hunters, and they contrived to meet "by accident" in the forests of eastern Poland. The rendezvous never took place, but the intention of the Bolsheviks was achieved, for Pilsudski did not take to the field to support Denikin.[9]

But with Denikin liquidated as a threat and with his successor, Wrangel, apparently bottled up in the Crimea, Pilsudski and the Poles acted before the Bolsheviks could consolidate their gains.

Even though the Western allies, on whom Poland was heavily reliant for food and other support, had declared that it would become the capital of a newly independent Lithuania, Vilna was Pilsudski's first target. On April 19, 1919, Polish troops burst into the city. For the rest of the year, the Poles pushed forward all along the Russian frontier. On August 8, they occupied Minsk, the capital of Byelorussia. By that time, the frontier had been extended to follow the strategic line of the Berezina River. Throughout this time, however, Markhlevsky pursued his peace feelers and the Poles lived up to their bargain of not extending overt help to the Whites. It was a curious kind of hot and cold war. But in December 1919, Chicherin made one more try to make a deal. In proposing immediate resumption of the talks that had been temporarily adjourned, he said: "The Soviet Government is convinced that all differences between [Russia and Poland] can be removed by a friendly agreement."[10] The Poles did not reply, although they subsequently acknowledged receipt of further, similar proposals made in the ensuing weeks. On March 27, 1920, Warsaw informed Chicherin that it was ready to begin peace talks, and went so far as to suggest that they begin on April 10 in the city of Borisov.

Despite this gesture, there was no mistaking the belligerent ambitions of the Poles. So much so that the Western allies, especially the United States, which had been providing the food that kept millions of Poles from starving and the medicine that controlled the serious outbreaks of typhus, were appalled at the monster they had apparently created in Eastern Europe. There was particular concern for Poland's large Jewish population because there were constant threats of pogroms from anti-Semitic groups in the new Poland.[11]

But Pilsudski was oblivious to these problems. For him, a once-in-a-lifetime opportunity had arisen from the restoration of Poland's former imperial glory, and he was not going to miss it. Ostensibly he was promoting an anti-Bolshevik federation of the Baltic states, Poland, Byelorussia, and the Ukraine; but there was no doubt he intended Warsaw to dominate it.

Not that Pilsudski was alone in pushing events toward a confrontation. There was also some on the Russian side—and Lenin was the chief among them—who saw in the Polish situation a chance to further world revolution, and they were quick to urge that Pilsudski be taught the lesson administered to Kolchak and Denikin. On the surface, however, the Russians were still open to compromise. To Pilsudski that must have seemed a confirmation of Moscow's weakness and further evidence that the time had come to strike.

Thus, in April 1920, over the objections of some of his colleagues, including the influential Joseph Haller, who was close to the French, he reached agreement with the nationalistic but now anti-Bolshevik regime in the Ukraine headed by Semyon Vasilyevich Petlura. On April 26, Pilsudski, backed by Petlura's ragtag forces, struck suddenly into the Russian-held area of the Ukraine. The Bolsheviks, still mopping up the remnants of Denikin's supporters in the Kuban and preparing to finish off Wrangel in the Crimea, were caught off guard. The Polish armies advanced with spectacular speed. One calvary brigade was said to have advanced 180 kilometers in two days, and by May 9 the spearhead led by General Ridz-Smigly was in Kiev.[12]

The Russians could do little to stem the Polish advance. The country's transportation system and industry remained in chaos. The people were hungry and already disillusioned that the utopia promised by the Bolsheviks had not arrived. The peasants were rebellious and the minorities—particularly the Ukrainians—wanted that independence already achieved by the Poles, Latvians, Estonians, Lithuanians, and Finns. The Bolshevik hierarchy was divided over present problems and future policy.

The pro-war group in the Russian leadership erred, but Pilsudski was mistaken in his optimism over an anticipated easy success in gaining his objectives. Blinded by his chauvinism, he neglected to take into account the possibility that his lunge into the Russian heartland would evoke very similar emotions among the inhabitants there. The Poles learned little politically from the Whites. To the Ukrainian peasantry there was no attraction in replacing Russian landlords with the Polish variety. Indeed, in tsarist times many of the landlords in the Ukraine had been Polish, and few Ukrainians did not revere the memory of Bogdan Khmelnitsky, the Ukrainian patriot who in 1654 had chosen alliance with Moscow rather than subjugation to Poland. There was also an underlying religious aspect to the situation; to the still heavily Orthodox population of the central Ukraine, the overlordship of Roman Catholic Poland was highly undesirable.

The Polish adventurism provoked nationalistic feelings in another, surprising direction. Even the Russian tories like the tsarist general Brusilov, to whom allegiance to the Bolsheviks had previously been as palatable as a partnership with the devil, rallied to the motherland in her time of danger. The Moscow leadership was grateful for the assistance, but it did not sit easily on their revolutionary conscience. To them the struggle with Poland was seen less in nationalistic terms than as an opportunity to open the window of Europe to Communism. They too were caught up in their own propaganda, mistakenly believing that the Polish workers would rally to the cause of international worker solidarity rather than to the narrow ethnic loyalty of the Pilsudski group. Lenin, as Trotsky could not resist pointing out, was perhaps the most enthusiastic of all in this regard. Trotsky and Stalin—at least until the latter saw how Lenin was tending—were not.

As Trotsky wrote later in his biography of Stalin, in May 1920 he had warned: "That the war will *end* with the workers' revolution in Poland there can be no doubt; but at the same time there is no basis for supposing that the war will *begin* with such a revolution. . . . " He said he was opposed to a march on Warsaw "because, considering the weakness of our forces and resources, it could end successfully only on condition of an immediate insurrection in Poland itself, and there was absolutely no assurance of that."[13]

He was not alone in these beliefs. In fact, those in the Soviet leadership who should have known best were against a wholesale invasion of Poland. Julian Markhlevsky, the man who had achieved the Polish truce of the previous autumn, said there was little chance of success. His view was supported by Dzerzhinsky, head of the Cheka but also a Pole, and by Karl Radek, born in Poland of German parentage. Like them, Stalin understood that it was one thing to fight the Poles on non-Polish soil but another, much more difficult thing, to do so on their own territory. "The rear of the Polish armies is monolithic and nationally united," Stalin wrote. "The dominant sentiment is the feeling for the Fatherland."[14]

But despite the protestations of Stalin and the others, Russian preparations for the war were pushed ahead. In the south, Budenny's cavalry was detached from the front facing Wrangel and moved against the Poles in the Ukraine. And in the north, young Tukhachevsky, the conquerer of Kolchak and Denikin, was removed from planning a new offensive to cement Soviet control in Turkestan and named to head the Western Front on April 29, 1920.[15]

His promotion to the new command was one of several decisions taken by the Central Committee that day, decisions that set in motion the second phase of the 1920 struggle between Russia and Poland. The meeting also gave approval to the plan for the Polish offensive drawn up by the general staff, but with considerable input from Lenin and Ephraim Sklyansky, a close associate of the Soviet leader. This anticipated a two-pronged blow at the Poles, the prongs largely divided north and south of the Pripet Marshes in the northern Ukraine and Byelorussia. The main attack, by Tukhachevsky's Western Front command, would be concentrated in Byelorussia and Polesia, north of the marshes. The second attack would be made by the Southwestern Front, commanded by A. I. Yegorov. Stalin was appointed to the Military Council of the Southwestern Front and Dzerzhinsky was named "chief of the rear"—an ominous sign that any opposition or malingering would be ruthlessly eliminated.[16]

The main attack was set for May 14 in Tukhachevsky's sector, with the Southwestern Front assigned to a general supporting role that failed to take into account the swaggering ambitions of Budenny or the more calculated opportunism of Stalin.

Bred by the spectacular successes against Kolchak and Denikin, an air of lighthearted optimism pervaded Moscow on the eve of the campaign. On the night before he left Moscow to take up his new command, Tukhachevsky was entertained at the home of the commander in chief, Sergei Kamenev. As a special gesture, Kamenev's wife played Schubert's *March Militaire* on the piano. It was a festive evening.[17]

The following day, Tukhachevsky left for the front, where he replaced V. M. Gittis, who had been transferred to Tukhachevsky's former post in the northern Caucasus. On his arrival, Tukhachevsky immediately took charge with characteristic forcefulness and individuality. He saw that the battle plan, drawn up by Lenin and the Supreme Command and initiated by Gittis, had a basic flaw, and he quickly set about to remedy it. He did this even though Sergei Kamenev had traveled to the Minsk area to confer with Gittis on the possibilities before the program was set. Like the later part of the campaign, the planning for the spring offensive was to be the subject of much criticism, but at the time Tukhachevsky had good reason for making the changes.

Tukhachevsky had two principal armies under his command: the 15th, commanded by A. I. Kork, in the northern sector of the front, and the 16th, commanded by N. V. Sollogub, in the center. To the south was a smaller formation, the Mozyr Group, commanded by E. N. Sergeyev. Facing them were, in the north, the Polish First Army and, to the south, the Polish Fourth Army. Political commissars with Tukhachevsky were Ivan Smilga and Christian G. Rakovsky.

The original plan had been for the 16th Army to strike in the direction of Minsk, where the Polish Fourth Army was based. To advance on this part of the front would have presented a major difficulty, as Tukhachevsky quickly noted. Any advance there would have meant forcing a crossing of the Berezina River, whose left bank had been heavily fortified by the Poles. He decided there was an easier route. So on May 1, he telegraphed a change in the plans to his subordinate commanders. The main action would now be directed to the Vitebsk-Polotsk region, in the 15th Army's sector. This drive would be directed northward toward Vilna. Sollogub's 16th Army would make a diversionary attack on the Berezina. Sergeyev was charged with crossing the Dvina River and then moving rapidly to strike at the Polish rear.

But Tukhachevsky was already looking beyond the immediate goals. "The plan for the offensive," he wrote later, "foresaw the breakthrough in the approaches to Smolensk, the destruction of the left wing of the Polish Army and the entrapment of the remainder in the marshes of Pinsk."[18]

The commander of the 15th Army, Kork, was a 32-year-old former lieutenant-colonel in the Russian Imperial Army. But in May 1918 he had switched allegiance to the fledgling Red Army, and he had played a prominent part in the defense of Petrograd in 1919 as commander of the Seventh Red Army. This was his first period of close association with Tukhachevsky, but it was by no means the last.

However, even Tukhachevsky's change of plan was not wholly realistic. The simple fact was that the Soviet Union at that time was ill prepared to fight a major war. Between March 10 and June 1, 1920, the leadership in Moscow had done its utmost to strengthen the Western Front. In that period, 40,000 infantry, artillery, and cavalry troops were dispatched to join the forces already there. Of them, 8,000 joined the 15th Army and 18,000 the 16th Army. The remainder were assigned to the reserve.[19]

Additional manpower was not the entire solution, however. The long distances involved, the chronic impediments of Russian railways, and shortages of war matériel from the still chaotic industries meant that supplies often were misdirected, were late in arriving, or did not arrive at all. There were also personnel problems; not every Russian shared Lenin's and Tukhachevsky's enthusiasm for the coming campaign. That meant that Communist Party political work among the troops and behind the front had to be greatly intensified.[20]

So, when Tukhachevsky altered the direction and location of the attack, the whole Soviet supply and reinforcement system was thrown out of synchronization. Most of the heavy artillery had been concentrated in the center of the 16th Army's sector, and in this area were stationed the bulk of the Soviet reserves.[21] Inefficiency on the part of Tukhachevsky's staff did not help the speedy transfer of men and matériel from the center of the front to its right flank, where it would be most needed.

It was obviously with this confusion in mind that, on the eve of the offensive, Tukhachevsky issued what was to become one of his more controversial orders. He instructed his subordinate commanders that in the initial attack, they were to commit their entire commands, not holding anything in reserve. He had done the same thing in the campaign against Denikin, but in some regards it was a gambler's move. It was later criticized by Tukhachevsky's enemies, of whom there were soon to be many.[22]

It was probably inevitable that the activity on the Russian side would come—or be drawn—to the attention of the Polish command. It therefore decided to "pluck off" the Soviet offensive before it started, according to one Soviet description. To do this, the Poles moved one infantry division from the Ukrainian Front (lightening the opposition for Yegorov and Budenny) to reinforce the Polish Fourth Army. Pilsudski's idea was to drive through the 16th Army of the Reds and, if all went well, to seize the city of Mogilev; from there he would outflank the Russians and cut through their already flimsy supply lines. The beginning of the operation was set for May 17.[23]

But on May 14, Tukhachevsky launched his own drive into the Polish front. The Northern Group had been assigned to push forward on a line connecting Opochna, Disna, and Yanopol (just north of Vitebsk). Kork's 15th Army had been assigned the front south from Yanopol to the town of Lepel. On the east bank of the Berezina, as far south as the town of Rechitsa, was Sollogub's 16th Army. At the outset of the offensive, not counting one rifle division that had been detached to watch for a possible Latvian intervention on the side of the Poles, Tukhachevsky had slightly more than 92,000 men. They had a decided advantage over the 66,000 troops in the Polish First and Fourth armies, but the Poles were much better equipped, thanks to supplies rushed from France. The Poles had 1,550 machine guns, 340 heavy artillery pieces, and 20 airplanes, all of which were scarce on the Russian side. In addition, the Russian armies consisted mainly of infantry and therefore lacked the mobility of the enemy, since they had comparatively few cavalry units and no tanks. Further, the Russians' concentration on the main sector of the attack, in the direction of Vilna, meant that they were especially vulnerable in the southern extremity of the front, near Mozyr.[24]

The lack of cohesion on the Russian side became apparent when the Northern Group went on the offensive in the early hours of May 14. As the right flank of the Russian Army moved, the left flank (the 16th Army) was still getting organized and did not attack at once. And, on a wider scale, there was a lack of coordination with the Southwestern Front that was to cost the Russians dearly later in the war. In reviewing the campaign later, Tukhachevsky underscored this when he wrote: "Before the start of the Polish campaign there arose the problem of liaison between the Western and Southwestern fronts. At that stage the High Command had judged that such unification was premature and did not intend to carry it out until the advance had reached the line running through Brest-Litovsk." Tukhachevsky explained that the reason for this caution was that the great extent of the Pripet Marshes between the two fronts made communications difficult, but between the lines he was also implying that the fault lay with Sergei Kamenev and Trotsky for not being assertive enough.[25]

So the 15th Army moved out. It advanced in zigzag fashion, moving northwest until May 16, and then turning to drive southwest. It was meeting heavy resistance, and by the time the 16th Army finally entered the action on May 19, the advance of Kork's men was beginning to stall. Sollogub's troops crossed the Berezina by May 21, but such was the opposition that Tukhachevsky quickly realized he had to have more strength if his forces were to prevail. Already there was some criticism in the Soviet command that the offensive had been undertaken prematurely.

That criticism seemed to be borne out when the Poles counterattacked in force on June 1. Even Lenin's optimism seemed to fade at the lack of early success. On June 2, he telegraphed Stalin, who was with the Southwestern Command at Kremenchug: "The situation on the Western Front is worse than Tukhachevsky or Glavkom thinks." The purpose of Lenin's message was to tell Stalin that reinforcements requested from his front must be diverted immediately to the northern sector. Lenin promised to speed up the delivery of new troops from the Crimea to the Southwestern Command.[26]

The principal reinforcement that Lenin had in mind was the First Cavalry Army, which had traveled from the Kuban by way of Rostov on its way to the Southwestern Front. Since its significant role in the destruction of Denikin, Budenny's army had been considerably strengthened. It now numbered more than 16,000 troopers, well armed with machine guns and supported by 38 heavy artillery pieces. In addition the famous Chapeyev Division, now commanded by I. S. Kutyakov, and some smaller cavalry units were moved to the Southwestern Front under Yegorov's command. With the inclusion of the 14th Army, commanded by Uborevich, the hero of Orel, and the Fastov Group, including the 45th Division of Yona E. Yakir, Yegorov's force totaled 22,400 infantry, 24,000 cavalry, 1,440 machine guns, and 245 artillery pieces.[27]

On May 9, the supreme commander, Kamenev, had sent Yegorov a directive setting out instructions for the offensive in the southwest. The 12th Army's first objective was to be Kiev. The 14th Army would protect the spearhead's right flank, while Budenny's cavalry would use its mobility to drive into the Polish rear and harass the area behind the enemy's lines. Kamenev arrived in Kharkov on May 10 to discuss the campaign directly with Yegorov. During the next two weeks the plan was refined by the front command, and on May 26 — when the northern offensive had already reached full fury — the attack in the south was finally launched.

In the initial conflict, the 12th Army, still not completely ready, was unable to beat through the Polish defense. There apparently was some indecision on the part of the army commander, Mezheninov, and on May 31 Yegorov had to order the 12th Army to make a direct, frontal assault on Kiev. The Poles were able to withstand this second attack and, in addition, were holding off Budenny's cavalry. The horse soldiers were unable to cope with the Polish infantry's use of trenches to impede the cossack charges.

In the face of these setbacks, the Soviet Southwestern Front reorganized for a new assault. One principal change was that Mezheninov lost his command. When the new drive opened on June 5, under heavy artillery and machine gun fire, Budenny's cossacks were in the vanguard. By June 9, the cavalry had broken through, threatening to overrun the Polish Third Army, and had moved on Kiev. The impetus of the cavalry was such that the

Poles reeled before it. By June 20, the Ukraine was again under Soviet control as far as a line running from Zhitomir to Kazatin to Vinnitsa. At that stage, because the rapidity of their advance had stretched them out unduly, the cavalry was split into two groups. Budenny remained in charge of the 6th and 11th Cavalry divisions, while Voroshilov now commanded the 4th and 14th divisions.

Simultaneously, in the north, Tukhachevsky's forces were having their first real successes. On June 18, the Poles fell back from the town of Mozyr, and the Soviet forces under T. S. Khvesin moved in to replace them. Tukhachevsky was eager to press this advantage, and reopened a general offensive. The third phase of the Russo-Polish War was about to begin, and as it progressed, alarms would sound in Paris and London with an intensity not experienced since the darkest days of 1917 on the Western Front in France.

On the surface, events were going entirely favorably for the Russians. Both Tukhachevsky and Yegorov seemed to be about to roll back the Polish invasion. But there was ominous occurrences that even in the early stage of the hostilities signaled their eventual outcome. First, and probably more important, the Soviet High Command was unable to coordinate the two wings of its pincer; both Tukhachevsky and Yegorov seemed intent on fighting their own wars. Second, although they were both able to discomfit the Poles, neither was able to strike a really decisive blow. Tukhachevsky was unable to force the Poles southward into the marshes that had trapped armies from time immemorial; Yegorov's hammer, Budenny, maneuvered seemingly at will but always found the enemy re-formed in front of him. Third, on June 6, on what had been the almost forgotten Crimean Front, Baron Wrangel's Second Corps struck at I. K. Pauka's unsuspecting 13th Red Army. The Whites were able to follow up the advantage won in this attack despite a counterattack ordered by Yegorov on June 10. In that engagement, Wrangel's rested and seasoned troops scattered the Red cavalry. By the end of June, Wrangel had enlarged his territory to include most of the northern Tauride and had created a nasty threat to the rear of the Soviet forces engaged against the Poles.

Not all the troubles, however, were on the Russian side. The Polish military setbacks had aggravated political disharmony in

Warsaw. Pilsudski may have been the undisputed strongman of the country at this period, but there was great confusion over who filled what post under him. Until June 9, 1920, the prime minister had been Leopold Skulski, but on that day he resigned after a protracted quarrel with Vincent Witos, the peasant leader in the Sejm. Witos tried to form his own government but failed, and a new regime led by Stanislas Grabski was formed. Its establishment, however, did not quiet the political quarrels among the Poles.

Meanwhile, events were increasing pressure on the Soviet High Command to execute a quick master stroke against Pilsudski. And speedily that master stroke came to be defined as a lunge at Warsaw itself. Because of the Wrangel breakout and because of a threat that Rumanians might mobilize to intervene on the side of the Poles — not to mention the troubles in the Russian rear, where the transportation system was buckling under the demands of the war — the Soviet situation did not look bright. Even on the front there were serious troubles. Desertion among the common soldiers — that old bugbear of Russian armies — was mounting to crisis proportions. The 16th Army, for example, reported that between May 14 and June 15 there had been no fewer than 24,615 desertions. Two-fifths had been apprehended, and the remainder had mostly changed their minds and returned to the ranks voluntarily.[28]

These threats were, however, balanced by one positive factor: the reemergence of the Germans, who made no secret of the fact that they would relish any humiliation the Russians might inflict on the obstreperous Poles. In November 1919, the new commander of the German Truppenamt (Army Bureau) — the equivalent of the former imperial General Staff — was 54-year-old Hans von Seeckt. After the failure of the Kapp-Luttwitz putsch of June 15, 1920, von Seeckt became the chief of the army command. The new military leader was no stranger to Russia or to Poland. He had served in East Prussia against the Russians in the offensive of 1915. But he was chiefly occupied with building up a new, modern German army, despite the limits imposed on Germany by the Western allies at Versailles. Communist Russia, similarly an outcast from the family of nations, could prove to be very helpful to fulfillment of that ambition, and he was unlikely to antagonize Moscow by siding with the Poles. In early

July, Berlin announced its neutrality in the Russo-Polish conflict, although, as was widely suspected at the time and as documents have since made clear, it was to be a pro-Moscow neutrality.[29]

Against this background, the Russians had built up their forces for the big offensive. Tukhachevsky's Western Front command now consisted of the Fourth Army, commanded by E. N. Sergeyev; Kork's 15th Army; the Third Army, under V. S. Lazarevich; Sollogub's 16th Army; and the Third Cavalry Corps, commanded by Gai. Tukhachevsky had 105,075 active troops under his command. Perhaps because of this buildup, he—and Kamenev behind him—had made a strategic commitment that, with the benefit of more than six decades of hindsight, seems overly ambitious. They had gambled on a knockout punch at Warsaw, in the belief that the Poles were incapable of effective resistance.[30]

Finally everything was ready, and on July 6 Tukhachevsky started his offensive. According to one account, Budenny, on hearing the news of the northern offensive, muttered: "Son of a bitch, he is finally moving."[31]

Tukhachevsky's men seemed to have benefited from the delay. The Poles fell back, allowing the Russians to cross the Berezina River. Tukhachevsky's sweeping movement to the northwest threatened them with encirclement, and Pilsudski's men were forced to retreat even further, to avoid being trapped in the Pripet Marshes. The Russians poured into Vilna on July 14, and within a week they had crossed another natural barrier, the Nieman River. Brest-Litovsk fell to the advancing Russians on August 1, and they did not pause until they had covered 300 miles and were approaching Malkin. In the south, the Poles had been more successful, but in Warsaw there was an air of foreboding. Only Pilsudski seemed hopeful. The major weakness of the Russian situation was already apparent to him, and the turn of events was to increase the weakness rather than lessen it. Instead of functioning as a coordinated pincer, the two concentrations of Russian forces became two wildly waving arms, directed by the ambitious young men who led them with little apparent regard—and indeed with some scorn—for the high command that supposedly supervised them. Tukhachevsky went his own headlong way in the north, while in the south, Stalin and his cronies Budenny, Yegorov, and Voroshilov did likewise. Disaster was almost preordained. But at the outset victory for the Russians seemed at hand.

As Tukhachevsky's armies rolled back the Poles, there was great jubilation in Moscow. One eyewitness described the scene thus:

> Lenin, in a small room just off the grand, gold-panelled hall of the Imperial Palace. A throne had been bundled away here, and next to this useless piece of furniture a map of the Polish front was displayed on the wall. The rattle of typewriters filled the air. Lenin, jacketed, briefcase under arm, delegates and typists all around him, was giving his views on the march of Tukhachevsky's army on Warsaw. He was in excellent spirits, confident of victory. Karl Radek, thin, monkey-like, sardonic and droll, hitched up his oversize trousers, (which were always slipping down over his hips), and added, "We shall be ripping up the Versailles Treaty with our bayonets."[32]

From July 5 to 16, as Tukhachevsky's offensive was gathering strength, the Allied Supreme Council had been meeting in the Belgian resort of Spa, and the Polish leader Grabski hastened there to plead for increased help for Poland. The reception was less than cordial. British Prime Minister Lloyd George, in particular, was impatient with what he saw as Warsaw's foolish dreams of imperial glory. He told Grabski that Poland should abandon all ideas of adding to its territory by conquest, withdraw all Polish armies behind the Bug River, surrender most of eastern Galicia, including Lvov, and submit the Danzig question to arbitration by the Supreme Council. Lloyd George even proposed all-inclusive peace talks involving the Baltic states, Poland, and Russia in London. In return, the British prime minister promised full Allied support in protecting Poland's independence. As a result of the Spa meeting, the Allies decided to send a mission, including Lord d'Abernon and General Maxime Weygand, to Poland; the group left hurriedly on July 22. They reached Warsaw three days later, to find the Polish capital in the middle of yet another political crisis. That day a new government of national unity, with Witos the leader this time, had been formed. Its first task was to vote confidence in Pilsudski, although his prestige had been considerably shaken by the rapid advance of Tukhachevsky's armies in the north.

Despite Lenin's continued optimism, Tukhachevsky's haste was causing divided feelings in Moscow. The rapidity with which his men were overrunning Polish territory brought elation, but the split that was opening ever wider between the Western and Southwestern fronts was causing apprehension. Sergei Kamenev therefore acted to fill the gap. On July 23 he ordered Yegorov to move his forces in a direction that would bring them in full contact with the southern extremity of Tukhachevsky's group. But the directive was ambiguous. In particular, it said that the First Cavalry, that precursor of World War II Panzer divisions, should merely proceed "in the properly decided direction." Unfortunately for the Russians, that left Stalin, Voroshilov, and Budenny too much personal leeway.

On July 19, Kamenev had visited Tukhachevsky's headquarters at Smolensk with more specific orders for the Western Front, but the visit also obviously caused Kamenev to be affected by the optimism of the youthful commander and his aides. The High Command ordered that Warsaw was to be captured by August 18.[33] Not that Kamenev made things easier for Tukhachevsky. On July 31, the High Command asked Tukhachevsky to detach his 48th Division for use by Yegorov's Southwestern Front against Wrangel. Two days later, Kamenev, at Yegorov's insistance, demanded two more divisions. Tukhachevsky, not too politely, refused. But Yegorov was adamant, and the units were detached. And that wasn't all. At the same time, Kamenev extended the actual fighting area of the Western Front to include some of the territory for which the Southwestern Front had previously been responsible, thereby further speading out Tukhachevsky's already thinly spread southern flank. There was no doubt that Kamenev faced monumental problems in coordinating his two fronts—actually three, if Wrangel is considered separately—but his inability to impose his authority certainly did not help the Russians' chances. Not that the whole blame should rest with him; throughout the Civil War the army commanders—and Tukhachevsky perhaps more than most—had achieved their greatest victories by doing exactly what they were doing now: waging their own war with emphasis only on their own immediate objectives.

So on August 3, Tukhachevsky launched a maneuver that

was to be a cause for recrimination even long after his death. In an effort to outflank the Poles and strike hardest in the northwestern extremity of their line, where they were least expecting such an attack, he moved his Fourth Army—what was called his "secret army," since it was not directly engaging the enemy and was moving somewhat behind and under cover of the other Russian armies—sharply north and slightly west, toward the frontier of East Prussia. He did this even though it turned the emphasis of his front even further away from Yegorov to the south.

The Soviet High Command was all too aware of the lack of cohesion on the Polish Front, especially since it had begun to receive reports of a Polish buildup in the area south of Warsaw, not north of it. On the Russian Front it was clear that no one was in total charge. Therefore, on August 6, Moscow acted to remedy that fault. Tukhachevsky was named the overall commander. Yegorov was ordered to replace the First Cavalry on the Galician sector with infantry, thereby freeing the cavalry to join the action to the north.[34]

But there was continued difference of opinion in the Russian command, especially between Tukhachevsky and Kamenev. Kamenev, like Pilsudski—and General Weygand of the French army, who by this time had joined the Poles—saw an inherent flaw in Tukhachevsky's rapid northern sweep. The further he moved northwest, the more he opened his flank to a counterattack from the Polish right. Tukhachevsky didn't exactly ignore the warnings; instead, he insisted that he must mobilize all the strength possible on the extremity of the Polish left flank. He had two reasons: that was where the Poles were weakest, and that was where he could most easily sever their vital supply line for Western munitions. To him it seemed the easiest route to Warsaw.

And things seemed to be going Tukhachevsky's way. His troops plunged deep into Polish territory. Before the ferocity of his advance, the Poles were unable to make a stand. Each day brought spectacular new advances. At that time, the second congress of the Communist International was being held in Moscow. And the debates on how to further the world revolution were submerged in the triumphant news from the Polish front. At any moment it seemed that Warsaw would fall to the Reds. Lenin was the most enthusiastic cheerleader, positioning himself daily in front of his map to give the foreign delegates his comments on Tukhachevsky's advance. Trotsky was more restrained, but his caution was generally overlooked.[35]

Pilsudski, too, was impressed by the achievements of Tukhachevsky and his men. Writing of the events of 1920 some years later, he said:

> The movement of Tukhachevsky's troops, after the Fourth Army and the cavalry had opened the way, was uninterrupted. The distances covered daily, almost to Warsaw and its suburbs, reached at least 20 kilometers almost as a daily march. These long marches, interrupted by fighting, were of a kind that brought honor to the armies as well as to their leaders. . . . The influence of this advance was enormous. Tukhachevsky suggests the comparison in one of his strategic essays to the advance of the German armies on Paris. In effect, this movement continued to draw out the mass of the enemy forces, interrupted from time to time by a kind of leapfrog. This movement, which lasted several weeks, produced the impression of something irresistible that advanced like a monstrous, heavy cloud that recognized no obstacle. There was in it something desperate that broke the resistance of the men and the people. I recall a conversation at that time. One of the generals with whom I had to confer frequently began his conversation and his report . . . with the words: "Ah! What a campaign! Ah! What a campaign!"
>
> There was something about it that held the admiration and the flavor of impudence. On the military, this had the effect of some enormous kaleidoscope in which every day brought a new situation, with a melange of news, names of geographic points, of regimental and divisional numbers, a new use of time, a new estimate of distances. And this enormous kaleidoscope unreeled its images slowly, while its irresistible and steady advance engendered, after a certain time, a frightening chaos of combinations not achieved and of counter combinations, of orders not executed and of reports that bore no relation to the actual situation.
>
> Under the impression of this cloud filled with hail, the [Polish] state broke down, characters were destroyed, the heart of the soldiers became putty. Everywhere around me, I was faced with the effect of this advance. . . .
>
> The process of decomposition of moral force, the wound-

ing of our will power, was, to my mind, the greatest triumph that can be attributed to Tukhachevsky.³⁶

But, looking back from the vantage point of his own success, Pilsudski was also able to say: "All these ventures had effectively the same character and changed nothing in principle regarding our strategic position."³⁷

Pilsudski was convinced that the key to victory in the north still lay in the south, and that "the motor of the war in the south was Budenny's cavalry and I didn't think that he would give me difficulty." As a basis for this conclusion, the Polish marshal compared the relative advances of the two Soviet fronts, noting that between July 4 and 20, Tukhachevsky's men in the north had advanced between 295 and 395 kilometers, while in the south the Russians had moved only between 80 and 130 kilometers.³⁸

Pilsudski may have been phlegmatic in the face of Tukhachevsky's advance, but in the West there was real apprehension that the end of the new Poland was near. "Defense Crumbles as Foe Nears Warsaw; Soviet Rule Set Up in Occupied Poland," said the *New York Times* on August 4. Five days later, the main headline in the *Times* read: "Bolsheviki Only 36 Miles From Warsaw — Crisis Viewed by Premiers as Only Less Grave Than That of 1914." In most circles those 36 miles, given the speed with which the Russians were able to plunge forward, seemed hardly to exist. It was almost a foregone conclusion that the Red flag would soon wave over Warsaw.

Ironically, in those doomsday accounts in the West Tukhachevsky's name was never mentioned. Instead, the headlines were reserved for Trotsky and Budenny. Trotsky was the cold, almost demonic Bolshevik who had engineered this disaster. Budenny was the rapacious semi-Asiatic cossack who, bloodied saber in hand, was the Mongol at the gates of Warsaw. No matter that Trotsky was less than lukewarm about the war or that Budenny was actually several hundred miles from Warsaw, going in another direction.

Few Western correspondents were able to get firsthand looks at the Russian armies. They were used to the relatively static fronts of World War I. But one who did get to meet the Russians at this stage was Eugene Szattamary, a German journalist who wrote for the *Chicago Tribune*. When he first encountered some of Gai's cavalrymen near the East Prussian border on August 3, he could only say to himself: "My wonder is increasing how the Russians have won the war." Szattamary's Lithuanian friends had warned him not to expect the Russian counterparts of Britain's Horse Guards or the Prussian Uhlans, but even so, he was shocked to discover that the Russians were such "a ragged, starved, disreputable looking crowd as they are."

> One of the cavalrymen was dressed in mufti, while his companion was in a uniform. I saw round hats, bearskin hats (the temperature is about 80 degrees Fahrenheit), derbies and slouch hats and those peculiar caps the Polish Jews wear.
> I saw one British uniform and seven Polish hats and uniforms on the first few Russians I met. Surely it was a nondescript lot, but they had one thing in common—the red star insignia of the Red Army, which each wore on his blouse or his cap.
> The men were dirty and ragged and the small Cossack horses were not groomed, but were caked with the mud of a thousand miles. I saw 300 horses and their riders, but not a one of them was dressed or fitted according to the standard of either side of the war in France. Only rifles and ammunition were in plenty and one Cossack showed me a Japanese carbine and bullets and even a knapsack, a proud souvenir of a Bolshevik raid in Siberia.
> An iron discipline everywhere prevailed. The officers were well-dressed in uniforms. With them was a civilian commissar who is really superior to the officers and watches them. When the Russians pulled out of Grajavo [the town where Szattamary met them] they requisitioned supplies, but they paid in Soviet rubles and did not plunder or confiscate anything. Only one car of flour was broken into.
> On looking over the Russian Army I cannot understand what has been urging them from victory to victory throughout the last two years. Perhaps it is their discipline. Perhaps it is the fear of starvation if they do not win. I know the men feel they have to conquer new territory in order to obtain food because there is none at home. That is why I was doubtful if the army will quit conquering when an armistice is signed and word is given to return to Russia.[39]

Szattamary was under the impression that he had met Budenny's cavalry, even though they were hundreds of miles to the south in Galicia. But his dispatches and similar reports emanating from Warsaw helped to create an aura of invincibility for the Red Army. By this time, too, Tukhachevsky apparently had fallen under his own spell, and increased the pace of his arcing, flanking movement. Even much later, when disaster had overtaken him, he remained convinced that his scheme had been correct, if only because of the need to bypass the main concentration of Polish forces in front of Warsaw.

"A central attack in the direction of Warsaw was beyond our forces," he said. "There remained the crushing of a flank, the right or the left. In falling on the left flank of the enemy, we would threaten at the same time the [Polish] communications with Danzig. Given that the revolutionary movement in Germany had interrupted the normal transport of arms and munitions from France to Poland, then the links with Danzig constituted an extremely important artery. . . . " He added a further reason for his choice: that, given the existing disposition of his forces, the attack on the Polish left did not require an extensive realignment of his armies, which would have taken a great deal of time and would have further strained his already chaotic transportation arrangements.[40]

The state of affairs seemed to support Tukhachevsky's argument.

Warsaw was in tumult. There was talk of evacuating the government to Poznan. There were rumors of a Bolshevik coup d'etat. Suspicion fell on everyone, particularly the Jewish population, since so many of the new Russian leaders seemed to be Jewish. The government was desperate for help from the Western allies, but Socialist trade unions in Britain and France threatened to prevent the shipment of any munitions or supplies to the beleaguered Poles. In Germany the workers were mutinous.

But not all the Poles were pessimistic about the struggle that was about to reach a climax. Lord d'Abernon, for example, reported that early in August "the Prime Minister [presumably Witos], a peasant proprietor, has gone off today to get his harvest in."[41] The British diplomat was a sagacious witness to the war. He saw that comparisons of the Polish campaign and the great battles of World War I were wide of the mark. "Both the Polish and Soviet Armies," he said, "were 18th Century rather than modern in many aspects, particularly in this, that there was no special animosity or rancour between the mass of combatants on the two sides." They were merely engaged because they had been told to do so.[42]

Thus, although there was confusion among the Polish military leadership and among the politicians, the great mass of the Polish people were largely unmoved by the swirl of events around them. Like Witos, they were preoccupied with the difficult task of feeding themselves, and they had been too recently freed from Russian, Austrian, or German suzerainty to worry very much about returning to it. Nationalism was a thing very much for the aristocrats like Pilsudski. As for worker solidarity, there was no such thing. This explains why Lenin's hoped-for rising of the Polish workers never took place.

In his understated British way, Lord d'Abernon noted that although the Polish military leaders were desperate for French arms and ammunition, they were much less eager to take advantage of the counsels of the French military delegation that had been sent to help them. The Western allies has expected that the celebrated General Weygand would be made commander in chief of the Polish forces. But Pilsudski had greatly different ideas. He meant to hold that role himself, despite Weygand's not very subtle suggestions otherwise. It was only after some behind-the-scenes maneuvering by d'Abernon and other diplomats that Weygand was admitted to the Polish war councils, and even then he was snubbed mercilessly. For example, at a two-and-a-half-hour meeting, Weygand was forced to sit and fume while the discussion was conducted entirely in Polish. Pilsudski did not address so much as a single word to the French general. Other French officers were even more harshly treated by the Poles. On one occasion, two Frenchmen were sent to the northern sector, where the Red offensive seemed most pressing. They drove to meet the Polish unit to which they had been assigned, only to have their automobile seized; they were forced to return to Warsaw discomfited and on foot.[43]

This was not always the case, however. A notable exception was Tukhachevsky's old prison companion, Charles de Gaulle. Soon after his release from prison camp, de Gaulle had volunteered for service with the unit General Haller was raising in France. During 1919 he was an instructor with the Polish forces at Rembertow, a suburb of Warsaw. As the war situation worsened, he was called to active duty, and displayed conspicuous bravery in the fighting on the Zbruca River, for which he was awarded the Virtuli Militari, Poland's highest such award.[44] It was here that he refined his theories about the use of tanks in close alignment with infantry and air power, producing the views that made his reputation as one of the leading military thinkers of the French army.[45]

During this interval, Lord d'Abernon had several opportunities to obtain a close look at Pilsudski, and his opinion was scarcely favorable to the Polish general. Said the crusty British diplomat about the equally crusty Polish marshal: "A pronounced skeptic about orthodox methods, whether applied to military affairs or politics, he loves danger, his pulse only beating at a normal rate when he is in imminent personal peril—at other times at forty to the minute. In appearance so striking as to be almost theatrical. None of the usual amenities of civilized intercourse. . . . " D'Abernon also provides an anecdote about Pilsudski's political opinions. "In November 1918, he [Pilsudski] received a Socialist delegation who came to greet Comrade Pilsudski, in the following terms: 'Gentlemen, I am no longer your comrade. In the beginning we followed the same direction, and took the tramway painted red but I left it at the station—Poland's independence; you are continuing your journey as far as the station—Socialism. My good wishes accompany you, but be so kind as to call me Sir."[46]

D'Abernon was everywhere. He cajoled the Polish general staff to pay more attention to Weygand. He importuned London for vital munitions. He even found time to visit the front. On the way he was surprised to find relatively few Poles fleeing before Tukhachevsky's advance, but he did meet one worried group of Polish prison officials. They had abandoned their charges and fled, since they knew that in other areas the first victims of the Bolshevik executioners were police and prison officials.[47]

Lord d'Abernon also found that morale among the Polish troops was abysmally low. North of Warsaw, he reported, the mere approach of Gai's cavalry was enough to send the Polish troops into panic. Only the threat of immediate execution kept them at their posts. Finally, on August 13, the situation was judged so grave that all foreign diplomats were ordered to leave Warsaw for Lodz. Only Monsignor Achille Ratti (later Pope Pius XI) and the British ambassador remained in the besieged capital.

By that time, Tukhachevsky had begun preparations for what the Russians believed would be the final offensive against Warsaw. On August 10, he had issued a directive setting out the plans for the campaign. It was to be a triple-pronged assault. The main northern push would circle to the north of Warsaw, cutting the Polish capital off from the Danzig source of Western munitions. At the same time, the 16th Army would drive across the Vistula to the south of Warsaw. The smaller Mozyr Group would move still further south, toward Deblin. Tukhachevsky, apparently ignoring the transportation obstacles involved, had expected that the 12th Army would sweep north to protect the flank of the 16th Army from the Polish forces massed between Warsaw and Lublin. But the Soviet High Command knew better. The 12th Army had been weakened in order to send help against Wrangel, and would not have strength enough for the task Tukhachevsky had set for it.

On August 11, the High Command in Moscow hurried to remedy the weakness. Yegerov was ordered to break off an attack aimed at Lvov by the First Cavalry Army and swing it to the north, toward Zamosc. The rest of Yegorov's forces were directed to shift north as well, to attack in the direction of Lublin. But there were inconsistencies in this order, too. Timoshenko's Sixth Cavalry Division, regarded as the elite of Budenny's army, was to be detached for service against the ever-growing threat from Wrangel; the 14th Army was suggested as a replacement for Budenny's men in the assault on Lvov. In the confusion, and aggravated by a dispute between Tukhachevsky and Yegorov over who was in command of portions of the Southwestern armies, the First Cavalry found itself removed from the battle and then reengaged in a furious fight near Brody.

In the face of this uncertainty, the High Command tried to assert its authority. It told Yegorov that from noon on August 13, the 12th Army and the First Cavalry would be placed under Tukhachevsky's command, with the exception of the Eighth Cavalry Division. But there intruded a series of incidents that were to doom the Russians' chances and to provide fuel for rancorous debates for half a century, long after most of the participants were dead. On August 14, Yegorov forwarded the directive about the change in command to the First Cavalry, but the following day, when Tukhachevsky instructed G. K. Voskanov, the new commander of the 12th Army, to initiate actions that would coordinate his army's moves with those of the Western Front, Budenny refused to recognize the validity of the order. The document in question was apparently a copy of the original, and as such bore only Tukhachevsky's signature and was not countersigned by a commissar. By the time the original document caught up with the headstrong Budenny on August 17, his men were heavily committed in the battle for Lvov. It took three days for the cavalry to be pulled back, and by that time events elsewhere had moved ahead momentously; the First Cavalry's opportunity to play a decisive, distracting role in the campaign for Warsaw was negligible.

On August 16, Tukhachevsky's armies had reached the Vistula, almost within sight of Warsaw. At this juncture, the long-hoped-for uprising of the Polish proletariat was to have occurred. In the preceding weeks, Markhlevsky and others, sometimes including Tukhachevsky, had been staging rallies in Byelostock and other towns, trying to encourage the Polish workers to join the cause of the Red Army in the same way that workers in Chelyabinsk had joined in the Civil War. Dzerzhinsky, Markhlevsky, and Felix Kon had established themselves in the town of Vischkova to form the Polish provisional government that would direct the uprising. The uprising never materialized.[48]

On August 16, even as his left wing was in danger of being annihilated by Tukhachevsky's arcing attack in the northwest, Pilsudski struck at the weakened hinge of the Russian armies. Disaster followed disaster for the Russians—and for Tukhachevsky. Not that a Polish victory seemed certain at the time. During the previous weeks, Pilsudski had quietly been gathering a force of five and a half divisions, south of the capital, for the flank attack he had been planning. But even he was not very optimistic about success. He describes some of the misgivings when he went off to the battle area:

> Finally, in taking leave of General Sosnkowski, I drew his attention to the lack of order which reigned in the general staff and in the organization of the troops as well, and I charged him with the impossible: to root out all the groupings, groups, undergroups, overgroups, advance groups, rear groups, which, in spite of all my efforts, were still in such

great numbers that they had not only plenty of commanders and chiefs of staff, but were so lacking in soldiers that on certain occasions 100 soldiers were divided into three groups commanded by generals. I recommended to him for a start to force himself to keep a watchful eye on the generals who quarreled among themselves continually and were perpetually in argument and to put a finish in some manner or other to the anarchy in the command that I believed forceful.[49]

After leaving Warsaw, Pilsudski went directly to his headquarters at Pulawy. Although he must have noticed such things before, he later recorded his surprise at the state of his army. Some had French rifles, some had German Mausers, some had Austrian Mannlichers. In the 21st Division, nearly half the men on parade were barefoot.[50]

The Polish commander had planned to launch his massive counterattack on August 17. But on August 14, "The situation deteriorated for me. From Warsaw there came anguished telegrams. The initial attack by the Soviets had broken our resistance and Radzymin, in the suburbs, had been under assault. The dispatches told of the alarm in the capital. I gained a certain amount of surprise in learning that the main thrust of Tukhachevsky's troops was increasingly in the direction of Plock and even Woclawek and Brodnica." In response to the pleas from Warsaw, Pilsudski advanced the timing of his attack by one day.[51]

Pilsudski was well aware of the dangers he faced. If the sweeping maneuver by Gai's horsemen and the Fourth Red Army should overrun the Polish left flank and turn back behind it, into the Polish rear, there would be no hope for Warsaw; and without Warsaw and the Danzig supply line, there would be no hope for Pilsudski.

"Because of the presence of the cavalry on the extreme right wing of the Soviet armies, these matters took the proportions of real defeats, the imagination was stunned with the rapidity with which the countryside was occupied by the enemy," he was later to recall.[52]

But Pilsudski gave the order to attack, and so began the fourth and final phase of the Russo-Polish War. At first, the outcome seemed uncertain. The two armies were almost like battered boxers swinging wildly, with the decision depending on which landed the first solid punch. On the Polish left, General Wladyslaw Sikorski was in danger of being outflanked. For a short time it seemed that Tukhachevsky's strategy had worked. And, as Pilsudski later pointed out, there was still the danger that his own flanking movement would be outflanked by a lunge from Budenny's army in the south.

What surprised Pilsudski most, however, was the fact that his troops met almost no resistance in their initial attack. In fact, there were almost no Russian soldiers to be seen, "except for a few skirmishers" who fled when confronted with the mass of the Polish armies. By the end of the first day, the Poles had been able to thrust more than 30 kilometers into the Russian lines.[53]

Pilsudski did not have to wait long for the first real clash between the armies. "I remember, as if it were today," he wrote three years later, "the moment when, drinking a cup of tea near my wagon, getting ready for bed, I jumped up when at last I heard the sound of life, the sound of reality, the deep growl of the artillery, coming to me from the north on the night air. The enemy really did exist."[54]

If Pilsudski had been somewhat at sea, Tukhachevsky was in even worse straits. The news of Pilsudski's counterattack did not reach him until two days after it had begun. And when it did come, it was relayed by the harried commander of the Soviet 16th Army, who had not comprehended the full extent of his predicament until a day after the Poles had launched their attack. In the circumstances, Tukhachevsky did the only thing he could; he advised the 16th Army to begin a strategic retreat. But by then the command structure had fallen apart, and the Russian soldiers were fleeing for their lives.[55]

The full scope of the Russian disaster quickly became apparent. The breakdown of Russian transportation had prevented Tukhachevsky from bringing into position 60,000 reinforcements that the High Command had belatedly provided. The Fourth Red Army, which was to have delivered the coup de grace to Polish hopes, somehow got out of communication and did not receive its orders until too late; it was now surrounded. Worst of all, it was not until August 20 that Budenny managed to break off the attack on Lvov, and by that time it was too late for him to create a diversion in the rear of the Polish right wing. At this point, Pilsudski had broken through the Russian 16th, 3rd, and

15th armies, and was plunging toward the border of East Prussia, thus cutting off the Russian retreat.

Pilsudski followed close behind his victorious troops, still astonished at the extent of their success. In his open car he drove into Minsk, stunned by the bodies of the dead Russians lying unburied by the roadside, their equipment abandoned in the haste of their flight.[56]

The Russian 12th Army in the south was the last to reel before the Polish onslaught. Pilsudski could not help gloating, some years later, about the extent of the Russian rout. "I remember the happy moment when I found on my portable desk the dispatch from the commander of the 12th Soviet Army, broadcast in the clear by radio and saying: 'Where are my divisions?'"[57]

By September 12, Sikorski on the Polish left had also rallied and launched a drive of his own that recovered much of the territory he had so recently been forced to relinquish. Even Budenny, in the south, found himself in dire trouble, finally being forced to fight his way out of a threatened Polish encirclement.

Pilsudski hammered home his advantage, striking heavily at the Russian Third Army. By September 20, it was in a state of disintegration. By September 26, the Poles had recaptured Grodno. In the northwest, the indefatigable Gai and his cavalrymen, their retreat cut off by Sikorski's thrust, battled tenaciously until they were forced to pull back into German territory, where they were quickly interned.

The Poles captured 65,000 prisoners, 231 artillery pieces, 1,000 machine guns, and 10,000 wagons of munitions and supplies. Another 30,000 men, mostly from Gai's and the Russian Fourth Army, were disarmed in East Prussia. Altogether Tukhachevsky had lost almost 150,000 men and a great storehouse of munitions and matériel that tattered Russia could ill afford.

As the Russian soldiers streamed back to their homeland, the humiliation was profound and the backbiting severe. Every one of the Russian leaders was trying to pin the blame for the debacle on someone else. Ivan Smilga came in for some of the criticism because he had been prominent in promoting the idea that the Bolshevik revolution could be transported across the Vistula. Tukhachevsky caught his share; indeed, he deserved it for overreaching himself and his resources. But he had other ideas about who was at fault. He wrote in 1923:

The commander of the Western Front, from day to day counting on the 12th Army and the First Cavalry Army being placed under his command, gave them in advance the task of carrying the left flank of the front, but the transfer was drawn out and the task remained in suspense.

The forces of the Southwestern Front did not cooperate with the forces of the Western Front; they replied with the evidence of the fact that the Southwestern Front had local tasks to carry out, a mission of capital importance, the occupation of the central point of Galicia, the city of Lvov. So it was in this direction that all the forces of the Southwestern Front marched, thus making an angle of 90 degrees from the forces of the Western Front.[58]

Tukhachevsky did not mention Stalin by name, but there was no mistaking that he held Stalin, Budenny, and Voroshilov responsible for the disaster that had befallen him when his triumph had seemed so close. There had been no love lost between them previously, and from then on, there was to be even less. As it turned out, Tukhachevsky had a long memory, but Stalin had an even longer one.

Over the years, the events of 1920 were examined and reexamined by many Soviet analysts. B. M. Shaposhnikov, who during the war had been on the High Command staff, in typical fashion came down squarely in the middle of the dispute. In his book *To the Vistula,* written in 1924, he stated that while Tukhachevsky had made mistakes, the real problem was a lack of strength on the Russian side.[59]

Another participant, V. K. Triandafilov, a year later gave a slightly different version. He placed the blame on the High Command, too, but added that part of the fault lay with the Southwestern Front command. He argued that the Lvov attack should have been promptly countermanded by the High Command and that the Southwestern Command should have been more responsive to the new directions for the First Cavalry Army.[60]

The Southwestern Front's rebuttal was given by Yegorov in the book *Lvov-Warsaw,* published in 1929. He minced no words, saying that "reproaches for the failure of the Warsaw operation lie exclusively in the command methods of Moscow and Minsk"—that is, with Sergei Kamenev and Tukhachevsky.[61]

At the time, despite Stalin's and Yegorov's protestations that the march on Lvov had been necessary because it was designed to prevent a newly mobilized Rumanian army from entering the war on the side of the Poles, Lenin sided with Tukhachevsky. In his uniquely cogent way he summed up the reason for the catastrophe by saying, of Stalin's and Budenny's procrastination in creating a diversion to offset Pilsudski's decisive attack: "Who on earth would want to get to Warsaw by going through Lvov?"[62]

6
COUNTERREVOLUTIONS IN KRONSTADT AND TAMBOV

ON OCTOBER 12, 1920, the Soviet government concluded an armistice with Poland. The Moscow regime was then free to turn its attention to ousting from Russia the last remnants of the White counterrevolution, Wrangel's army in the south. Steps had already been taken in that direction with the formation on September 21 of a new Southern Front under the command of Frunze, who had been serving in Turkestan. By the end of November, after an offensive in which Uborevich, Philip Mironov, and V. K. Bluykher played important parts, Wrangel was driven from the Crimea. The troublesome Ukrainian anarchist partisan Nestor Makhno was also dealt with during this period.

Now was the time for the Soviet regime to lick its wounds. And gaping wounds they were. True, the immediate threats posed by the White generals had been removed. Moscow was once again in control of the wheat fields of the Ukraine, the Donets coal mines and the vital Baku oil supply. Siberia and

Turkestan were under Soviet control. So Lenin and his colleagues began to turn to the task of reconstruction, and for this they looked abroad. On February 26, 1921, they concluded a treaty with the new shah of Persia, Riza Pahlevi. Two days later a similar agreement was signed with Afghanistan, and there were high hopes that a Russian trade delegation that had begun discussions with the Italian government on February 5 would obtain help for the battered Russian state. Help was urgently needed. Millions of Russian citizens had died. Industry was at a standstill because of the lack of raw materials and spare parts. Agriculture, because of the lack of manpower and the ravages of war—not to mention the effects of three years of confiscation under the policy of war communism—was in a shambles. The people were tired, hungry, and angry.

Their principal complaint involved food shortages, and there was also a constant outcry against the system of rationing imposed under war communism. Workers in war-related industries were given a daily ration of 800 grams of bread, while ordinary people had to make do with 400, or in some cases 200, grams. The effect of this was that less privileged workers began to seek their supplies on the black market and the price of food soared. During 1920, for example, the price of bread was said to have risen tenfold.[1]

On top of all this, as the long Russian winter closed in, supplies of fuel became very short. This was to be expected, given the damage done to the mines and the mangled state of the railroads. No repairs had been made since 1913, and they had not been notably efficient before the war.

The final point of friction was the character of the new regime. During the Civil War and the Russo-Polish War, chauvinism had obscured the differences between the political factions that still survived in Russia. But with the end of the fighting, some workers began to question the supremacy of Lenin and the Communist Party, as the Bolsheviks were now officially called. The old slogan "All Power to the Soviets," as distinct from the Communists, began to be heard increasingly. The difference concerned more than semantics; to many Russian citizens there still remained a vast difference between the democracy of the soviets and the dictatorship of Lenin, Trotsky, and the Communist leadership.

In the countryside this anger was reflected in peasant uprisings against Moscow. These affected many provinces, particularly in the crucial chernozem belt of the Ukraine. But it also infected the cities, where the workers, previously the main support of the Communists, now grumbled openly about their unhappy situation. The situation, in the city and the rural areas, was worsened by the rapid demobilization of nearly half the Red Army; about 2.5 million men had been released from service by the spring of 1921.

As the winter snows swirled, the railroad system became strangled to the point of collapse, and food supplies in the main northern cities became almost nonexistent. So, on January 22, 1921, the regime was forced to announce that the bread ration in the cities would be reduced by a one-third. The problems of the transportation system did not impress the hungry population.

The bread cutback was quickly followed by mutinous meetings in Moscow and Petrograd. When party emissaries were dispatched to the worker gatherings, they were usually hooted down. Workers took to the streets with banners demanding an end of war communism, the provision of larger rations, and occasionally the revival of the Constituent Assembly. There was a vicious undertone of some of the protest banners, alluding to the ethnic origin of some of the Communist leaders: "Down With the Communists and the Jews."

The outbreaks in Petrograd had begun shortly after the disruptions in Moscow. But in Petrograd they were aggravated by reports—indeed, a general belief—that higher-ups in the party were not taking their fair share of the privations. This form of discontent was to persist throughout the turbulent days that followed, and surfaced again in the upheavals in Hungary and especially in Poland in the 1980s.

There were plenty of people with time to protest. Lack of fuel had forced many of the factories in Petrograd to close. Their idled workers quickly took to the streets. One particularly angry group of workers assembled on February 23 in the Trubochny metalworking factory. They passed a resolution demanding an immediate increase in the food ration, and the distribution of all the shoes and winter clothing in government stores. The following day, the workers assembled on Vasili Island, by the Neva River. Workers from other factories and students from the nearby Mining Institute joined them until there was a crowd of about 2,000 on hand, yelling their general disagreement with the government. A party official sent to try to get the mob to disperse was dragged from his automobile and beaten. Things were getting out of hand when Grigory E. Zinoviev, the Petrograd party leader, sent a company of military cadets to break up the assembly.

But the following day the Trubochny employees were back in the streets. This time they were joined by workers from other plants, many of them attracted by rumors that some of the protesters had been killed in the previous day's melee. Appeals from Zinoviev and his colleagues that to desert the factories would only aggravate the city's sorry state, went unheeded. Even warnings that the Whites and their British and French backers would take advantage of the unrest to renew their intervention did not diminish the anger of the protest.

On February 24, the Petrograd authorities set up a special Committee of Defense to organize suppression of the disturbances. Named to the new committee were M. M. Lashevich; N. M. Anzelovich; and Dmitri N. Avrov, the 31-year-old commander of the Petrograd Military District. This troika was mirrored by the formation of similar committees for each section of the city and region. Each had a representative from the party, the government, and the military; and each was charged with policing its own territory so that the state of siege proclaimed by Zinoviev could be enforced completely.[2]

By February 26, the regime was becoming very worried. At an emergency meeting of the Petrograd soviet, N. N. Kuzmin, who since the age of 20 had been a party activist and now, at the age of 42, was commissar of the Baltic Fleet, warned that the strike fever was beginning to infect his sailors. It was a sober warning, the more so since these were the very sailors who had played such a pivotal role in the early days of the 1917 Revolution and in the final overthrow of the Kerensky regime.

During the remaining days of February, all attempts by the authorities to end the disturbances proved futile. Every day more plants joined the protest. The tone of anger was also intensifying and changing. Whereas, in the beginning, the complaints had dealt mostly with food and shelter, now political demands were beginning to predominate. This change was accentuated by the work of the remaining Menshevik and Social Revolutionary factions, which, although greatly depleted by arrests and emigration, still functioned. On February 27, one of their manifestos appeared, containing a frontal attack on the Bolsheviks. The broadside called for release "of all arrested socialists and non-party workers; freedom of speech, press and assembly for all who labor; abolition of martial law; free election of factory committees, trade unions and soviets." The workers were urged to hold meetings, to pass resolutions, and to petition the authorities.[3] Other leaflets were not so orderly, calling openly for insurrection against the Communists. But after about a week of protests, the agitation in Petrograd began to subside.

The change was hardly spontaneous. The Communists had struck back at the dissent by locking the workers out of the factories, thus depriving many of them of their rations. In addition, the Cheka started a wholesale roundup of Menshevik and Socialist Revolutionary leaders and sympathizers. Military reinforcements were rushed to Petrograd, just in case the worst should happen. In addition, Zinoviev acceded to some of the protesters' demands. They would be allowed, for example, to leave the city to seek food in the countryside. Special trains would even be scheduled to help them in this quest. Further, the party chairman announced, the government had managed to buy coal overseas, which would soon arrive to help ease the fuel crisis. By March 3, the result of these actions was apparent; nearly every factory in Petrograd was back in operation.

The immediate threat to the Soviet regime seemed to have faded. But events were soon to prove that the events of late February had been only the prologue. The Petrograd disturbances had been largely dispelled without bloodshed. True, there had been numerous arrests, but Zinoviev's firm handling of the situation had paid off. He was to be less sure of himself when new troubles arose at the giant naval base of Kronstadt.

Seen from the shore of the Baltic at Petrograd, or from the grounds of the summer palace at Petrodvorets, the island of Kotlin, on which Kronstadt stands, on most days in hardly more than a smoky blue line on the horizon 15 or so miles away. In the winter, when the sea freezes solid, it is barely distinguishable. But since Peter the Great first fortified it in the eighteenth century, Kronstadt has provided a strategic barrier for his capital.

Kotlin is about six miles long and about three miles across at its broadest point. The fortress was reinforced by a line of batteries placed on rocky islands across the Gulf of Finland. On the northern shore of the Baltic two more forts, at Sestroretsk and Lisy Nos, were built; and two more were on the southern shore, at Oranienbaum and Krasnaya Gorka. The latter fortresses served a double purpose; they could help repel an invasion and, more important, they could neutralize Kronstadt if Kotlin fell into the wrong hands. In 1905 and in 1917, the Kronstadt garrison had provided crucial components of the revolutionary forces. Now that threat was to surface again.

Unrest had been simmering in Kronstadt for a long time. The sailors' complaints were largely political, involving dissatisfaction with the military specialists appointed by Moscow to supervise what the sailors had previously thought of as their sovereign domain. According to Ida Mett, this dissatisfaction had produced pronounced disillusion with the Communist Party, and in late 1920 and January 1921, 2,000 of the 4,000 party members at the base had resigned.[4]

A contributing factor was undoubtedly the distaste for the machinations of Trotsky and Zinoviev for control of the Soviet Navy. Trotsky, as the regime's dominant military figure, thought that this was his purview, but Zinoviev, as chairman of the Petrograd soviet, thought it was his. The result was that inside the base there were rival factions, some supporting the two leaders, but others wanting nothing to do with either of them.

By the middle of February, as the Petrograd workers were beginning their demonstrations, the sailors of Kronstadt were also voicing irritation with the Communists. Reports from Petrograd added to their anger, and when rumors reached them that protesting workers on Vasili Island had been shot by Zinoviev's troops on February 26, they staged a mass meeting that decided to send a delegation to the mainland to find out what had gone wrong. What they saw there left them aghast. Factories were ringed with troops, and even inside the plants, armed soldiers watched for trouble. After the delegation's return to the fleet on February 28, another meeting was held on the battleship *Petropavlovsk*. The gathering issued a proclamation that became the rallying point for the uprising that was soon to follow.

The 15-point document was a catalog of complaints against

the Communist Party. It called for new elections to the soviets, with freedom to campaign granted to all parties. It also demanded freedom of speech and assembly for all parties. It attacked the Communist Party directly by demanding an end to Communist-controlled political departments in the military and a cessation of state support for Communist Party functions. The document also called for recognition of the right of the peasants to keep their own cattle and to till their own plots, as long as they did not hire outside labor. In addition, all political prisoners were to be freed.[5]

Zinoviev had already acted to meet some of the demands, by removing the roadblocks barring travel from the city to the countryside, but the political nature of the other points seemed designed to strike a deathblow at the Communists' hold on power. On those points, Lenin, Zinoviev, and their colleagues could give no ground.

On March 1, another meeting was held in Anchor Square, the heart of Kronstadt. More than 16,000 of the garrison's residents turned out. From Petrograd came Kuzmin and Mikhail I. Kalinin, respected in Kronstadt and elsewhere for his worker-peasant origins. They were greeted with a military honor guard and music, but as soon as the *Petropavlovsk* resolution was put before the meeting, such courtesies disappeared. Kalinin rose quickly to speak against adoption of the resolution. There was an immediate outbreak of heckling from the now angry crowd. They taunted Kalinin with the charges that they suspected were true of all the Communist leaders: that they drew pay from several jobs and that the special arrangements for government and military leaders provided them with extra supplies of warm clothing and food. Kalinin could not make himself heard above the din. Kuzmin then intervened, but the chorus that greeted him was even nastier. There were shouts of anger about his activities as commander of the Sixth Army on the Northern Front during the Civil War, including the charge that he was responsible for having many good comrades shot during the fighting there. Kuzmin, after having spent almost half of his 38 years in often dangerous party work, was not fazed. "The working people have always shot traitors to the cause," he shouted. "And they will continue to shoot them. In my place you would have shot every fifth man, not every tenth."[6]

The resolution was then voted on, being approved by all but Kalinin and Kuzmin. As a last act, the gathering voted to send a delegation to Petrograd to inform the citizens there of what had transpired. Kalinin was then allowed to depart.

During the night, hasty elections were held in all the ships and units in Kronstadt to select delegates who would choose a new soviet for the base. The election of soviet members was held the following day, under the chairmanship of Stepan Maksimovich Petrichenko, a 20-year-old sailor from the *Petropavlovsk* who was emerging as the dominant figure among the dissidents. Despite — or because of — his heavy Ukrainian accent, he was already a leading figure among the sailors, many of whom, like him, came from peasant backgrounds.

On March 3, Kuzmin made one more effort to dissuade the dissidents from the course on which they were so obviously embarked. He reminded them that no formal peace treaty had been concluded with Poland, and that any sign of disunity among the Russians might well induce Pilsudski to break the precarious informal truce. Kuzmin's tone was defiant, even threatening, and that was his mistake. The threats merely served to stiffen the resolve of the sailors and their allies to push to the utmost for the realization of their demands. The upshot was that Kuzmin and Vassiliev, president of the Kronstadt soviet, were immediately arrested. From then on, there was no turning back for either side. The Kronstadt rebellion had begun.[7]

When word of Kuzmin's arrest reached Petrograd, Zinoviev and his colleagues wasted no time in striking back. Airplanes from the city flew over Kronstadt, dropping leaflets saying: "The Committee of Defense announces that it has imprisoned the families of sailors as hostages for the return of Communist comrades arrested by the insurgents of Kronstadt and in particular for the commissar of the fleet Kuzmin and the president of the Kronstadt soviet Vassiliev. If a hair falls from their heads, these hostages will lose their heads."[8]

The leaflets worsened an already inflamed situation. Rumors flew through Kronstadt, starting during the March 3 meeting, when there was a report that 15 truckloads of armed Communists were being sent to the island to break up the assembly. Those present quickly elected a Provisional Revolutionary Committee to take charge of what was expected to be a defense against a general assault on the island. Rumor piled on rumor, including one aired by Petrichenko that 2,000 Communists were being rushed to the island. The Provisional Revolutionary Committee set up its headquarters on the *Petropavlovsk* and prepared to do battle with the invaders. They were quickly well enough organized to begin publishing their own newspaper to air their grievances against the Communists in general and Zinoviev in particular.

Who were these sailors who dared to challenge the authority of Lenin, Trotsky, and Zinoviev? What were the concerns that had brought them to open rebellion against the Soviet powers? As later Soviet writers have pointed out, there had been a substantial change in the makeup of the garrison at Kronstadt since the early days of the 1917 Revolution. The sailors who had provided a spearhead for the rebels against the tsar and against Kerensky had frequently been co-opted for service elsewhere by the new regime. Many of them had seen service against Kolchak on the Volga. Their places at Kronstadt had been taken by young peasants recruited from the provinces, giving the great naval base a completely new population. This perhaps explains why Petrichenko, who spoke the same language as so many of the new sailors, was so quickly able to gain such widespread popularity. It also perhaps explains the anger that was so easily aroused in the garrison. The young peasant sailors had heard all the lurid tales of forced confiscation of grain and livestock from their families at the hands of Trotsky's and Dzerzhinsky's subordinates, and they did not like what they heard.

The confiscation was a frequent theme in the dissidents' newspaper, the *Kronstadt Izvestia*. In one issue the editors declared: "Comrades, peasants, you, more than anyone, were misled and robbed by the Bolshevik Government. Where is the land you had wrested from the squires, land you have dreamed of for hundreds of years? It was given to the communal farms or taken for Soviet farms and you can only look on and smack your lips. From you was taken all that could be carried away. . . . With hungry bellies and gagged mouths, barefoot and naked, you are forced to do the will of the new nobility." In the last issue of the paper there appeared an editorial that said in part: "Here in Kronstadt we have laid the first stone of the third revolution, have knocked off the last fetters of the toiling masses and have opened up a new, wide road of socialist creation. . . ."[9]

The Communists charged that a leading role in the uprising had been played by renegade tsarist officers, particularly the artillery general Aleksandr N. Kozlovsky. On March 3, Radio Moscow broadcast this message: "For the struggle against the White Guard plot, the mutiny of the old general Kozlovsky and of the ship *Petropavlovsk*, as the other insurrections of the White Guard have been organized by the spies of the Entente. These developments the newspaper *Le Matin* has published, two weeks before the revolt of General Kozlovsky. It is clear that the Kronstadt revolt is directed in Paris." It is certainly true that Kozlovsky and some other former tsarist officers did remain in the fortress during the turbulent days of March, and it is also true that they participated in the defense against the attacking Communist forces. But there is also little doubt that the leading rebels were Petrichenko and other low-ranking sailors who felt free to ignore Kozlovsky's advice. For example, Kozlovsky is said to have urged the mutineers to stage a preemptive attack against the Communist garrisons at Oranienbaum and elsewhere, but Petrichenko and his colleagues would not do so. Of course, there were numerous former tsarist officers on Lenin's side, not the least of them Mikhail Tukhachevsky. And as for external influences, they played an insignificant part in the Kronstadt events. Victor Chernov, the Socialist Revolutionary leader, radioed from his exile in Reval an offer to come to Kronstadt and to send supplies. It was politely and firmly refused by the mutineers.[10]

From the beginning, the Communist authorities were determined to stamp out the rebels. They felt it was essential to deal a death blow before the dissidence spread. This attitude was reinforced by events on the night of March 2, when delegates from Kronstadt slipped across the ice to the fortress at Oranienbaum and persuaded the rank and file of the First Naval Air Squadron to join their cause. When Zinoviev was alerted to this, he at once called on all Communists at Oranienbaum to take arms against the new rebels. In the predawn hours, a detachment of *kursanty*, military cadets, and some military units were sent to back up the Oranienbaum Communists. The airmen were quickly subdued, and within hours 45 of their leaders were summarily executed.[11]

Alarmed by events in Oranienbaum and similar incidents in the suburbs of Petrograd, the authorities hastily gathered reinforcements from Moscow and elsewhere. Zinoviev set up his headquarters in the elegant Hotel Astoria, opposite St. Isaac's Church, and ringed it with machine gun posts. All loyal Communists in the area were mobilized and issued arms. Young Communists were dispatched from all over Russia. Special Cheka detachments were hurried to the scene.[12]

On March 4, Zinoviev summoned a special meeting of the Petrograd soviet to discuss the action to be taken against Kronstadt. It was a stormy session. Zinoviev and Kalinin denounced the rebels as stooges of the Whites. But others at the meeting angrily responded that the real villains were the Communist leaders. Zinoviev was branded an autocrat indifferent to the starvation and privation around him. According to Emma Goldman, who was present, one worker even went so far as to warn: "Barely three years ago, Lenin, Trotsky, Zinoviev and all of you were denounced as German spies. We, the workers and sailors, had to come to your rescue and saved you from the Kerensky Government. It was we who placed you in power. Have you forgotten that? Now you threaten us with the sword. Remember you are playing with fire. You are repeating the blunders and crimes of the Kerensky Government. Beware that a similar fate does not overtake you." The mood grew uglier. But Zinoviev had apparently expected as much. The platform was heavily guarded by *kursanty*, and Cheka soldiers with fixed bayonets stood between it and the unruly audience. Zinoviev at times seemed on the point of nervous collapse. Several times he rose to speak but sat down without doing so. When eventually he did speak, his head jerked from side to side in a nervous tic and his voice, Emma Goldman says, always adolescently thin, rose to a high-pitched shrillness.[13]

Despite the opposition, the gathering passed a resolution urging the rebels to cease and desist. With this legal nicety attended to, the Communist authorities immediately sent a proclamation to the dissidents:

> The Workers and Peasants' Government has decreed that Kronstadt and the rebellious ships must immediately submit to the authority of the Soviet Republic. Therefore I command all who have raised their hand against the Socialist fatherland to lay down their arms at once. The obdurate are to be disarmed and turned over to the Soviet authorities. The

arrested Commissars and other representatives of the Government are to be liberated at once. Only those surrendering unconditionally may count on the mercy of the Soviet Republic. Simultaneously, I am issuing orders to prepare to quell the mutiny and subdue the mutineers by force of arms. Responsibility for the harm that may be suffered by the peaceful population will fall entirely upon the heads of the counter-revolutionary mutineers. This warning is final.

> TROTSKY
> Chairman, Revolutionary Military Council of the Republic
>
> KAMENEV
> Commander in Chief[14]

This was followed by a threat from Trotsky, who had arrived in Petrograd on March 5, to the mutineers: "I'll shoot you like pheasants." As might have been expected, the reaction from Kronstadt was entirely negative. The rebels insisted on their demands being met, particularly for changes in the makeup of the Petrograd soviet, changes that would have mandated that no more than 15 percent of its members could be Communists.[15]

The Petrograd authorities had given the rebels 24 hours to give up their struggle. It would expire on March 6, but in the interval sweeping changes were being made in the command of the regime's forces, necessitated largely by the uncertain allegiance of the military units on which Trotsky, Zinoviev, and the others would have to rely. Avrov was unceremoniously dumped as the commander of the Petrograd Military District. He had seemed one of the rising stars of the Red Army but now his career was over; he died a year later.

His successor was Tukhachevsky, now officially designated commander of the Seventh Army but in fact the overall military commander of the Petrograd area. As one of his subordinates, Aleksandr Tipolt, recalled later, the new assignment seemed to promise nothing but trouble, but Tukhachevsky took it eagerly, perhaps out of a desire to atone for his recent humiliation on the Polish Front. Tipolt had served with Tukhachevsky in the Semyenovsky Guards and had been a member of the young general's staff on the Western Front, so he knew him well. His recollections provide an unusual glimpse of the youthful Tukhachevsky—he had turned 28 just two weeks before.

As usual, Tukhachevsky was filled with confidence. He knew that one of his more serious problems was to restore confidence in the command, shaken by signs of dissent—what the Communists called a "demobilization mood" among the troops—and to convince the worried officers that they could successfully deal with the storm around them. The same mood that had caused Zinoviev to surround his person with Cheka guards and to surround the Astoria Hotel with machine guns had caused the previous district commander to shift the military headquarters into the isolation of the Peter and Paul Fortress. Tukhachevsky immediately moved it to a building formerly used by the Russian General Staff on Palace Square, not far from the Astoria. It was a move designed to exhibit confidence that apparently succeeded, for the staff, according to Tipolt, began working with unaccustomed vigor. The new commander had assigned the staff to come up with all the available details of Kronstadt's layout, but what they showed him was not encouraging. All inspections of the plans revealed that Kronstadt was almost impregnable. However, Tukhachevsky gathered up the plans and disappeared with them. In a short time, according to Tipolt, he returned, obviously in a more cheerful frame of mind. He believed that he had found Kronstadt's weakness.

The first attack was scheduled for dawn on March 7. Tipolt describes the scene in the hours just before:

> We stood by with weapons at the ready in the staff headquarters. Others waited for the order in Oranienbaum—and in Schlisselburg. The time of the ultimatum was running out. Silence reigned. In deathly silence we heard the thunder of the artillery. Krasnaya Gorka fired; the mutineers answered. It had begun.[16]

The attacking force, wearing long white coveralls as camouflage on the windswept ice of the Baltic, moved out under covering fire from the batteries on the mainland. Kronstadt replied with artillery fire, and the machine guns of the rebels mercilessly raked the vulnerable troops out on the floes. Seeing this, some of the Red soldiers refused to venture out to what seemed certain death. But others, mostly *kursanty*, pushed ahead. However, the first assault wave was unable to break into the fortress. A second assault suffered even greater losses from the rebel fusillade. Artillery shells broke up the ice, and many of the attackers plunged to their deaths in the freezing, black waters of the Baltic. Even the threat that the faint of heart would be shot by their commanders was not enough to spur on the attackers. Some of them went over to the mutineers.

In the first attack from Oranienbaum, the Red soldiers were persuaded to begin the advance only with difficulty. And, as soon as they neared the enemy, the second battalion surrendered. The officers and a few loyalists had to return to base. The third battallion behaved in the same way.

> Everyone surrendered, except the commissars and 3 or 4 soldiers who had to retrace their steps back across the ice alone. The same situation arose in the Northern Sector. Uglanov, the commissar on the Northern Sector, reported on March 8: "Among the *kursanty* there reigns a feeling of peril and despair at the idea of going to attack on the ice. This state of mind continues this morning, the day of the attack against the numbered forts. They are quite ready to leave the attack to the Communists and the brave nonparty people. It is only thanks to the commander, to the urgings of the political workers and the officers that the *kursanty* set in process the assault which opened under violent artillery fire from the forts and Kronstadt. This attack will end with the occupation of Fort No. 7. We will have to abandon the others today, because of the state of depression of the troops. It is impossible to send a second time the army to attack the forts. I have already spoken of the state of the *kursanty* to Comrades Lashevich, Avrov and Trotsky. I must signal to them the following tendencies: They want to know what the Kronstadians want and would like to send delegates to Kronstadt. The number of political commissars in the sector is insufficient." [17]

The failure of the Northern Sector's forces to occupy more than one of the numbered forts showed that the assault plan, prepared in haste, had been faulty. Moreover, because of the refusal of a considerable number of the Red troops to take part, it had been insufficiently manned. The lesson would not be wasted on Tukhachevsky.

As the attackers retreated and returned to their bases, he was already drawing up a new assault plan. This time there would be no mistakes.

To replace the recalcitrant members of the Seventh Army, new reinforcements were rushed in from other parts of Russia, among them Kirghiz and Bashkir units who had no fraternal feelings with the mutineers. They were quickly set to training for the maneuvers on the ice. As the snow pummeled them, they were moved out from barriers on the frozen sea. They were instructed on the layout of Kotlin Island and how to take cover behind the ridges on the ice. Most important, new political workers were distributed throughout the attack forces, instructed to watch carefully for all signs of counterrevolutionary feeling or activity. Three hundred and twenty delegates to the Tenth Party Congress, which had opened in Moscow on March 8, hastened to Petrograd. Among them were Voroshilov and A. S. Bubnov, prominent for their political work on other fronts, and the military specialists Ivan Fedko, Yan Fabritisius, Pavel Dybenko, Aleksandr Sedyakin, and Tukhachevsky's close friend Vitovt Putna.

On March 9, *Pravda* published an interview with Tukhachevsky that followed the official line that the revolt was inspired by White Guard sympathies and that the privations of which the mutineers complained were no worse than those endured by the bulk of the population that was not protesting. It also revealed something about the personal feelings of the young general. In speaking of General Kozlovsky, who was generally believed by the Communists to be the main military mind behind the uprising, Tukhachevsky commented: "General Kozlovsky always was reputed among those colleagues least capable among the military specialists." In another section of the interview he referred to the artillery commander as "incompetent." Lack of confidence in his own ability was never one of Tukhachevsky's weaknesses.[18]

But that did not mean that the battle was over or that Kronstadt would be easily taken, as Tukhachevsky fully realized. Therefore, his preparations for the next assault were carried out with deliberate haste. There was reason to hurry: The advent of March meant that the spring thaw would not be long in coming; the ice would melt and the liquidation of Kronstadt would be much more difficult.

The fratricidal conflict seemed certain to intensify, with more bloodshed the inevitable outcome. But there were some in Petrograd who still were trying to prevent such an outcome. Particularly prominent in such efforts were the anarchists Aleksandr Berkman and the redoubtable Emma Goldman. They sent a plea to Zinoviev, urging restraint. But the Communists were determined to silence the rebels in Kronstadt. Tukhachevsky's plans were pushed ahead.[19]

Tukhachevsky was apparently occupied with inspecting his command. In the March 11 issue of the Petrograd *Pravda*, he was reported to be in Oranienbaum, where he was doing his bit to add to the already furious propaganda campaign being conducted by the Communists, aimed at undermining outside support for the rebels on Kotlin. As he had in the earlier interview, Tukhachevsky took pains to emphasize his contention that the White generals were the real instigators of the uprising and that the common people of the island were eager for an armistice. According to Tukhachevsky's report, a refugee from Kronstadt had told the Communist authorities that the White officers were . . . in very good humor.

> They don't care about the bloodletting that they have provoked. They dream of the delights that await them if they take Petrograd. 'Once Petrograd is in our hands, there will be at least a half-pood of gold per man. And if we lose, we will save ourselves in Finland where they will greet us with open arms.' This is what these gentlemen declare. They feel totally masters of the situation. And, in effect, they are. Their attitude toward the sailors is no different from that of the old tsarist times. That is, these are the real leaders, not like the Communists, blinding the eyes of sailors. They have not lost their 'gold epaulettes.' We bring to the attention of these gentlemen, the White Guard officers, that they cannot count too much on an escape to Finland and that they are going to receive, not gold, but a good portion of lead.[20]

It was ten days before Tukhachevsky was ready for a second assault. One reason for the delay was the need to make sure that the troops involved in the operation were totally reliable. The seriousness of this question was vividly illustrated three days before the attack was scheduled to begin: The celebrated 27th

Omsk Division, which had first won fame in its decisive victory over Kolchak's forces on the Eastern Front, mutinied at Oranienbaum. The men refused to join the attack against Kronstadt. Troops loyal to the Communists surrounded the mutineers and arrested the principals, some of whom were shot. Among them was the former commander of the regiment, a one-time tsarist officer who was thoroughly disillusioned with the new regime. Just before he was shot, he said: "I waited years for this moment. Murderers of Russia, I hate you. I have lost the game, and now life means nothing to me." Putna was placed in command of the unhappy regiment and charged with whipping it back into line. And the events at Oranienbaum were not isolated. Even the *kursanty*, both those from Peterhof and those brought recently from Moscow, were affected by desertions and discontent. The crews of the naval vessels in Petrograd were threatening to join the Kronstadt rebels.[21]

In this desperate situation Tukhachevsky rushed his preparations for the second assault. This time there would be no halfhearted attack and, he hoped, no mistakes. In the first attempt to overrun Kronstadt, it has been estimated that perhaps 25,000 troops were involved on the Communist side. For the second attack, reliable estimates place the number at a minimum of 50,000.[22] In addition, they were directed by the best men Tukhachevsky and the Communist leadership could find. The Northern Group was commanded by E. S. Kazansky, while the Southern Group was commanded by Sedyakin, with the help of Putna. Sergei Kamenev was involved, if at a distance. To boost morale among the attackers, Tukhachevsky made sure that each man was given a two-day ration of bread and two cans of meat. There were to be no complaints about a lack of food. Special Cheka units were brought into action to guard against the desertions that plagued the first attempt. But despite the repression and the reorganization, morale was still shaky. On March 14, one unit refused to fight, saying: "We do not wish to go into battle against our brothers, those who come from the same *stanitsas*" or villages.[23]

On March 16, Tukhachevsky issued his order of battle:

To the commander of the Northern Group, Kazansky, and the commander of the Southern Group, Sedyakin, copy to Glavkom. Petrograd. March 15, 1921, 11:45 P.M.:

> I order the fortress of Kronstadt to be taken by an all-out attack during the night of March 16–17. With this end in view: 1. Artillery bombardment is to begin at 2 P.M. on March 16 and to continue until night. 2. The northern column is to move out at 3 A.M. and the southern column at 4 A.M. on March 17. 3. The Northern Group will attack the northeast sector. The Southern Group will attack the northwest and southwest areas of the town. 4. Both groups should restrict themselves to the occupation of those forts the greatest obstacles to their advance. 5. The commander of the Southern Group is to appoint a single leader to direct the fighting in the streets of Kronstadt. 6. The commander of the Southern Group is to concentrate his effort on the capture of the northwest part of the island of Kotlin within the time set. 7. The lines of the columns are to be strictly maintained. 8. Receipt of this order and reports of actions taken are to be notified.
>
> Tukhachevsky[24]

The artillery barrage designed to soften up the fortress began more or less on schedule, and in the early morning hours the two-pronged offensive by the infantry got under way. As the men moved out, shrouded in white camouflage suits, their movements were further covered by the winter fog that cloaked the Baltic ice.

The Northern Group, mostly cadets, moved out in two files from Sestroretsk and Lisy Nos. Their aim was to pick off forts Totleben and Kasnoamyets, and the seven numbered forts that were strung out across the gulf of Finland. Tukhachevsky insisted that the initial movement must be kept as quiet as possible. Conversation was forbidden. Wherever possible, given the poor visibility, orders were flashed by light. Even smoking was forbidden, lest the light give away the movements of the troops.

The men crept forward, and by 5 A.M. the Northern Group had reached the outermost of the numbered forts, 5 and 6. Outside the forts were thick entanglements of barbed wire, and the cadets were cutting their way through when the searchlights of the forts suddenly burst upon them. The startled *kursanty* immediately charged forward, but were briefly driven back by machine gun fire. Again and again, however, the cadets pressed their offensive, until they prevailed.

The Southern Group had been given a special task—to penetrate the Kronstadt weakness that had brought a smile to Tukhachevsky soon after his arrival—according to Tipolt's account. Under Dybenko's leadership, the 80th Brigade was to advance toward Kronstadt's military harbor and the Petrograd Gate. While the ice remained in the harbor, that was Kronstadt's Achilles heel. A breakthrough there could be quickly decisive. Putna was leading the 79th Brigade—the one sound brigade of the 27th Division—toward the southern part of the town.

By the time the first of the northern forts had fallen to the Communists, day was breaking. Now fortune seemed to smile on the defenders, for March 17 proved to be a cloudless, sunny day. The attackers, despite their white camouflage suits, stood out vividly on the ice. Shells from the rebel-held forts now began to thunder down on the ice around the attackers, breeching small lakes into which, on several occasions, groups of the attackers were hurled to an icy death. But by the middle of the afternoon, all the numbered forts were back in Communist hands. Fort Totleben, however, proved more difficult. It was not until after midnight on March 18 that it finally surrendered.

The Southern Group had left the base at Oranienbaum an hour later than its northern counterpart. Pulling machine guns and light artillery on sleds behind them, they trudged across the ice, aiming for the harbor. It was still dark as they reached the approach to the harbor, a darkness that was made eerie and dangerous by the searchlights that played out from Kronstadt. The attackers showed remarkable courage—no more so than the defenders, however—but some tried to turn back, only to be executed by their commanders.

Just before dawn, the Communists managed to break into the city near the Petrograd Gate, where, if anything, the fighting became fiercer. Machine gunners and riflemen on the rooftops poured a murderous fire onto the attackers. At ground level the Communist troops were also meeting heavy resistance, and had to force their way forward with bayonet charges. Communist losses were exceedingly heavy. The defenders, too, were taking heavy casualties, and soon the dead and wounded were lying everywhere. From street to street the battle advanced. Tukhachevsky's men had to grope their way forward. At 4 P.M. on March 17, the rebels staged a furious counterattack and would have driven the Communists back onto the ice had not fresh reinforcements, a cavalry unit from the reluctant 27th Division and a detachment of Communists from Petrograd, arrived on the scene. At 8 P.M., the Communists renewed their attack, now joined by horse artillery brought from Oranienbaum. The shells fell thunderously into the rebel-held areas of Kronstadt, causing heavy casualties among the civilian population. During the evening, the Northern and Southern groups managed to link up, and together swept into the center of the city.

At this point, it had become certain that Kronstadt could no longer hold out. Its fall was only a matter of time. In that realization, and knowing well that certain execution would follow their capture, most of the leaders of the uprising slipped off the island and headed for sanctuary across the Gulf of Finland. Petrichenko and Kozlovsky were among them. Altogether, in the following day and night, 8,000 of the mutineers managed to slip through the Communist lines. Only a few pockets of resistance held out. The crews of the *Sevastopol* and *Petropavlovsk* laid down their weapons and offered no resistance.[25]

At 10 minutes to midnight the Communists were able to send a message to Petrograd: "The counterrevolutionary nests on the *Petropavlovsk* and *Sevastopol* have been liquidated. Power rests in the hands of sympathizers with Soviet authority. Urgent measures are being taken to stop the officers who have fled toward the Finnish frontier."

During the afternoon of March 18—ironically, the fiftieth anniversary of the Paris Commune—the last resistance was smothered. Tukhachevsky's plan had worked. The Communist regime had annihilated a major threat to its existence, but at a terrible cost.

A distraught Emma Goldman recalled the scene.

> The stillness that fell over Petrograd was more fearful than the ceaseless firing of the night before. It held everyone in agonized suspense, and it was impossible to learn what had happened and why the bombardment had ceased. In the late afternoon, the tension gave way to horror. Kronstadt had been subdued—tens of thousands slain—the city drenched in blood. The Neva a grave for masses of men, *kursanty* and young Communists whose heavy artillery had broken through the ice. The heroic sailors and soldiers [of Kronstadt] had

defended their position to the last breath. Those not fortunate enough to die fighting had fallen into the hands of the enemy to be executed or sent to slow torture in the frozen regions of northernmost Russia.[26]

Officially, the Communists placed the toll at 700 dead and 2,500 wounded, but most independent sources place their losses much higher. Harold Quarton, the United States consul at Viborg and an unbiased source of information on the attack, suggests the total casualties among the Communists—dead and wounded—was probably around 10,000. The rebels lost around 600 killed, 1,000 wounded, and about 2,500 taken prisoner. Many of the latter were executed or transported into exile.

Like Emma Goldman, many foreign socialists who had been enthusiastic about Lenin's and Trotsky's policies now recoiled in horror at the bloody lengths to which the Communist leaders were willing to go to quash dissent. Tukhachevsky became, to these disillusioned liberals, nothing less than a ruthless butcher.

Ida Mett said:

> In 1921, the revolution found itself at a crossroads—to take the democratic route or to follow the dictator's way. In putting bourgeois parliamentarianism and workers' democracy in the same bag, the Bolsheviks condemned both. They decided to create socialism from above. . . .[27]

For Tukhachevsky, the Kronstadt affair had several important ramifications. Coming so soon after the Polish failure, it had redeemed his reputation as a military commander. For the first time in history, infantry troops had reduced a naval fortress by attacking across the ice. Despite the high casualties—it is doubtful they could have been fewer in the circumstances—his plan had been well thought out. He had found Kronstadt's weakness and broken through it. Politically he had cemented his position as a loyalist who put the welfare of the Communist regime above all else. There was no doubt of his allegiance after Kronstadt, and he was soon to be called on to fill his new role: the gendarme of Lenin's revolution.

As the mopping up was being completed at Kronstadt and Trotsky was staging an ill-timed victory parade in sullen Petrograd, Tukhachevsky returned to Moscow. After less than a month, he was given a new assignment: to deal with what had become a chronic revolt against the Soviet regime centered in Tambov Province, led by a Social Revolutionary of long standing, A. S. Antonov. The Tambov rebellion was just one of 50 such uprisings that occurred against the Lenin government at this time, but in size and duration it was by far the most serious.[28]

The circumstances under which Tukhachevsky was delegated to take care of the Antonovschina are somewhat uncertain. According to Todorsky, Tukhachevsky was waiting in Moscow after the Kronstadt events, with nothing much to do. He got into conversation with Gusev and aired his dissatisfaction with being idle. Gusev suggested that he approach Lenin directly, to see what the leader had to offer. In this version, Tukhachevsky did call on Lenin, who told him: "It is necessary to have done with the Antonovites in Tambov Province. How would you like to undertake this task?" Tukhachevsky agreed with alacrity, and soon had joined Vladimir Alekseyevich Antonov-Ovseenko, who was already working in the area.[29]

But in the Trotsky papers a much different and far less casual version is implied. In the archives, dated in April 1921, there is a message in the handwriting of Efraim Markovich Sklyansky: "I would consider it desirable to send Tukhachevsky to put down the Tambov uprising. There has been no improvement there of late and here and there even a deterioration. This appointment would produce something of a major political effect. Especially abroad. Your opinion?"

There follows a notation in Lenin's handwriting: "Pass to Molotov for P/buro for tomorrow. I recommend appointing him without publicity at the Center—without gazetting it."[30]

Sklyansky apparently wanted to use Tukhachevsky's new reputation for ruthlessness, one prominent result of Kronstadt, to influence opinion overseas, particularly among the Socialist Revolutionaries, who had deep roots in the Tambov area. Lenin was more cautious.

Tambov was the heart of peasant Russia. Antonov-Ovseenko noted the region's character in a report to Lenin:

> As compared with its 3¼ million rural population there are only about 250,000 townsfolk (about 8 percent). Industry is extremely poorly developed. . . . The province is reckoned

to be a productive one and sent out up to 60 million poods of agricultural products per annum, of which up to 26 million poods were for abroad. Tambov, Rasskazavo and Kozlov were major grain markets with turnovers of many millions of rubles. This remote province, farmed by peasants and landowners, had also long been the domain of the Socialist Revolutionaries. For a long time it had been a place of administrative exile; no small number of the local peasants had been removed to more distant places. As early as 1895 the Socialist Revolutionary organization embraced five *yezds* [at that time a congress of these *yezd*, or governmental district groups took place at Borisoglebsk]. . . . from there came such prominent members of the Socialist Revolutionaries as Sletov, M. Spiridonova and V. M. Chernov.[31]

The first recent uprising among the peasants of the area had broken out in September 1918, but it was swiftly put down by the Soviet authorities. The dissidence, however, continued to simmer, with guerrilla bands of peasant soldiers operating throughout the area, 200 or so miles southeast of Moscow. In September 1920, the revolt flared again, aggravated by peasant dissatisfaction with the forced confiscations of grain and livestock under Moscow's policy of war communism.

The uprising in Kronstadt had also played a part in helping encourage the Tambov peasantry to renew their rebellion. When the news of the events in Petrograd reached the Tambov area, it seemed to confirm the peasants' belief that the Bolsheviks were mishandling the affairs of the country.[32]

Understandably, to Lenin and Trotsky, the chief danger in the Tambov rebellion seemed to lie in the possibility that it would provide a base for the Socialist Revolutionaries, who by this time were the only real political opposition. The activities of Spiridonova, who was a great heroine in the region, had caused them particular concern. Also, to a great extent the Antonovistas did use Social Revolutionary slogans to try to rally the peasants to their side. Moreover, in the first years of the century A. S. Antonov had been at least nominally a member of that party. But there were other political strains present among the rebels, including remnants of the Land and Liberty movement, Republicans, and even adherents to Kerensky and the Constituent Assembly.[33]

Before Tukhachevsky's arrival in the region, the Bolshevik authorities had exerted strenuous efforts, even brutal methods, to try to subdue the unrest. One of their first actions, beginning early in March 1921, was to deport whole villages of the rebels. And Cheka units, already active in the area, were systematically executing known sympathizers with the rebels, and even some who may not have been rebel sympathizers, in a terror campaign to choke off the uprising.[34]

There was no doubt that the uprising had the support of the local population. Even Tukhachevsky, writing about it some months later, was impressed by that fact:

> The local peasants and bandits designate their revolution and even date events from the time of its occurrence (they say for example: "This was before the revolution, this after it" and so on). . . . The causes of the uprising are the same as throughout the RSFSR, i.e. dissatisfaction with the policy of food requisitioning and the clumsy and exceptionally harsh enforcement of it by the food requisitioning organs on the spot.[35]

The unrest spread quickly from Tambov to cover most of the province, and even into neighboring provinces. Tukhachevsky says that when Antonov first took to the field in 1918, he had about 150 diehard followers; by early 1920 that number had increased to perhaps 500; by the end of the year the total had mushroomed to about 6,000; and by May 1921 Antonov's strength had grown to between 8,000 and 10,000 troops, divided into two armies. One army, commanded by Antonov, was operating near the city of Tambov. The other was near Kirsanov.[36]

As Moscow was preoccupied with the Polish war and then with the Kronstadt uprising, the peasant forces had grown. The exceptionally severe winter of 1920–21 added to the countryside's misery, and recruits to Antonov's forces were easy to come by. Deserters, and then recently demobilized soldiers from the Red Army, added to the rebel ranks, until by the summer of 1921, part-time adherents brought their numbers to 50,000. That figure must, however, be viewed as being very elastic; the total varied greatly from week to week and place to place. For this reason Tukhachevsky estimated that Antonov's forces totaled about 21,000 men at the peak of the campaign.

Like most guerrilla opposition movements, the Tambov forces were organized along the same lines as the Red Army, with political departments, revolutionary tribunals, and internal security organs, complete with a network of informers (much like Dzerzhinsky's Cheka). Supervising the whole creation was an elected committee of the Workers and Peasants Union, which had oversight of a headquarters staff that ran military affairs. The troops were recruited on a territorial basis, and each guerrilla army was divided into local regiments that drew on specific areas for reserves of men and horses.

In August 1920, the Moscow government had proclaimed a state of siege in Tambov Province, and in January 1921 had sent 21,000 troops there to bring the peasantry under control. But, as had been the case with Nestor Makhno in southern Russia, the will-o'-the-wisp nature of the guerrilla units made their suppression difficult. The Red Army was unable to deliver a decisive blow to a foe that came and went almost at will, disappearing when it needed to among the sympathetic population.

Subduing the Antonov partisans would be no easy task for Tukhachevsky, who had brought Uborevich as his deputy military commander, with Fedko and G. I. Kotovsky as assistants. The leader of the rebels, the schoolteacher son of a locksmith from Kirsanov, had a long history as a revolutionary agitator in the area. He had been exiled by the tsarist authorities in 1905 and had not returned until 1917, when he had taken command of one of several revolutionary militia units operating in the province. In that capacity he had gained access to supplies of rifles and machine guns, which had been concealed in strategic locations unknown to the Communists. During 1918 and 1919 he had waged his own private war against the Soviets, burning government warehouses, assassinating leading Communists, and attacking isolated Red Army detachments. As Denikin had driven toward Moscow in the summer and fall of 1919, Antonov had made contact with the White forces, even sending delegates to a political gathering at Balaschov and placing 2,000 of his sympathizers in alliance with Mamontov during the latter's sweep through the region.[37]

As the summer of 1921 approached, the Antonov movement was beginning to spread to neighboring provinces and Lenin decided it had to be subdued. From their strongholds on islands in the region's rivers and lakes, the guerrillas would sally out, using information supplied by their clandestine agents, to attack the weakest units of the Red Army, then scatter before retribution could be meted out. This was the situation Tukhachevsky found when he arrived on May 6.

It did not take Tukhachevsky long to realize that this was a very different kind of rebellion from the one he had faced at Kronstadt. This time, the solution was obviously not purely military, but just as much political. Both politically and militarily, the Kronstadt sailors had been naive, if valiantly stubborn. That could not be said of Antonov. All those years of political and military struggle had given him a formidable background for the contest with Tukhachevsky. The battle against him would not be confined to one ice-locked fortress, but would range over an area as big as Belgium in which the population was decidedly in sympathy with him.

And Antonov meant to try, as the Kronstadt sailors had done, to sway the Red Army and Communist forces to his point of view. After an important congress of his sympathizers in Tambov Province in May 1920, he issued a proclamation, which not only set out to convince the Red soldiers to switch sides but also cataloged the population's complaints:

> Comrades, citizens, Red Army brothers, workers and sailors. Taking power by trickery and brute force in 1917, crushing the All-Russian Constituent Assembly, the Bolsheviks promised the people peace, bread and liberty. Instead of this, the people received an obscene peace with Germany, civil war, violence and hunger.
>
> Instead of liberty, the people received punitive detachments of the Cheka in the towns. The Bolsheviks destroyed freedom of speech, the press; they destroyed the churches and they wiped out the clergy.
>
> Comrades, brothers of the Red Army and sailors.
> Now they send you to suppress the "White Guard and kulak uprising" in Tambov Province. Look at them: Against the Bolsheviks and Soviet authorities have rebelled the peasants who drove out the landlords who controlled their land. Truly, we are not White Guards and kulaks; that is why the White Guards went instead with Kolchak and Denikin and the peasants did not travel that route.

In Tambov Province and in all Russia they rebelled against the Bolsheviks' peasants and workers intelligentsia, they revolted against them and the People's Will.

Refuse, brothers, to turn your weapons against the peasants of the Antonov detachments. Arrest your commissars and the Bolsheviks, send your delegates to communicate with the peasant detachments.

Red Army men, sailors and workers must not be the executioners of the working people.

Yes, welcome the Russian People's Republic.
Yes, welcome the Constituent Assembly.
Yes, welcome the Peasants and Workers Union.
Down with the Bolsheviks and commissars.[38]

Tukhachevsky summarized the strengths of the rebels under three categories: the powerful Socialist Revolutionary network built up in Tambov Province, the clever tactic of developing the Union of Workers and Peasants (which the Socialist Revolutionaries dominated, at least in the early stages) as a clearinghouse for peasant grievances; the large stock of weapons and ammunition cached by Antonov during his term as a militia leader.[39]

After arriving in Tambov on May 6, Tukhachevsky had plunged into the business at hand. He quickly took stock of the region's military resources and, by visiting the army units, discovered what he could of the rebels' tactics. Then, with Uborevich's help, he set up three cavalry brigades and special motorized units to harass the main rebel units. These highly mobile units, armed with machine guns, were designed to fall quickly and stealthily upon the Antonovistas, to attack them before they could respond, but would avoid pitched battles. As Uborevich said later: "So, really by stealth, we conducted this extraordinary, unpleasant campaign."[40]

Tukhachevsky also offered both a carrot and a stick to entice the Antonovistas to switch sides. On May 12, 1921, the Tambov Military Command issued a decree in which the peasants were offered an amnesty if they handed in their weapons and turned over the ringleaders of the rebellion to the Communist authorities. The decree promised that those who did so would be protected from the vengence of the rebels. At the same time, the soldiers of the Red Army, as well as the Cheka and political workers, were ordered to avoid provoking the inhabitants.

Then, after a short interval, came the stick. A decree issued on June 11 warned the peasants who persisted in continuing to shelter the guerrillas that they would have to suffer the full consequences.[41]

Tukhachevsky was no stranger to the area. The Penza area where he had spent his boyhood, a hundred or so miles east of Tambov, was inhabited by the same kind of rural peasantry. Indeed, on his mother's side, Tukhachevsky was one of them. Not that that made any difference to him.

With the Civil War now behind them, the Communists had provided Tukhachevsky with the pick of the Red Army to wind up this resistance to their overlordship. Among those sent to Tambov was a young officer, Georgi K. Zhukov, who had already made something of a name for himself as a cavalry commander. He described his first meeting with his new superior officer thus:

> We had already heard many good things about Mikhail Nikolaevich Tukhachevsky, particularly about his strategic ability, and the troops were pleased that they were to be led by this talented commander.
>
> I first saw Tukhachevsky in the village of Zherdyevka in Tambov Province, when he visited the base of our section of the 14th Cavalry Brigade. I was able to be present for his consultation with the brigade's officers. In a speech, Tukhachevsky displayed great erudition and experience in guiding operations on a large scale.
>
> Later, in a discussion that went on about the operations of the brigade, Mikhail Nikolaevich chatted with the soldiers and the officers. He was interested in learning about where it had been beaten and in the frame of mind of the units and the inhabitants, what political work we were engaged in among the country people.[42]

As the carrot-and-stick policy showed, Tukhachevsky and Anton-Ovseenko set themselves to driving a wedge between the peasants and the rebels. While the three brigades under Uborevich actively pursued the rebels, the great bulk of the 50,000 troops under Tukhachevsky's command were used for what was essentially police work. As he himself put it in his report to Lenin:

The principal and most difficult task was the conquest of the territory, the occupation of the sources of recruitment of the bandits and the Sovietization of them. . . . Sovietization was to be enforced by the following measures: elimination of the bandit element, institution of revolutionary committees, splitting up the peasantry by means of arming it against the bandits while providing it with material interest in the shape of property confiscated from the bandits, application of terrorist measures to bandit sympathizers, rounding up of Union of Working Peasants committees, labor help by the Red Army for the population, and proper organization of Soviet work.[43]

In other words, Tukhachevsky and Anton-Ovseenko would use the political carrot and the Cheka stick to achieve their objectives. The combined resources of the Cheka and the Red Army were gathered in a campaign of terror. Villages suspected of being rebel strongholds were singled out for particularly harsh treatment. In such places the entire adult male population was placed under arrest. Families of those suspected of helping the Antonovistas were placed in prison camps. Some were transported to more remote provinces. Door-to-door searches were conducted for weapons. When weapons were found, the senior member of the household was shot. But these tactics were not one-sided. Antonov's men were using the same methods against Soviet sympathizers.[44]

The Soviets had the greater power, and their campaign paid off. By the middle of July, most of Antonov's partisans had been run to ground. According to Tukhachevsky, only 1,200 diehards still followed the rebel leader by that time. But there had been no spectacular successes on the battlefield, and Lenin was getting nervous at the lack of news from the scene.

> How are things with Tukhachevsky? Hasn't he captured Antonov yet? Are you putting pressure on him? When is the report to the Politburo?[45]

A few days later Tukhachevsky's optimistic report was in Lenin's hands. It suggested that the worst days of the uprising were over. But it also contained some blunt warnings:

> The peasantry has been compromised in the eyes of the bandits and is looking to the Red Army for protection against them. But at the same time the peasants do not believe in the sincerity of the decree about the tax in kind. Rumors are current among them that by autumn our troops will be withdrawn from Tambov Province and that then the bandits will go into action again, and, finally, here and there district committees of the Union of Working Peasants are still in evidence.[46]

The young general went on to urge that the Moscow authorities not reduce the considerable military presence now in the district. Indeed, he urged that, if anything, the military and political cadres be reinforced throughout the winter, when fresh disturbances could be expected. Finally, in what can only be taken as an oblique reference to what he considered the root of the problem, he suggested that no new taxes of any kind be levied on the long-suffering population.

Antonov was to survive as a hunted man for another year, escaping first with the remnant of his band toward Penza and then crisscrossing the Tambov region before being run to ground and killed by the Red Army in June 1922.[47] His insurrection had been nullified long before that, and its conclusion and the elimination of Makhno's separatist movement further south brought an end to significant opposition to the Lenin regime. Like so many other aspects of this period in Russia's history, it had been a brutally painful experience, and those who had suffered the greatest pain were the unfortunate peasants of Tambov. According to one estimate more than 200,000 peasants had died from hunger and from the fighting during the uprising.[48]

The end of the Antonov campaign was also a benchmark in Tukhachevsky's career. It was his last duty as a combat soldier, and during it he was transformed into much more of a political creature. It was a transformation fraught with great difficulties for Tukhachevsky and for Russia.

Tukhachevsky in Paris in 1936. (United Press International Photo)

The first five marshals of the Soviet Union. Front row, from left: M.N. Tukhachevsky; K.E. Voroshilov; A. Yegorov. Rear: S.M. Budenny; V.K. Bluykher. (Brown Brothers Photo)

Kirov's funeral. The funeral procession of S.M. Kirov passes through Moscow's Sverdlov Square. Stalin and Voroshilov are immediately behind the gun carriage. Tukhachevsky is behind and between them.

The Kronstadt survivors. Fugitives from the ill-fated 1921 rebellion in Finland. S.M. Petrichenko, is third from left in sailor's uniform.

Marshal Tukhachevsky in 1933. (Sovfoto)

Tukhachevsky's last public appearance, at the May Day parade in Red Square in 1937. Front row, from left: Tukhachevsky, I.P. Belov, Voroshilov, Yegorov, Budenny. Stalin is at left rear; Molotov, third from right, at rear.

7
A PARTNERSHIP WITH FRUNZE

WITH THE SUPPRESSION of the Antonov revolt and of similar movements throughout the nation, the Soviet military leaders were able to turn their full attention to an internal debate that had been in progress for some time: the question of whether Russia should develop a militia army or maintain a standing army for the defense of the republic. Tukhachevsky was to be an influential figure in the debate, and for the first time he was to show himself in vociferous opposition to Trotsky. Since many Communist leaders—not least of them Trotsky—regarded Trotsky's opinions on military matters as virtually holy writ, this was no small step for the young commander.

Behind the military debate was an even more momentous struggle, the battle to succeed Lenin as leader of the revolution. Zinoviev's behavior at that stage of Soviet history was particularly motivated by a desire to emphasize his preeminence among Lenin's associates. But, behind the scenes, Stalin and others were maneuvering to press their claims. It was new and dangerous ground for Tukhachevsky.

The militia question had first been raised at the Eighth Party Congress, and again at the Ninth Party Congress, held from March 29 to April 5, 1920. At the latter gathering, Trotsky had pushed through his ideas on how the socialist military would operate. The plan was that the militia would function in the closest possible conjunction with industrial and agrarian enterprises. Thus a militia division might be operated in conjunction with a very large industrial enterprise. Smaller enterprises would provide a basis for a brigade or a regiment. In addition, according to the Trotsky plan, the "best elements" of the industrial or administrative cadres would fill a parallel role in the military. For example, a leading trade union officer might at the same time be a leading military commander. The idea was simply to maintain the working-class overlordship of the military.

This was where Tukhachevsky came into direct conflict with the war commissar. Despite the defeat of his armies before Warsaw, Tukhachevsky maintained that it was indeed possible for the Red Army to assist, or even impose, revolution abroad by force of arms; and to do so would mean the retention of a standing army. Trotsky's proposal was a utopian concept, and Tukhachevsky and his colleagues quickly suggested that in the twentieth century, when waging war was becoming increasingly mechanized and complicated, the idea of the yeoman-soldier was no longer feasible.

In January 1921, Tukhachevsky wrote a pamphlet on the subject that was influential not only in Russia but, particularly, also in Germany, which was wrestling with some of the same problems, though under greatly different circimstances. It was not by accident that Tukhachevsky's pamphlet, *The Red Army and the Militia,* was quickly translated into German.

The adventurist nature of the young general shows clearly throughout the work:

> The adherents of the militia system take absolutely no account of Soviet Russia's present military mission of disseminating socialist revolution throughout the world. The rich varieties of socialist life and the socialist revolution cannot be forced into any particular framework. They will spread

irresistibly over the whole world, and their expanding force will endure as long as there is a bourgeoisie left anywhere.

What is the way in which they will best achieve their aims? It is the way of armed insurrection within every state, or the way of armed socialist attacks on bourgeois states, or a combination of both ways. No one can make definite prophecies, for the course of the revolution will show us the right way. One thing, however, is certain: If a socialist revolution succeeds in gaining power in any country, it will have a self-evident right to expand, and will strive to cover the whole world by making its immediate influence felt in all neighboring countries. Its most powerful instrument will naturally be its military forces.

The structure of an army is determined on the one hand by the political aims it pursues and on the other hand by the recruiting system it employs. It is self-evident that a proletariat which has emerged victorious from a class war cannot recruit its army in the ordinary form of national compulsory military service. The obligation to serve in it must affect the working classes alone.

We therefore see that the Socialist Revolution has created a new recruiting system for its international class army, thus forming a contrast to the bourgeois revolutions which evolved national and democratic armies.

The characteristic features of a militia army are its vast size and its comparatively small war efficiency. Large armies which lack the nuclei of permanent military formations can receive no thorough training with regular units in time of peace, since they are assembled only by mobilization orders. Their war efficiency is therefore bound to be small.

This defect must be remedied in some way or other, and the most suitable way is by the method of war technique. The success of a militia system is dependent on an extremely well constructed network of communications which permits the transport of men by railway, motor vehicle and waterway. It can become a source of great strength—but only when the state in question has practically all its land under cultivation and possesses great wealth and highly developed industries. A militia army is not worth a brass farthing if it lacks these vast reserves of manpower and a military technique which can be applied to the utmost limits. In our case, the introduction of the militia system would be tantamount to a crucifixion of Soviet Russia.[1]

Although he was still something of an ideological neophyte, Tukhachevsky spared no scorn in pushing his argument. He called the militia system "an antiquated idea, or more correctly, antiquated superstition dating from the period of the Second International."

Despite Tukhachevsky's self-assurance, the defeat of the Russian armies in Poland had pointed to the urgent need for military reform, and seemed to provide ammunition for Trotsky and his sympathizers, who saw Russia's chief need militarily as obtaining the means to defend the revolution, not to extend it. Undaunted, Tukhachevsky persisted that quite a different lesson could be learned from the Polish experience. Contrary to Trotsky's view, Tukhachevsky maintained that revolution could indeed be carried abroad militarily, but only with a well-trained army, suitably equipped and suitably attuned politically.

He had first promoted this idea in the middle of the Polish war, writing from his headquarters at Smolensk to Zinoviev, suggesting immediate action on establishment of an international socialist military command that would further world revolution.

In phrases uncannily prescient of the still far-distant Warsaw Pact, Tukhachevsky said:

> Considering the inevitability of world civil war in the very near future, we must now set up the General Staff of Comintern III. The staff's mission—to consider in advance the forces and means of the adversaries in a future civil war in countries even as yet ruled by capitalism.
>
> To avoid those difficulties and crudities, from which we suffered at the creation of our Red Army, it is vital to work out beforehand a plan for the mobilization of the working class, worker Red officers must be trained in advance, both senior combat chiefs and staff workers must be prepared beforehand.
>
> World civil war need not come as a complete surprise. The working class must be trained for it, so that with the seizing of arms it can be quickly formed into a regular Red Army.
>
> By the way, taking into account the difficulties of training officers from workers in bourgeois countries, it is essential for us in Soviet Russia to open a series of military instruction centers and academies of the General Staff to train

command staff from workers and Communists of all nationalities in their languages.²

Complicating the debate were the structure and composition of the Red Army command as it stood at the end of the Civil War. The years of fighting had produced a number of Bolshevik commanders, military figures who had begun primarily as political revolutionaries. Frunze was the most notable of these, and Voroshilov was another. There was a second group, mostly men who had been noncommissioned officers in the tsarist army and had risen to command rank in the new military. They were experienced in military matters but educated to a very limited degree, and scarcely capable of molding a war machine of the size that the Soviet republic would need. Budenny, Timoshenko, and the likes were in this group. Third, there was the group of which Tukhachevsky was the prime example: young men—many were still in their twenties—who had been very junior officers in the tsarist army and had swung their allegience to the Communist cause. They were knowledgeable in military science—perhaps not as knowledgeable as they themselves thought—and they were sophisticated enough to take charge of the Red Army if they were given the chance. Finally, there were the older commanders, former tsarist generals and colonels, men like Vatsetis and S. S. Kamenev, who had spent their lives in wars of one kind or another. Although they had enlisted in the Communist service, they were not entirely politically reliable, and their disposition was perhaps too conservative or too old-fashioned to cope with fashioning a revolutionary army for the middle of the twentieth century. All these groups strove to exert their influence on the shape of things to come; their struggle for dominance would eventually lead to fratricidal bloodshed.

And beyond the military rivalries, there were the even more virulent political feuds. There always had been theological disputes among Lenin's followers, but at this stage of the Soviet Union's development a new kind of ward-heeler politics was beginning to engulf the young republic, pitting Trotsky against Stalin and just about every other pretender to Lenin's leadership.

In the resulting quarrel, Trotsky was not without allies in the military. The older military specialists, such as Vatsetis, who believed that they owed their present fortunate circumstances to

Trotsky, were quick to support him. But the more political officers, including Voroshilov, who were allied with Stalin and Zinoviev, had potent arguments against the militia plan. It was pointed out that a similar Trotsky scheme, adapted to the transport trade union, had failed and had finally led to his removal from control of the operation. By extension, Zinoviev and Stalin said, a similar military plan would be doomed to failure.

At this stage, Gusev and Frunze entered the debate with a proposal of their own. Originally the 21-point Frunze-Gusev program was to have been brought before the Tenth Party Congress in March 1921, which coincided with the Kronstadt mutiny, but Trotsky's adamant opposition and Lenin's behind-the-scenes maneuvering forced cancellation of that schedule. However, Kronstadt and the events in Tambov and the Ukraine showed the urgent need for better execution and planning in the military apparatus. Even Trotsky realized that it would no longer suffice to pluck Tukhachevsky from this command or Frunze from that assignment to direct operations as crises arose. In both Kronstadt and Tambov, the discipline of the military had been a crucial factor. In Petrograd some of the Red Army units had functioned only at the point of the commander's pistol. Even worse, the navy had been at the very heart of the uprising. And in Tambov, many of Antonov's supporters were peasant-deserters from the Red Army.

The unease in the nation had been aggravated by the rapid demobilization of the army. At its greatest strength, the Red Army had mustered 5,300,000 men. By December 1921, this total had been slashed to 1,595,000. By December 1922 it would fall to 610,000, and by the end of 1923 to 562,000.[3]

On July 25, 1921, Tukhachevsky returned from the Volga districts to take up a pivotal position in the continuing debate; he was named to head the Military Academy of the Soviet Union, which at that time was still staffed by the highest officers of the tsarist regime.[4] Among the instructors were General A. I. Verkhovsky, a former tsarist minister of war; Major General A. A. Svechin; the cavalry expert Gatovsky; and the controversial former commander in chief of the Red Army, Vatsetis. Even the location of the academy seemed to imply conservatism; it was located in the former building of the Moscow Hunt Club.[5]

As the debate over the future of the Red Army gained intensity, an effort was made by the political apparatus to weed out the undesirable or untrustworthy elements in the military. The purging process could be brutal on occasion, but sometimes it was a pro forma affair.

For example, Alexander Barmine, a young officer studying at the academy in October 1921, recalled the show-and-tell performance through which Tukhachevsky was forced to pass. The commandant of the academy was called before one of the purge commissions operating at the time.

> He took his stand before the judges, a young man with a square-cut, energetic face, dressed in a private's tunic, dignified, unconcerned, with not the least suspicion of pose in his attitude. The sole decoration he wore was the recently instituted Order of the Red Banner, given only for valor on the field of battle. The simplicity of his appearance pleased us, for we had already had enough of amateurs in resplendent uniforms among our colleagues and in the higher ranks of the military.
> It was in a tone of almost complete detachment and in brief sentences that Tukhachevsky spoke of his past record to an absorbed and silent audience.
> Entered the Red Army in 1918; parentage aristocratic; formerly subaltern in the Imperial Guard; captured by the Germans; escaped. While in the Red Army commanded first a division, then an army on the eastern front. By special order of the day of Comrade Trotsky, President of the Revolutionary War Council, was decorated with the Order of the Red Banner for having inflicted a decisive defeat on Kolchak. Was later commander in chief on the western front. Before joining the Communist Party had been a member of no political organization. Since joining the party had been subjected to no disciplinary action. . . ."
> The members of the commission put a few questions which Tukhachevsky answered in the same laconic manner. One or two nods were exchanged and then the president announced the board's decision: "Michael Tukhachevsky, a member of the party since 1918 and head of the General Staff College, is declared worthy of his membership."
> Tukhachevsky then came down from the platform amid general applause.[6]

In March 1922, the dispute over the future of the Russian military gained a new intensity with the appearance of Frunze, freshly returned from a top-level but more or less clandestine assignment in Turkey, at an assembly of the commanders and commissars of the Ukrainian and Crimean units of the Red Army. Frunze's address was cautious. It made appropriate bows to the need for unity in the Red Army and was tactful in dealing with the theoretical argument on the virtues of "maneuverability" as compared with "positional" strategy for the new Russian defense system. "Maneuverability is not an end in itself," Frunze said. "It is only one means of achieving the fundamental goals," which he defined as overcoming and capturing the resources of the bourgeois enemy states. He continued: "Maneuverability by no means excludes positional military formations. Quite the opposite, correct maneuvers are unthinkable without broad utilization of positional methods of battle," particularly in important border areas.

However, recalling his experiences fighting Kolchak and Wrangel, Frunze could not help including criticisms of the ultraconservative strategists personified by Vatsetis. He concluded by enumerating 15 points on which development of the Red Army, in his view, would have to be based. First, it was essential, even in the era of demobilization of the bulk of the soldiers, that training be resumed. Likewise, political work had to be increased and to be consistent in its doctrines. The principle of maneuver would be supreme in military strategy. There was obvious need for technical improvement in the Red Army. Finally, the primacy of the offensive would be emphasized. It was a program that could only draw applause among the commanders raised to prominence during the Civil War, among whom Tukhachevsky was one of the more notable. And it provided a strong foundation for the case Frunze and his allies were to make at the Eleventh Party Congress, which opened in Moscow on March 27.[7]

Frunze's advocacy of offensive operations was countered principally by Svechin. Citing the success of the British blockade of Napoleonic France, he held that a defensive posture was a better guarantee of success. He held that in Russia's case, correct utilization of the vast spaces of the country, with its forests and marshes, would provide the best defense against an enemy, even one with superior technical means at its disposal. This was particularly important, he argued, since the state of Russian industry did not seem to hold much promise of immediate technical help for the Red Army.[8]

At the Party Congress, Trotsky vehemently attacked the theses put forward by Frunze, seconded by Voroshilov. Trotsky was particularly scornful of one point in the program that was close to Tukhachevsky's thinking. It saw future Red Army actions in "revolutionary war" terms, either in repelling an attack on the Soviet Union or in joining in the support of an outside revolution. Trotsky argued that the largely peasant-based Red Army could not be induced to fight other people's wars.

In the debates, Tukhachevsky defended the offensive doctrine as outlined by Frunze, but on some points he differed from his former colleague. As John Erickson suggests, Tukhachevsky's fascination with Napoleon's campaigns still permeated his thinking, as did his earlier suggestion for an international military command, created under the aegis of the Comintern, even though that plan had already been rejected.[9]

Despite Trotsky's vigorous defense of his views on the military, the congress was the beginning of his decline as an eminent leader of the Soviet Union. For, in addition to the military affairs debate, the gathering named Stalin to be general secretary of the party, his first independent power base and the point from which his later dictatorship arose. His assistants in that key post were to be Vyascheslav M. Molotov and Tukhachevsky's former sponsor, Valerian Kuibyshev. Another threat to Trotsky's place in the Soviet hierarchy was soon to arise from a different direction. On May 26, 1922, Lenin suffered the first of the series of strokes that eventually killed him. Such was Lenin's all-important place in the leadership that news of his illness was kept from the Russian people for nearly ten days.

Events outside Russia were also affecting the Soviet leadership's attitudes. On October 24, 1922, Benito Mussolini's Fascist Party staged a congress in Naples that was in effect a prelude to the seizure of power in Italy. At the time, Mussolini seemed as much a political ogre to the statesmen of Europe as any of the Soviet leaders, even though in Moscow, too, he was regarded with apprehension. A week after the Naples congress, Mussolini added to the anxiety by staging his march on Rome. The crude display of muscle by the black-shirted Fascists was such that on October 31, the Italian king asked Mussolini to form a government, setting the stage for Italy's two-decade political nightmare.

Russia remained an outcast among the European nations, and Moscow was eagerly searching for a friend. Throughout the summer, secret negotiations had been held with Germany, and on August 7, a thoroughly surprised Europe was told that the two pariahs, Germany and Soviet Russia, had signed a pact of friendship and cooperation, the Treaty of Rapallo. Four days later, in Moscow, the Red Army and the Reichswehr signed a provisional agreement on collaboration in training and technical matters. Von Seeckt's *Ostpolitik* had been made formal. Under the terms of the treaty, the Germans gained access to facilities for training and weapons testing, including weapons that were theoretically forbidden to them under the terms of the Treaty of Versailles: planes, motorized infantry units, and chemical warfare. In return, the Russians received payment for the use of the bases and full access to the results of the testing and training.[10]

The pace of this cooperation quickened greatly. In the autumn of 1922, the German general Otto Hasse held long discussions in Moscow with P. P. Lebedev, the Soviet chief of staff, on furthering the partnership. There were other German visitors to the Soviet capital, all traveling clandestinely; among them was the influential Major Kurt von Schleicher, who had been a key figure in the first German-Soviet overtures. Karl Radek was involved in the activities, too, holding his second conference with von Seeckt at Berlin in December 1922.[11]

Nor was the parade of high military officers entirely from Berlin to Moscow. The diary of von Seeckt's adjutant, von Selchow, records a secret visit by "high Russian officers" to Berlin as early as February 27, 1922.[12] Another writer mentions that Zhukov and Tukhachevsky were at the War Academy in Berlin immediately after the signing of the Treaty of Rapallo.[13]

It would have made sense for Tukhachevsky to have been involved with the Germans at this time. Officially he was now commander of the Western Military District, bordering Poland, and the Poles were very much a matter of concern to both Berlin and Moscow.[14]

These developments were overshadowed by Lenin's second stroke on December 16, 1922. It proved to be so severe that he was, for all purposes, removed from his dominant role in the affairs of state. His absence allowed Stalin to move in two directions to increase his hold on power. First, politically, he formed an alliance with Zinoviev and L. B. Kamenev that became the triumvirate that actually ruled the country. Second, in the purely military field, his associates Frunze and Voroshilov came to be the dominant army figures. In both areas, Trotsky was the target, and in both areas Trotsky was the loser.

During this period, Lenin was not totally oblivious to the way matters were going, and he did not like what he saw. As a result he wrote his so-called Testament with its strictures against Stalin's crudities. And, according to Trotsky, he went out of his way to propose to Trotsky that they should form a bloc to have Stalin removed from his new position of influence. But it was not to be.

At the beginning of the Twelfth Party Congress on April 17, 1923, Stalin was still not publicly head of the triumvirate. Zinoviev, backed by a majority of the Politburo and the Central Committee, occupied that position. But Stalin, through his overriding influence on the Central Control Commission, where his followers were in the majority, was able to change all that. The Control Commission rode herd on the party membership—even its highest members—and that was power base enough for Stalin. Zinoviev was a much weaker personality, as events at the beginning of the Revolution, and later at Kronstadt, had demonstrated. By the end of the congress, there was no doubt as to who was the leading figure among the triumvirs.[15]

But Zinoviev was a plotter, too. Soon after the Twelfth Congress, in September 1923, he initiated a conference at a retreat in Kislovodsk, in the Caucasus, to chart Stalin's replacement. Those gathered for the discussions, in addition to Zinoviev, were Nikolai Bukharin, Lashevich, Grigory Evdokimov, Ordzhonikidze, and, of all people, Voroshilov, who had been summoned from his headquarters at Rostov. It was a symptom of Zinoviev's naiveté that two of the participants, Voroshilov and Ordzhonikidze, were now among Stalin's closest collaborators. Needless to say, Stalin dismissed the suggestions from the meeting when they were presented to him by Ordzhonikidze.[16]

As Stalin's star was in the ascendant during this period, so Trotsky's was in decline. He was dogged by ill health and was quickly becoming isolated in the party, where so many regarded him as an interloper. In December 1923, Trotsky wrote a letter to the Central Committee attacking the growth of bureaucracy in the Soviet state—a euphemism for Stalin's consolidation of his power—and in return was greeted with angry denunciations.

Zinoviev even went so far as to accuse Trotsky of treason and call for his arrest. This squabbling intensified during the first few days of 1924, particularly at the Thirteenth Party Congress, January 16–18. The denunciations still ringing in his ears, the ailing (the illness seems, at least partly, to have been officially diagnosed by his enemies) Trotsky left Moscow for Sukhum on January 18.[17]

Three days later, while Trotsky was still en route, he received word that Lenin had died. With Trotsky opportunely out of the way, Stalin was the chief mourner at Lenin's funeral on January 27. It was his first public performance as the dominant political figure of the Soviet state.

Stalin was also moving against Trotsky from another direction. Since June 1923, the Central Control Commission had been conducting a full-scale inquiry into the Soviet military. In August this inquiry had been directed by one of Trotsky's more ardent military opponents, Gusev. On February 3, 1924, Gusev delivered his findings to the Central Committee, almost all of them critical of the way Trotsky and his subordinates handled the defense of the nation.

The report singled out for exceptionally scathing criticism two of Trotsky's close associates, Sklyansky and P. P. Lebedev, the chief of staff. The alignment of the anti-Trotsky forces at this time is particularly interesting because it included some of the men who were later to gather around Tukhachevsky in pushing for further reforms in the Red Army. For example, in delivering his report, Gusev read a letter from Uborevich, recently stationed in the Far East. Uborevich criticized the "benumbing spirit of the old Tsarist specialists." Frunze joined in the attack, declaring that supply and organizational aspects of the military were being totally ignored.

The campaign against Trotsky had been waged with an unusual amount of propagandistic overkill by Stalin and L. B. Kamenev (the latter was Trotsky's brother-in-law). Late in November 1924, *Pravda* would devote 20 columns of space to Stalin's and Kamenev's reports on Trotsky's offenses. Stalin accused Trotsky of trying to usurp Lenin's mantle and of favoring bourgeois factions in the regime. The carefully orchestrated campaign was peppered with almost daily resolutions from provincial branches of the party calling for Trotsky's ouster.[18]

But long before November, Trotsky's power base had been

greatly eroded. On February 4, the Revolutionary Military Council empowered Frunze to begin the task of reshaping the Red Army, as president of a special commission set up for the task. On March 3, Sklyansky was removed as Trotsky's deputy; eight days later, Frunze was named to succeed him. With Trotsky out of the way in the Caucasus, Frunze was now the effective chief of the Red Army. More changes soon followed. Voroshilov was appointed commander of the crucial Moscow Military District, and later in March the staff of the Revolutionary Military Council was shaken up. New appointees to the staff included numerous close associates of Stalin: A. S. Bubnov, Budenny, Sergei Kamenev, Ordzhonikidze, I. S. Unslikht, Frunze, and Voroshilov were among them. Tukhachevsky was still on the periphery, even though many of his views coincided with Frunze's. Tukhachevsky, significantly, was still no friend of Stalin. The old sores of the Polish war were not easily healed.

While the long knives were being sharpened in Moscow, Tukhachevsky was serving in Smolensk as commander of the Western Military District. An article giving some insights into how he spent his time appeared in the newspaper *Sovetskaya Rossiya* in 1982. The item was based on a document, found in the party archives at Smolensk, that deals with questions he was asked in connection with political lectures and work.

Many of the 60 questions deal with biographical details, but others deal with political and social attitudes. In the biographical section he dealt modestly with his background in the military and with his fluency in French and German. But characteristically he gave pointed replies to some of the other inquiries. One question asked, for example, if he knew the conditions of peasant life and the party's program for dealing with the middle peasants. The man whose mother was of peasant stock, the man who so recently had sternly put down the peasant uprising in Tambov, answered "Abstractly."[19]

But not all of his time was taken up with military and political matters. Although the exact details are somewhat vague, about this time Tukhachevsky fell in love with Nina, the woman who was to become his second wife. Although she was apparently a simple country girl when they married, and Tukhachevsky must have been a difficult husband, she stood by him steadfastly to the tragic end.[20]

But the quiet days in Smolensk were soon to end. By the early summer of 1924, Tukhachevsky had been recruited to the center of power. On July 18, 1924, he was named assistant chief of staff and staff commissar — in other words, Frunze's deputy. He was succeeded as commander of the Western Military District by his deputy, A. I. Kork.

From this time until his death, Tukhachevsky was to be recognized, even when he was removed from the center of the military leadership, as the intellectual fount of the Red Army. Moreover, the men associated with his ideas, the men who would rise and fall with him, were likewise placed in strategic positions throughout the Red Army. In addition to Kork in Smolensk, Uborevich, who had been commander of the celebrated Fifth Army, was in the Western District as Kork's deputy. Eideman was commander of the Siberian Military District, and from 1925 was commandant of the Moscow Military Academy (later the Frunze Military Academy). Even Putna, who had had his differences with Tukhachevsky in Poland and who had sided with Trotsky in 1923, but also had shared the rigors of Kronstadt and generally held many of Tukhachevsky's views, was commandant of the Moscow Infantry School. N. V. Kuibyshev, who had helped bring Tukhachevsky into the Red Army and the Communist Party, was commandant of the Vystral Higher Infantry School. (In 1925, after a brief period as commander in Turkestan, he went to China, to replace Blukhyer as adviser to Chiang Kai-shek.) N. N. Shvarts, who had been deputy to Tukhachevsky in the Polish campaign, taught tactics and warfare at the Moscow Military Academy. Feldman, who was to work with Tukhachevsky on revising the military regulations, after 1928 was the commandant of the strategic Leningrad Military District.

The relationship of these men to Tukhachevsky was important, but perhaps even more important was the relationship of the man they regarded as their leader to Frunze. In the early days of the Civil War, in the fighting on the Eastern Front against Kolchak, Tukhachevsky and Frunze had worked together harmoniously. They had then evidenced a kinship in disputing what they saw as the hidebound conservatism in the strategy being pushed by Trotsky and Vatsetis. Tukhachevsky's adventurism had been nicely balanced by Frunze's caution, a caution learned in long years of revolutionary effort during which he had spent long periods in exile and had even been sentenced to death.

The friendship that had developed between Tukhachevsky and Frunze in the Urals, blossomed anew within the confines of the Moscow military establishment. Tukhachevsky had provided Frunze and Gusev with much of their theoretical ammunition in the polemics with Trotsky, but now the professional association developed into a real camaraderie, so much so that in the first few months of Frunze's tenure as effective commander of the Red Army, Tukhachevsky became his closest friend. Frunze had undoubtedly become a perceptive military thinker in his own right, but he was also a politician of long standing. Where Tukhachevsky was brilliant, if sometimes erratic, Frunze was cool and collected. Where Tukhachevsky, despite the correct political content of his writings at this time, could be naive amid the Communist backbiting, Frunze was politically astute. Frunze had ready access to and the full confidence of Stalin, which Tukhachevsky never did. Tukhachevsky's domineering, even impudent manner and his sophistication in art and literature always outshone the uncouth former seminarian from Tiflis. Tukhachevsky made Stalin uncomfortable; Frunze reassured him.

If Tukhachevsky's sister-in-law is accurate, at this time both Frunze and Tukhachevsky became part of a compact social circle that also included Valerian Kuibyshev. On the rare occasions that Stalin ventured to join it, he made the others uncomfortable while the convivial Frunze, ever ready to provide a couple of extra bottles of vodka, was just another of the friends.[21]

Frunze and Tukhachevsky wasted no time in undertaking their reforms. The older military specialists—the Vatsetises and the Sergei Kamenevs—were either forced out entirely or confined to largely administrative positions. In his writings, notably *Maneuver and Artillery,* Tukhachevsky was also providing material for discussion in the revamped military leadership. The planning processes and the creation of the new Red Army were Frunze's responsibility, but the army's intellectual makeup was largely inspired by Tukhachevsky and, to a lesser extent, by Shaposhnikov. But developing this new army would not be easy.

In the first place, the army would be much smaller than Frunze and Tukhachevsky had envisaged. In their view, the regular army should have numbered somewhere between 1 million and 1.5 million. Instead, by the end of 1924 it was only half that size, and even that figure was deceptive, since militia units accounted for 52 percent of the infantry strength. To offset this preponderance of part-time soldiery, Frunze and Tukhachevsky maintained a solid base of permanent cadres—about 16 percent of the total—that was kept on a war footing. And even this was difficult, because there was considerable peasant reaction to serving in the military. During the mobilization of the militia in 1924, there were angry peasant demonstrations against the army policies. Because of these outbreaks, the geographical dispersion of the militia units was largely confined to the more industrialized sections of the country. Thus, in the Moscow Military District there were 13 territorial units, while in Siberia there was only one.[22]

Not all the reforms were of a purely military nature. Much of Frunze's work was of a political variety. Because of the peasant attitudes and the changes that were being made in the commands, political indoctrination of the military was given a high emphasis. Furthermore, as Stalin sought to increase his power in the country, it was necessary for him to cement his hold on the army. In this effort, Stalin's long-time crony Voroshilov was the leading stalking horse. Finally, on January 17, 1925, Trotsky was forced out of his position on the Revolutionary Military Council. Nine days later his place was taken by Frunze, who became titular as well as effective head of the Red Army.

These hectic events tended to obscure the sub rosa cooperation with the Germans, but it proceeded apace. The first fruits of the arrangement were aircraft manufacturing plants established by Junkers at Fili (near Moscow) and in Kharkov. Since 1922, German officers had been training in Russia. Everything seemed to be working to von Seeckt's satisfaction. There had been further expansion of the collaboration in 1923, when a tank school was opened at Kazan and a school for fighter pilots at Kharkov. An antigas training center was opened, and Russian and German officers carried out joint exercises on the training grounds near Kiev and Lipetsk in Russia, and at the German base in East Prussia.[23]

There was also political fallout. The change in the Revolutionary Military Council had not been achieved without Byzantine political skirmishing. In one last effort to thwart Stalin's ascent to absolute power, Zinoviev had sought to have Stalin take Trotsky's place as war commissar. This would have forced Stalin to resign his other posts. But Stalin did not fall for the bait, and the last serious challenge to his authority failed.

Frunze and Tukhachevsky plunged ahead with their work of reshaping the military edifice. Training, especially for the new Red command, was pushed with the utmost speed. This was no easy task, for by far the bulk of the new defense leadership had no formal military training. They also had sought to separate, however slightly, the military commanders from control by the state's political apparatus. To some extent this had been achieved. Under a directive issued in March 1925, the Red Army command was freed from supervision in matters of a purely combat or military administrative nature. Documents dealing with those areas could be signed by a military commander alone. But this directive did not apply to the naval forces or the so-called national forces. The memories of Kronstadt and disturbances in Georgia were still too fresh.[24]

In the middle of this feverish activity, Frunze fell ill. According to Trotsky, among others, he was the victim of a Stalinist plot. In the Trotsky version of the episode, Frunze was suffering from an acute case of ulcers. His doctors declined to operate because they believed his heart was weak and he could not stand the effects of an anesthetic. Frunze therefore was said to have refused to undergo an operation. Stalin then commissioned a doctor from the Central Committee to pick a medical committee to examine the ailing defense chief. Their decision was that an operation was imperative. Frunze, faced with a decision of the Central Committee, as a loyal Communist had no choice but to submit to the surgery. He died on the operating table.[25]

Frunze's funeral provided Stalin with a unique opportunity to display publicly the new alignment in the Soviet leadership. The scene in Red Square would have been worthy of the Romanovs. An estimated 250,000 people moved solemnly past the red-draped coffin placed just behind the relatively new Lenin mausoleum. On the day of the funeral, 30,000 soldiers from the Moscow garrison were assembled in the great cobblestoned square. At the foot of the Kremlin wall, black-coated Soviet and foreign diplomats assembled. The dead general's ashes lay on a catafalque, surrounded by palms and lilies. At the head and foot of the coffin were two privates in the Red Army. Stalin himself delivered the main eulogy, speaking for the first time from the plinth of the Lenin tomb. After referring to Frunze as "the purest, most honest and most fearless revolutionary of our time," Stalin said: "The Communist Party mourns the loss of a most loyal and devoted member; the Soviet Government mourns the loss of a daring and efficient servant; the Red Army mourns the loss of a fearless and popular chief." A small group of the Soviet leaders, with Stalin in front, carried the coffin to its final resting place in a grave under the Kremlin wall, and the artillery of the Kremlin roared out a 100-gun salute.[26]

The loss to the Red Army was enormous. But to Tukhachevsky it was worse. Frunze had been his comrade in the darkest days of the Civil War, and in peacetime they had become the closest friends. They thought alike on most military matters. Frunze had picked Tukhachevsky to be his right arm. It was only a matter of time before Frunze's death brought Tukhachevsky another reverse in his already checkered career.

Tukhachevsky immediately perceived the danger in his situation. But he had learned enough of the new Russia's political ways to try to make the best of the position in which he found himself. He knew that Stalin would never place him in full command of the Soviet military machine but, according to a person who was close to him in that period, he suggested that another of his wartime comrades, a man with whom he was developing a renewed close relationship, be given the task. The man Tukhachevsky suggested was also a long-time associate of Stalin, Sergei Ordzhonikidze. But that would have given the fiercely independent Ordzhonikidze too much power, so Stalin opted for the much more pliable Klementi Voroshilov.[27]

8
INTERVAL IN LENINGRAD

AS FRUNZE'S DEPUTY, Tukhachevsky became, for the first time, one of the recognized leaders of the Soviet state. He was very much the man about Moscow. A striking figure, in the prime of life, he quickly won a reputation as something of a rascal.

His new wife, the daughter of a Smolensk official, had been 17 when he married her. Tukhachevsky had been 30 and much more experienced. It was natural that from the beginning the marriage had had its problems. Within a few months he and his wife had separated, although there was a reconciliation after the birth of their daughter, Svetlana. According to Tukhachevsky's gossipy sister-in-law, the immediate cause of the discord was an affair Tukhachevsky had with Tatiana Chernolizky, the sister-in-law of the veteran Bolshevik leader Anatoli Lunacharsky. But there were other reasons, including the vastly different backgrounds and aspirations of the young couple. As Tukhachevsky's sister-in-law was to note, he was married to the army as much as he was to any woman.¹

For Tukhachevsky military matters were vitally important but, unlike most of his fellow Soviet leaders, he was also sophisticated in culture and art. By all accounts, he was a dismal musician, but he eagerly sought the acquaintanceship of musicians more skilled than himself. His violinmaking hobby served as something of an entree with them. Tukhachevsky had also assumed the role of patron of the arts. For the 32-year-old general, it must have been a pleasant experience to be viewed as a venerable elder by young musicians in Moscow and elsewhere.

It was in this way that he met and grew friendly with a young Leningrad musician, Dmitri Shostakovich. In 1925, Tukhachevsky heard through friends that Shostakovich was writing a symphony, and he invited the young musician to visit him when he came to Moscow. Years later, in his memoirs, the composer recalled the event:

> When we met I wasn't even nineteen and Tukhachevsky was over 30. But the main difference between us wasn't age, of course. The main difference was that by then Tukhachevsky had one of the most important positions in the Red Army and I was just a beginning musician.
>
> But I behaved very independently. I was cocky, and Tukhachevsky liked that. We became friends. . . .
>
> Tukhachevsky was probably one of the most interesting people I knew. Of course, his military glory was irresistible. Everyone knew that at 25 Tukhachevsky was commander of the army. He seemed to be fate's favorite. He had fame, honors, rank. . . .
>
> Tukhachevsky enjoyed being attractive. He was very handsome and he knew it. He was always dressed flashily. I really liked that about him. When I was young I enjoyed dressing well myself. I really envied another of his qualities— his unshatterable health. . . . Tukhachevsky could put a man on a chair and then lift the chair, yes, lift the chair and its occupant by one leg with his arms outstretched. . . . His office in Moscow had a gym with beams, a horizontal bar and other incomprehensible equipment.
>
> . . .
>
> Tukhachevsky was very ambitious and an imperious

person. In these traits [he] resembled Meyerhold who adored military masquerades. . . .

That was Meyerhold's weakness, let's put it that way. Tukhachevsky's weakness was art. Meyerhold looked silly in a uniform, but many were impressed. Tukhachevsky looked just as silly when he picked up his violin, but many were charmed.[2]

Shostakovich was not the only musician in Tukhachevsky's circle. Another was Nikolai Zhilayev, a composer and music teacher who had known Tukhachevsky's family before World War I. In the early years of the Soviet regime, Zhilayev was one of the country's prominent musical authorities, but eventually he, too, was a victim of Stalinist vengeance, largely because of his relationship with Tukhachevsky.

Some idea of Tukhachevsky's standing in the Russian musical world can be gauged from a singular event involving Shostakovich toward the end of 1926. At that time the Polish authorities had established the Chopin Competition in Warsaw, and they had invited four young Russian musicians to compete. Shostakovich was one of them, the others being Lev Oborin, Grigori Ginsberg, and Yuri Bryshkov. Before leaving for Warsaw, the Russian pianists gave a public concert in the great hall of the Moscow Conservatory. Three of them—Shostakovich, Oborin, and Bryshkov—played privately for Tukhachevsky, who, it is said, "listened attentively, occasionally making quiet, tactful and pertinent comments."[3]

In this aspect of his life, Tukhachevsky revealed a side of his personality quite different from the one he showed as a formidable military commander. It was almost as if he were trying to escape. Shostakovich observed: "Tukhachevsky was alone. He had no friends, only fawners and companions for amorous expeditions."[4]

His sister-in-law saw him in much the same way, but liked him no less for what she saw. "Mikhail Nikolaevich had not the faintest idea of friendship," she wrote later. "According to his view, he could have friendship when and where he pleased. I suggested to him that he was a little truant." She had once encountered him on a Leningrad street, obviously under the weather, but when he was supposed to be with other top Soviet military commanders, reviewing important military maneuvers. He hailed her and promptly asked, "What would you like? Shall we go to the theatre? Do you want a drink?"[5]

This may have been an isolated event, for although Tukhachevsky was at the center of the cultural fervor that bubbled through Moscow and Leningrad, he usually did not allow such diversions to distract from his work with the army.

The advent of Voroshilov to the top command meant that Tukhachevsky's influence in the inner circles of the military establishment was at least temporarily in eclipse. There was little love lost between the two. It was only a few years since their unfortunate first encounter in the final days of the battle against Denikin. The hauteur displayed by Tukhachevsky on that occasion, reinforced by the events on the Polish Front in 1920, made friendship unlikely.

Whereas Frunze, toward the end of his career, was becoming more military than Communist, Voroshilov was the opposite. Moreover, whereas Frunze was becoming more independent of Stalin, as evidenced by his friendship with Tukhachevsky and his alignment with Kirov and Ordzhonikidze, Voroshilov remained very much Stalin's creature to the end of his days. In the mid-1920s that was an especially important difference, and it had a marked effect on Tukhachevsky.

Thus, in the early days of Voroshilov's appointment, Tukhachevsky's position in the hierarchy was in extreme doubt, the more so since the struggle for political supremacy among Stalin, Trotsky, L. B. Kamenev, Zinoviev, and others was still being waged with Borgialike venom. During this period, many formerly prominent members of the party fell. Most notable among them was the Soviet diplomat Adolf Joffe, who committed suicide in a dramatic but futile gesture of protest against Stalin's policies on November 17, 1925.

The conflict between Tukhachevsky and Voroshilov apparently broke into the open over the production of new field service regulations for the Red Army. This project had been launched under Frunze and entrusted to a commission headed by Tukhachevsky, with Yakir, Uborevich, Eideman, and V. M. Primakov, the organizer of the Red Guard in 1917, assisting him. According to one version of the dispute, Voroshilov had decided to remove Tukhachevsky from Moscow and post him to either the Western Military District or the Leningrad Military District.

Yakir and his associates protested, saying that they could not continue their work without Tukhachevsky's direction. Tukhachevsky therefore kept his position. Moreover, in the preface to the *Provisional Regulations for Field Service,* Tukhachevsky took sharp issue with those Red Army leaders, of whom Voroshilov was the most prominent, who believed that because of the backward condition of Russian industry, the Soviet military machine could not be expected to compete with foreign adversaries, but must depend on its "enthusiasm" to provide victory. Tukhachevsky derided such beliefs as "foolish chatter which helps the counterrevolution." He stated instead that "the superior technique of imperialist armies must be overcome by the Red Army's evolution and mastery of a still more powerful technique."[6]

During this period, the military cooperation with the Germans continued. In August 1925, German observers were present at the Red Army's maneuvers, and later that year Russian officers attended the exercises of the Reichswehr. For their visit to the Soviet Union, the Germans passed themselves off as German worker-Communists, while on the return visit the Russians pretended to be Bulgarians.

German documents captured at the end of World War II have shed some light on the extent of this cooperation, but even so, Tukhachevsky's exact role in them is difficult to judge, since the most prominent roles were filled by Voroshilov and I. S. Unslikht, a former officer of the OGPU and now Voroshilov's deputy. From other sources, it seems certain that Tukhachevsky was involved to some degree.

For example, in 1926 and 1927, several senior Russian commanders were sent to Germany for the course in general staff training. In 1926, Uborevich — one of Tukhachevsky's closest associates — was one of two Russians who took the course. In 1927, another Tukhachevsky associate, Eideman, was sent to Germany for training. In the spring of 1928, yet a third Tukhachevsky associate, Kork, was named Soviet military attaché in Berlin.

In the background of the German-Soviet collaboration was the unspoken fear that Poland would cause either or both of the struggling nations new trouble. This apprehension was heightened in May 1926, when Pilsudski again surfaced in Poland, deposing the Witos government and, although declining the position of president, again became the real ruler of the country.

Moreover, the relationship between Russia and Germany had been renewed by the signing on April 24, 1926, of the Treaty of Berlin, which was a reaffirmation of the earlier Treaty of Rapallo.

Changes were also being made in the organization of the Red Army. On July 12, 1926, the Red Army staff became the focal point for the Soviet armed forces in time of war. Also at this time, determined efforts were being made to weed politically unreliable officers out of the higher ranks of the army. The older military specialists were an obvious target. This apparently caused some apprehension in the army, enough for Voroshilov to address the officers of the Moscow Military District on the subject. In his explanation, the new defense commissar said that the main rationale for the recent dismissals had been the fact that there were too many officers in the Red Army. While the ratio of officers to soldiers in the tsarist army had been 1 to 18, in the Red Army it was 1 to 10. He added that a considerable saving was achieved by trimming back the officer corps. Citing as an example—although whether that was the actual number dismissed is uncertain—a reduction of 16,000 officers, Voroshilov said a saving of 16 million rubles would be realized. As a sop to the discontented, Voroshilov said special arrangements would be made for the return of the ousted officers to civilian life.[7]

At the same time, the Moscow authorities sought to widen the potential base for recruits to the army by initiating compulsory military training for all high school and university students. In addition, ever increasing emphasis was being placed on the development of the Soviet Air League (Osoviakhim), which by the beginning of 1928 had 3 million members.

Abroad, too, these were worrisome times for the Soviet regime. In the Far East, trouble always seemed to be breaking out. Russia's protégé, Chiang Kai-shek, turned and bit the hand that had fed him. The Japanese were constantly threatening the vulnerable Soviet territory in the area. In Britain, on January 12, 1927, there occurred the notorious Arcos raid. In this incident, defying the quasi-diplomatic status of the Soviet trade delegation, British police raided its building. Two weeks later, the Soviet Union severed diplomatic relations with the British. Relations with Poland, agitated by Pilsudski's return to power, took a more ominous turn with the murder in Warsaw, by a Russian exile, of the Russian ambassador, I. M. Volkov, on June 7, 1927.

And, inside the Red Army, the coolness between Voroshilov and the Tukhachevsky group was deepening into open antagonism. The chief item in dispute was the basic attitude to be adopted in Soviet military preparations for the war that everyone from Stalin down seemed to feel was imminent. Voroshilov apparently was arguing in favor of strictly defensive preparations. Tukhachevsky and his associates argued that to follow such a course was defeatist. The intervention of Trotsky did not serve to cool the dispute, even though by this time his influence in military matters was negligible. The matter reached a climax in July, when Yakir, Putna, and several other ranking officers closely identified with Tukhachevsky—although not Tukhachevsky himself—sent a secret report to the Politburo, contending that Voroshilov was incompetent and unfit to direct the Soviet war machine. This "in-army opposition" was well-organized, and soon its sympathizers were active in many key garrison centers—Smolensk, Minsk, Mogilev, Vitebsk, Kiev, the service academies, and the fleets—passing resolutions of support. A plenum of the Revolutionary Military Council was convened to hear the opposition's complaints. It was a serious threat, since it coincided with the political turmoil in the party related to the final ouster of Trotsky and Zinoviev from the party. That ouster came on October 23, 1927, and in January 1928, Trotsky was exiled to distant Alma-Ata.[8]

But Voroshilov stayed. Since he was Stalin's man, that was only to be expected. But Tukhachevsky did not stay. He was replaced on the command staff by the apolitical Shaposhnikov, another former tsarist officer, who had caused quite a stir in the summer of 1927 with the publication of the first part of a three-volume study, *The Brain of the Army*, which advocated the close alignment of the party and military commands. Although he was not yet a party member, his views were close enough to Stalin's and Voroshilov's to indicate that he would be less trouble to the Stalinist leadership than the stormy and adventurous Tukhachevsky. Tukhachevsky's sister-in-law, who knew Shaposhnikov well, had a felicitous description for the two rival generals: "the Volcano and the Iceberg."[9] Ten years older than Tukhachevsky, Shaposhnikov had considerably more formal military education, and he seems to have regarded his young fellow commander as something of an upstart. With Shaposhnikov's promotion, Tukhachevsky was relegated to the lesser post of commander of the Leningrad Military District.

There has been much speculation about the reason for Tukhachevsky's being removed from the command center of the Soviet military at this time. Field Marshal Wehrner von Blomberg, the German military leader, who met both men about this time, is reported to have offered two reasons. The first was that Stalin considered Tukhachevsky unreliable. The second was that Stalin and Voroshilov had disagreed with Tukhachevsky over the policy toward Poland. Tukhachevsky is said to have urged a preemptive strike against the Poles, while Stalin and the ultracautious Voroshilov strenuously opposed such a venture. But the answer could just as easily have been much simpler. Voroshilov didn't like Tukhachevsky; Stalin didn't trust him. At this stage of Soviet history, frequent comparisons were still being made between Tukhachevsky and the young Napoleon. Stalin never had much patience with potential Bonapartes.[10]

The icy Shaposhnikov must have seemed a much safer person to have control of the Red Army. The more so because of his views set out in *The Brain of the Army*. Shaposhnikov outlined a military machine controlled by a general staff, fully subordinated to the policies of the regime, that devoted itself entirely to a very rigorous planning. To Stalin, who was about to launch his monstrous experiment in state organization, the First Five-Year Plan, that must have seemed attractive. For this reason, stories that Stalin and Voroshilov personally attended Shaposhnikov's lectures at the Military Academy seem likely to be true.

In contrast with the new chief of staff, Tukhachevsky was much more venturesome. Nowhere is the contrast between the two men more vividly displayed than in Shaposhnikov's tome and Tukhachevsky's article "War as a Problem of Armed Struggle," published in 1928.

Where Shaposhnikov's long treatise was introspective, concerned with the defense of Russia, Tukhachevsky's short article retained most of his earlier internationalist objectives, although now they were tempered somewhat by his maturity. His idea of how future wars would be waged had also changed with the years. Maneuverability, the previous hallmark of Tukhachevsky's and the Red Army's thinking, was played down. As a result, he admitted the role of defense in future battles. Even so, offense was to be the main concern, since, as Tukhachevsky argued with no little logic, the aim of war is the defeat of the enemy. But where Shaposhnikov and Tukhachevsky differed most was on political matters. Shaposhnikov maintained the need for the closest possible alliance between the military and political organs, implicitly admitting the superiority of the latter. Tukhachevsky, although a party member for almost a decade, insisted that in the actual execution of battle plans, the commander should be supreme. As always, Shaposhnikov compromised where Tukhachevsky was independent.[11]

These were dangerous times in Russia. The fallout from the intraparty fighting in November 1927 still hung over the Soviet regime. Stalin was still preoccupied with consolidating his power. Even Voroshilov was not counted wholly on his side, although with the ouster of Trotsky and Zinoviev, there was nowhere else for him to go.

In Leningrad, Tukhachevsky was distant from the Sturm und Drang. He made the most of the situation, and seems to have enjoyed himself thoroughly. His friendship with young Shostakovich deepened. Years later, the great composer said: "We met often and went out a lot. He liked driving in the country and he used to take me with him. We would leave the car and go deep into the woods. It was easier to talk freely there."

The desire to escape apparently was still strong. Shostakovich says: "Tukhachevsky loved impersonating Haroun al Rashid. Actually the uniform became Tukhachevsky and he knew it. But he was recognized immediately in uniform and therefore he often went into town in blatantly civilian clothes. His suit would also be well made. Tukhachevsky loved the cinema. He could have seen the films in private screening rooms for the top brass. But he preferred putting on his civilian clothes and going to a seedy movie house. Alone, without a bodyguard. It was more interesting to him that way."

Tukhachevsky went other places incognito. Shostakovich relates another incident:

> Once Tukhachevsky and I went to the Hermitage to look at the paintings. Actually it was his idea. He was in mufti,

of course. First we wandered around the museum on our own, then we tagged along with a group. The group had a guide. A young fellow and obviously not very educated. Tukhachevsky began correcting the guide. He said two words to the guide's one, and, I must admit, to the point. The people finally stopped listening to the guide and listened only to Tukhachevsky. Finally, the guide grew angry. He wouldn't even talk to Tukhachevsky. He approached me and said, "Who is that?" Meaning why is he sticking his nose in my business?

Without blinking, I replied, "Tukhachevsky." It was like a lightning bolt. At first the guide didn't believe me. But then he looked closely, and of course recognised him. Tukhachevsky had an extremely distinctive face. Naturally this not very educated worker at the Hermitage got scared. He feared for his job, that his children would starve.

And they would have fired him if Tukhachevsky had ordered it, or if he had merely complained. As commander of the military district, Tukhachevsky had great power in Leningrad.

The guide's feistiness was replaced by terrible fear. He began thanking Tukhachevsky for his priceless information. Tukhachevsky replied benignly, "Study, young man, study. It's never too late." And we headed for the exit. Tukhachevsky was very pleased with the adventure.[12]

Shostakovich's warm memories of the young general include another incident that had potentially more serious overtones but that displayed the generous side of Tukhachevsky's nature. Tukhachevsky's bodyguards had found a drunk sitting in the general's car, trying to unscrew the shiny, nickel-plated door handles. The bodyguards apparently intended to take the unfortunate drunk to the police, who would teach him a lesson for trying to damage an important official's car.

Tukhachevsky intervened, however, and told the officers to let the man go home and sleep it off. The drunk turned out to be the composer Arseny Gladovsky, the creator of an opera about the defense of Petrograd in 1919. Gladovsky, to show his gratitude for Tukhachevsky's leniency, invited him to a performance of the work. Tukhachevsky sat through the opera but was not greatly impressed. Says Shostakovich: "Later he said to me thoughtfully, 'Maybe I was wrong in letting him go.' He was joking of course."[13]

During Tukhachevsky's period as commander of the Leningrad Military District, he was also occupied with more serious affairs, many of which produced effects decades after his death. But the whole period was exemplified by his driving energy and his eagerness to try novel experiments.

His first meeting with the staff of the Leningrad Military District set the tone for his command there. As one junior officer recalled, the garrison commanders inspected this relatively young soldier, already renowned for a decade of exploits in the Red Army "with unconcealed curiosity and profound respect" when he was introduced by Feldman. In a brief address Tukhachevsky gave them a not too subtle admonition to be on their toes. He suggested that one of his first tasks would be to check them all and that reassignments might follow.

The officer said of the garrison commanders, "They gained the impression from meeting him, to brace ourselves. And as was shown later, as we got to know him, we were not mistaken." According to several contemporaries, Tukhachevsky routinely put in 12-to-15 hour days and expected his aides to do likewise.

Without delay, Tukhachevsky ordered a report from his new aides on the background of the district's commanders and the status of the troops under their leadership. He carefully studied the reports and then summoned a conference of the commanders. He was not long in reaching his point: "You show a considerable lack of training and in preparation of military plans," he said. "We will have to work diligently. The authority of the military district must be reinforced in its basic knowledge and experience. Sometimes [the officers] will not be capable."[14]

Tukhachevsky was much occupied with basic military matters. Here again he displayed the qualities that made him so different from Shaposhnikov. Where Shaposhnikov was the epitome of the staff general, the remote figure concerned with maps and communications, Tukhachevsky was always a fighting soldier, a leader of men, concerned with trenches and weapons. Thus, when he arrived in Leningrad, he made a practice—and insisted that his subordinates follow his example—of touring the outlying areas of the district, particularly those near the frontier. What he saw there apparently caused him some alarm, especially the lack of air defenses.

"Don't you know, comrades," an associate remembers him saying, "that quite a few countries in Western Europe have planes capable of carrying a ton of bombs? Isn't it known that those countries have incendiary bombs as well?"

The colleague continues:

> And, as always with him, after giving the orders, concrete actions followed. He personally revised the layout of the Leningrad Military District, arranging for the increase of antiaircraft artillery, for more fighter aircraft and broadening the network of guard posts. And . . . at the time of the Great Patriotic War, right up to the siege [of Leningrad] itself, the defenses were not passed through by one plane, but they were kept well away, thanks to Mikhail Nikolaevich.[15]

Tukhachevsky's next concern was further afield, in the Karelian Peninsula, where he discovered there was almost no defenses against invasion from the east. To remedy this, he ordered construction of a series of troop bunkers and fortifications, which, in one of those ironies of history, served the Russian defenders well in their fight against the Germans in World War II, not many years after Tukhachevsky had been executed for conspiring with the Nazis.[16]

Tukhachevsky had visited the region, and during that trip he had grilled his junior officers extensively about the manning, the locations of the defenses, and even the smallest details. Apparently there had been plans for further defensive construction, but the work was going too slowly for Tukhachevsky. When he asked the reason for the delay, an aide replied that in the current year, 1928, the district officials had not allocated enough men for the task. With characteristic disdain for such matters, Tukhachevsky promptly insisted that more workers experienced in handling concrete be found and that the building program be speeded up. "We will hope that neither Narkom nor Sergei Mironovich will deny us," he chuckled. It was a measure of his considerable clout and his developing relationship with S. M. Kirov that they didn't.[17]

Despite this activity, to most outsiders Tukhachevsky

seemed to have been shoved into something of a backwater, although the Leningrad command was one of the most important in the country. He was still of interest, however, to the Germans. In September 1928, Blomberg undertook an extensive tour of the Soviet Union, and in the course of it made sure to visit Tukhachevsky in Leningrad. The future German commander in chief rated him "a personality worthy of notice," although not quite as impressive as the "English-officer type" Shaposhnikov.[18]

In fact, Tukhachevsky was far from being cut off from the center of power. He continued to be one of the instructors at the Military Academy in Moscow and, if anything, his output of articles in the military publications increased. He remained the mover and shaker, the leading theoretical spirit of the Red Army.[19]

When the Manchuria crisis threatened to embroil the Soviet Union in a war with Japan in the early summer of 1929, Tukhachevsky was quickly summoned to take over the operations section of the Red Army. The nominal point of friction was the Chinese Eastern Railway, the outlet from the Soviet Union to the Pacific, which was threatened by the Japanese-dominated Manchurian regime. And with General Giichi Tanaka, the man who had led Japan's intervention forces in Siberia at the end of World War I and now the prime minister of Japan, the enmity ran a great deal deeper. The Soviet regime had no interest in abandoning the railroad, but it seemed that it would be necessary to fight Japan, or at least the Manchurian army, to save it.

Blyukher, who had been supposed to become the Soviet military attaché in Berlin, was named to head the new Special Far Eastern Army, and by the fall it was engaged against Manchurian units. From then on, there was sporadic fighting until Zhukov's engagement at Khalkin-Gol a decade later decided the matter in favor of the Russians. After that, the Japanese stayed well clear of the Red Army.[20]

But the Far Eastern crisis ebbed, and Tukhachevsky returned to his work in Leningrad. He was soon occupied with his military experiments, but he was also cementing an important political alliance. Since 1926, the leading political figure in the old capital had been Sergei Mironovich Kostrikov, better known by his nom de guerre, Kirov. He was seven years older than Tukhachevsky but was regarded as one of the younger stars of the Soviet regime. They had worked together briefly during the campaign against Denikin, and in Leningrad their similar aims for the development of the defense-related industry made them ideal partners.

Kirov had proved himself politically adroit. During the height of the anti-Trotsky campaign, he had been safely out of the way on various assignments in the southern part of the country. In those tasks he had become closely identified with Stalin and with Ordzhonikidze, who at that time was regarded as essentially a Stalin crony. Thus, in November 1926, soon after he had taken over in Leningrad, Kirov staged a rally, attended by 4,000 delegates, at which he urged "merciless war" against the opposition led by his predecessor, Zinoviev, and L. B. Kamenev. In a gesture that was certain to please Stalin, Kirov maneuvered another gathering, held to mark the fifth anniversary of Zinoviev University (which had been founded by the man whose name it bore), to pass a resolution insisting that the school's name be changed to Leningrad Communist University.[21]

At the same time, Kirov was staking out an independent fiefdom for himself in Leningrad. When he was named to the Politburo in 1930, he was allied there with two other men close to Tukhachevsky, Ordzhonikidze and Valerian Kuibyshev. This association gave Kirov considerable clout in the upper echelons of the regime and, coupled with his position as the leader in Leningrad and the apparent regard in which he was held by Stalin, caused him to be regarded as the dictator's heir apparent and, in effect, the number 2 man in the Soviet Union.

That is not to say there was a distinct opposition bloc to Stalin in the Politburo. Rather, Kirov and the others shared like backgrounds and like ambitions. In fact, rather than opposing Stalin in the execution of the Five-Year Plan, they were his close collaborators and must share the blame for its excesses. Recent Soviet writers—or at least some from the Khrushchev era—blame the tragedy of this period exclusively on Stalin; but Kirov was, if anything, more zealous than Stalin in trying to root out obstructions to the plan. In the middle of the campaign, when Stalin's six theses for governing the plan—improvement of technical knowledge, respect for "labor discipline," rooting out of bureaucracy, equalization of wages, eradication of what was called "premature leftism," and strengthening of the "single command"—Kirov was one of the more voluble speakers campaigning for the official line. In January 1932, he was able to report that by applying the program to the great industrial plants of Leningrad, he had been able to eliminate 65,000 "superfluous" workers. Elimination did not yet have its later sinister meaning; rather, the affected workers were peremptorily shifted from the relatively civilized confines of Peter's city to new factories 2,000 miles away, in the rough-and-ready industrial centers, such as Magnitogorsk, that were springing up in Siberia.[22]

Kirov was particularly occupied with increasing the output of the defense-oriented heavy industries, and in this effort he worked closely with Ordzhonikidze, Valerian Kuibyshev, and, to a lesser extent, Anastas Mikoyan. All of them, at various times, had been engaged in revolutionary work in the south during the Civil War, forming what might be called a Caucasus Mafia in the higher reaches of the Soviet regime.[23]

Tukhachevsky was a sort of associate member of the group, for around him in Leningrad there gathered a subordinate military group with a similar background. These aides included Ivan Fedko, the son of a Ukrainian cossack, and the district chief of staff, Boris Feldman, both of whom had served in the south.

Kirov's strong attachment to the expansion of industry was not displeasing to Tukhachevsky, and the methods used to ensure it were certainly not alien to him. He too could be tough, especially when faced with incompetence. A unit commander who failed to do his job would promptly be replaced. But Tukhachevsky was equally concerned about fairness and correct behavior—after all the training at the Alexandrovsky Academy and the Semyenovsky Guards, that was to be expected.

One day, during an exercise, Tukhachevsky heard one of his divisional commanders "scold" some of the unit's junior officers.

"You always talk that way to subordinates?" Tukhachevsky asked.

The divisional commander tried to make light of the incident. "I wanted them to remember it for the rest of their lives," he said.

"The damage you do will also be retained for a long time, in their case," Tukhachevsky replied. "You have wasted the authority of the Red Army. Your big mouth and bad language were better kept for your friends. . . ."[24]

It was this forceful personality, leavened with a genuine concern for and interest in the welfare of his troops, that perhaps explains the affection with which Tukhachevsky was regarded in the Red Army. Even after all the vicissitudes of the Stalin purges, it has not been entirely extinguished.

Said one officer who served with Tukhachevsky in Leningrad:

> Mikhail Nikolaevich suffered no rudeness, lying or bootlicking or pretense. In return he liked and valued greatly anyone who, without fuss and jabbering, performed his tasks. . . . That is why people so willingly supported him. They put their whole soul into carrying out the tasks because they liked working with him. . . . He knew how to fit the allocation of tasks to particular circumstances. They were not onerous to carry out even if it appeared that they were unplanned.[25]

Fedko, Feldman, and many others looked up to Tukhachevsky as the chief spokesman for their ideas on modernizing the Red Army. Voroshilov also, at least publicly, favored many of their plans, and so did Stalin. But, like Tukhachevsky, they were all, to some extent, opposed to Stalin on political questions, particularly on the political independence of the army.

Therefore it was by no means taken for granted that the Tukhachevsky faction—if that was what it could be called—would prevail. In his usual fashion of dividing and conquering, Stalin was apparently developing an alternative to Tukhachevsky, and perhaps even to Voroshilov, in the military.

In the late 1920s, according to some versions, this alternative was centered on Yan Fritzovich Fabritsius, a Latvian who had been a member of the party since 1903. He had risen from private in the tsarist army to company commander; and after joining the Red Army he had served on the Northern and Polish fronts. He apparently ran into political difficulties in the uproar of 1927, but was quickly reinstated and appointed to the all-important Central Control Commission, and seemed destined for higher things. But on August 24, 1929, he was killed in a plane crash near Sochi, and whatever plans Stalin had for him were never fulfilled.

Fabritsius was an independent spirit—so independent, in fact, that it hardly seemed credible that Stalin would ever have seriously considered him for a top command. He was notorious for his disregard of party edicts and his contempt for bureaucrats. One story told about him related how, while swimming in a river in the Caucasus, he and his commissar got into a violent argument. Fabritsius thereupon threatened to drown the offending commissar "like a mangy pup." The man escaped by diving into the river and swimming to the other bank, where he was forced to stand naked on the shore until Fabritsius departed.

It was not surprising that he died in a plane crash; he had earned the nickname "Flying Dutchman" because of his fondness for ordering an aircraft and flying to Moscow, regardless of the weather, to protest some ukase or other that had emanated from the bureaucracy. And, as might have been expected, there were rumors that his death might not have been accidental. The basis for this talk was that, according to a doctor's report, the ebullient commander had not been killed by the crash, but had drowned when the plane fell into a shallow river.[26]

Whether or not Tukhachevsky was about to be shoved further into the background, his time in Leningrad did not diminish his restless drive to improve and modernize the Red Army, or at least the part of it under his control. He was constantly stimulating the development of new weapons, particularly in aviation and mechanized units.

Some of his ideas led Tukhachevsky down blind alleys. For some time he had been intrigued with the possibility of developing a "flying tank," a hybrid that would combine the maneuverability of the airplane with the armor of the tank. When that proved impractical, he turned to pushing for the development of larger planes, capable of carrying tanks wherever they were needed.

One important innovation to come from these experiments was the increased and better use of paratroops. It was scarcely by chance that Tukhachevsky was the first prominent commander, either East or West, to recommend using such forces on a large scale. The idea of dropping highly trained shock troops behind enemy lines, where they could link up with sympathetic partisans, fitted admirably with the ideas he had advanced as early as 1921 about the future course of international warfare. By 1929 he had led the first exercises with such troops, and about the same time he conducted a searching study of whether airborne troops could be sent to Germany to assist the proletariat in any uprising that might start there, a possibility that seemed very likely at the time.[27]

Tukhachevsky's interest in the uses of military aviation was further stimulated during his work on revising the Red Army's Field Service Regulations, on which he worked during his years in Leningrad. The revision involved considerable give and take between the authors of the various chapters and the committees that reviewed the work. Sometimes the discussions became acrimonious, and then Tukhachevsky would step in as arbiter. An aide later recalled one such instance: "In haste, after one such argument, Mikhail Nikolaevich ordered that material be gathered, ours and from abroad, about paratroops and that a paper be prepared on the theme 'The Handling of Airborne Infantry in Offensive Operations.'"

Tukhachevsky had set a two-month time limit for this task, and when the report was delivered to him, he went through it thoroughly, amending and revising it. From this beginning he quickly built the experimental airborne unit that was the first of its kind, antedating by many years the formation of paratroop detachments in the West.

Working closely with Tukhachevsky in this new branch of the military was another remarkable personality, Vladimir Ivanovich Bekauri. Bekauri was a Georgian-born and Georgian-educated engineer who had begun his career as a railroad technician, then had diverted his talents to revolution by making bombs for the movement. From 1919 on, he had been a member of the Red Army and active in modernizing Soviet weaponry and developing new equipment. He had received several awards and prizes for his inventions, and had donated the proceeds for famine relief in the Volga region. Similar prizes later came to him, and they too went to charity, for the construction of schools in the provinces or for a tractor for his native village.

The airborne experiment was something to which Bekauri could devote his whole energy. He assembled kindred spirits, and before long they were altering aircraft so that motorcycles and sidecars could be slung under the wings. When that seemed to work, they grew more ambitious, adapting a larger plane so that an automobile with a radio transmitter could be placed under the fuselage. From there it was a short step to placing a light tank in the same place.

A few months after this crude beginning, there was an airborne formation that, to its immediate commanders, seemed to be fully operational. But Tukhachevsky was not satisfied. However, when he saw that his criticisms had left his colleagues somewhat crestfallen, he hastened to reassure them: "We support you in this." He then ordered even more extensive experiments. By the fall of 1930 the experiments had been refined and expanded to the point that, at the Red Army maneuvers held near Leningrad, successful jumps by parachute units were an integral part of the operations. By 1931, similar units were functioning in the Byelorussian and Ukrainian military districts.

Such was Tukhachevsky's drive that the paratroop project was just one of several that occupied him in Leningrad. He was continually seeking new trends in military affairs, particularly those involving tanks and other modern weapons. With Bekauri and others he pushed for the making of new incendiary bombs and bombs with delayed-action fuses that would be used by the growing air force. In 1930, he equipped entire divisions of his troops with special mobile shelters for use in forested and marshy areas. The troops were also given skis and trained in using them. Cannons and howitzers were fitted with runners so that they could be moved easily during the long Russian winters; for warmer weather, he rushed the manufacture of special pontoon floats that could carry them across rivers.

"His creative brain worked without tiring," said an aide, "the fantasies were indeed infinite."[28]

According to General Todorsky, it was because of one of Tukhachevsky's initiatives that the Gazodynamichesky Laboratory was established in July 1928. From this collective a great deal of future Soviet weaponry was to come: jet aircraft engines, antitank guns, and the forerunners of the Katyusha and other rockets.[29]

"There was not in the army a man who was like Tukhachevsky; he foresaw and discovered exactly new things in military-technical affairs, such as the carefully defined trends in armaments and military equipment," said an officer who worked with him both in Leningrad and later.[30]

In one account, Voroshilov had become an enthusiastic backer of Tukhachevsky's plans for paratroops. In this version, during the 1930 field exercises, a small unit of airborne troops dropped behind the "enemy" lines managed to surprise and capture a corps headquarters. The story, which seems plausible, is interesting not only for the light it sheds on the concentration on aerial troop movements but also for the illustration it provides of the relative simplicity of the defense commissar's thinking. Tukhachevsky's abstract ideas about paratroops may not have impressed Voroshilov, but the practical proof did.[31]

The new branch of the military service was indulged with all the excesses of Stalinist Russia. Within a short time Osoviakhim, the territorial military organization, was devoting its attention to training as much of the population as possible in parachute jumping. More than 1,000 centers were established for that purpose throughout the Soviet Union, and the press was filled with the epic feats of endurance and skill of the tens of thousands of young Russians who took part in the exercises. One particular hero was the parachute champion Zhevdokimov, who let himself fall free for 142 seconds before pulling the release on his chute at 660 feet.[32]

During this time, Tukhachevsky had been embroiled in a furious dispute over the organization of the Soviet military, and over the merits of a defensive or offensive strategy. Inevitably the defeat before Warsaw was dragged up once more, being cited as a classic example of a foolhardy offensive, even being compared with the ill-timed Greek adventure in Smyrna in the 1920s, when the Turks finally drove the Greeks out of Asia Minor. The two main protagonists in the debate were Tukhachevsky, who favored a mass, highly mobile army tuned to offensive operations, and Svechin, who favored a strategy of attrition and the use of a smaller, elite army of well-trained specialists. Strongly supporting the Tukhachevsky view was Eideman, who had become head of the Frunze Academy in 1932.[33] In typical fashion, Stalin stepped in; Svechin and his colleagues at the academy, Snesarev and Verkhovsky, were arrested. Although they later returned to duty, they were to meet the same fate as Tukhachevsky.[34]

Tukhachevsky, however, was gradually returning to power, and in 1931 he was back to his former eminence as deputy to Voroshilov. Once again he was in a direct position to influence the modernization of the Red Army, and with his usual verve he plunged into his new duties.

9

AT THE PINNACLE OF POWER

WHILE TUKHACHEVSKY had been absent from Moscow, the country had been thrown into a madness that is scarcely credible to anyone who did not live through it. Stalin's First Five-Year Plan had developed into a disaster of proportions unknown in a modern nation, even though the official press continued to trumpet the glorious successes of the program in terms of increased coal, steel, and other production. In reality, peasant resistance to collectivization of the farms and bureaucratic inefficiency in many areas had brought much of the population to the point of starvation—and in many cases beyond it.

Soviet statistics are often considered unreliable, but it is possible to put some numerical proportions on the scope of the tragedy. In 1929, the average Russian city dweller consumed about 104 pounds of meat, including poultry and fats. The following year, as peasants slaughtered their livestock to prevent their expropriation and the meat supply for the cities shrank in consequence, the intake had fallen to 72 pounds. By 1931, it was down to 60 pounds; and in 1932, in the full depth of the disaster, it fell to 37 pounds (less than 2 ounces a day).[1]

The situation was worsened by the regime's decision to push grain exports in order to earn foreign exchange with which to buy machinery and tools for the industrialization program. There had been a bumper grain crop in 1930, but in the following years, the harvest was much smaller. However, the total amounts of grain exported remained at roughly the same level, even though some peasants were reduced to such straits that they were eating bark.[2]

Other figures measure the calamity from a different perspective. In 1928, the Soviet Union had 32 million horses; by 1934, the number had shrunk to 15.5 million. Before the collectivization began, there were 60 million cattle; by 1934, there were 33.5 million. The number of pigs dropped in the same period from 22 million to 11.5 million, and the total of sheep fell from 97.4 million to 32.9 million.[3]

The human dimension of the tragedy was equally stark. More than 5 million peasants classed as either kulaks or "wreckers" were uprooted and sent to distant exile—if they were lucky. The not so lucky starved or were executed for opposing the will of the Kremlin. Altogether, 100 million Soviet citizens were to undergo drastic changes in their way of life, and by the mid-1930s there were 20 million fewer peasants than there had been at the beginning of the First Five-Year Plan.[4]

Robert Conquest, whose book *The Great Terror* is the most complete dossier on the enormity of Stalin's crimes against the Russian people, estimates that 3.5 million people died during the collectivization. Even that horrific figure is dwarfed by Conquest's estimate that 20 million Russians died as a result of all of Stalin's purges.[5]

Tukhachevsky could not have been unaware of the political state of the country. There were plenty of signs all around him. One touched close to home when Ivan Smirnov, his long-time colleague from the days of the battles against Kolchak, was arrested and sentenced to 10 years' imprisonment for "antiparty activities." Smirnov was an obvious target for Stalin's displeasure because he had sided with Trotsky in the 1920s. His fate showed the complete indifference of Stalin to previous ties. Smirnov had been on the party's Central Committee with Stalin since 1912 and at one time had lived in exile with him. But in the end, the alliance with Trotsky was what mattered.[6]

The effect of the political turmoil in the country was echoed by changes in Stalin's foreign policy. And it was in this area that Tukhachevsky was chiefly affected. Until then, the Soviet Union had depended for its military buildup mainly on the sub rosa links with Germany. But by the summer of 1933, Stalin was obviously having second thoughts about relying so heavily on a nation that had been all too often in the past—and could so easily become in the future—antagonistic toward Russia. The basis for the military cooperation with Germany had been codified in protocols to the Treaty of Rapallo in April 1922 and in the Treaty of Berlin of April 1926. This second treaty remained in force for five years and was duly renewed on June 24, 1931, at a ceremony in Moscow. On this occasion it was renewed for three years, with a protocol providing that it would remain in force indefinitely unless either party revoked it.[7]

Tukhachevsky had, of course, been privy to the military ventures and, as we have seen, was reported to have visited Germany several times during the 1920s. But he had not been a principal in the undertakings. Instead, in the beginning, they had been directed by Trotsky and his immediate subordinates, and later by Voroshilov and Yegorov, for whom the Germans had a particularly high regard.

Tukhachevsky's close colleagues, however, had played integral roles in the Russo-German developments. Kork had been military attaché in Berlin until, following German Communist troubles in May 1929, he had been asked to leave. His post was quickly filled by another Tukhachevsky colleague, Vitovt Putna, who had held similar posts in Helsinki and Tokyo. Putna remained in Berlin until February 1931, after which he spent a further month in Germany, ostensibly on vacation with his children. However, according to the French, who were watching the Russo-German collaboration, Putna had more serious tasks in mind during this interval that involved military instruction.[8]

In September 1932, Tukhachevsky again visited Germany, at the invitation of Kurt von Schleicher, the ambitious minister for the Reichswehr. He arrived in Berlin on September 17 with five other high-ranking Russian military men: Feldman; A. I.

Sedyakin; Zhakovenko, who had replaced Putna as attaché; his deputy; and an unidentified person. They remained in Berlin until September 20, at which time they moved on to Frankfurt-on-Oder, to watch the German military maneuvers. From September 25 to October 7, they toured factories in the Ruhr and the Rhineland. On October 8, Tukhachevsky left Berlin for East Prussia, where he stayed until October 12. Only then did he return to Russia.[9]

Despite the apparent congeniality displayed toward Tukhachevsky and his colleagues, strain was showing in the relationship between Moscow and Berlin. The Germans had not failed to notice subtle shifts in Soviet foreign policy that seemed to indicate that Russia would now seek to use France as it had once used Germany to help it modernize its armed forces. By the early summer of 1933, they were reinforced in this belief by the enthusiastic reception given by Voroshilov and Budenny to French military visitors to the Russian capital. Even the strenuous protestations of continued friendship from the Russian military chiefs did not allay the German suspicions. For some time the Germans had sensed that they were giving more than they were getting in the arrangement. Russian officers were frequently at German installations, including the most sensitive, and their activities created tension. In 1929, a high-ranking German officer had been removed from his post at the Dresden Infantry School for objecting to the activities of the Russian officers, of whom Uborevich was one. The protesting officer had been upset by the Russians' "indiscretion, their desire to see and get to know everything, their propagandistic spirit."[10]

And while the Germans had developed a close rapport with Yegorov, and to a lesser extent with Voroshilov, they remained suspicious of Tukhachevsky. General Erich von Manstein, after a visit to Russia in 1931, reported his belief that Tukhachevsky was definitely pro-French. Even nonmilitary matters added to the uneasiness about Tukhachevsky. During a visit to Kiev the Germans had been introduced to the Russian commander and a woman identified as his wife. But later, at another dinner in Moscow, Tukhachevsky was accompanied by another "Frau Tukhachevsky." To the puzzled Germans, other Russians explained that the general had been married twice. The Germans, imbued with the spirit that had led to the curtailment of Blomberg's career when he married his secretary, were scandalized.[11]

Moreover, Manstein decided that Tukhachevsky was interested in gaining all the advantage he could from the Germans without giving up anything of value in return.¹²

German apprehension must have been further heightened by the signing on November 29, 1932, of a Franco-Soviet non-aggression pact, especially since it followed a similar treaty signed with Poland on July 25.

Then, on January 30, 1933, a new situation arose with Hitler's accession to power in Germany. Now was the time for the Reichswehr to reassure their Soviet counterparts that no changes were anticipated in German policy. But there were changes, although they could scarcely be called detrimental to the Russians. Colonel Kostring was replaced by Major Otto Hartmann as German military attaché in Moscow. Hartmann had met Tukhachevsky during a 1928 visit to Russia and during Tukhachevsky's visits to Germany. He spoke Russian. From these facts it would seem that at this time Hitler was acting cautiously, even though a hostile speech he made on March 2, 1933, drew a formal Soviet protest.[13]

The rise of Hitler seemed to fulfill many of Tukhachevsky's predictions, and at this time he seemed to have Stalin's support, so much so that on February 21, 1933, he was decorated with the Order of Lenin. The citation was brief: "For exceptional personal services to the revolution in the efficient organization of the defenses of the U.S.S.R. on exterior and interior fronts in the period of the Civil War and subsequently organizing measures to strengthen the Red Army."[14]

In response to the cordial reception he had received in Germany in 1932, Tukhachevsky had invited his counterpart in the Reichswehr, Lieutenant General Alfred von Bockelberg, to visit Russian units. He arrived in Russia on May 8. Both Voroshilov and Yegorov were still cordial, although they expressed anxiety about some of the new German regime's propaganda. During a dinner honoring the German visitor, Voroshilov took pains to emphasize his personal friendship toward the Germans and the fact that there had been no change in the official Soviet attitude.

Later in May, Tukhachevsky told Hartmann that the Soviet authorities had agreed to carry out joint chemical warfare experiments, although the required material had not arrived. Hartmann was not satisfied, for he had sensed that in other areas he was not being dealt with strictly on the level. He took up the matter with Tukhachevsky, but the resulting interview was even less satisfactory, from the German viewpoint. It was agreed that the chemical warfare tests should proceed, even if the new material did not arrive. Tukhachevsky was much more evasive on conducting further experiments in 1934. Citing money problems, he told the German attaché that just because it had been decided to continue the work in 1933, it should not be considered certain that it would continue in the future.[15]

By the end of June, relations between the two commands had visibly deteriorated, and on July 26, Hartmann had to tell his Soviet contacts that Russian officers would not be permitted to attend the German maneuvers that fall.

One by one, the bases where the joint experiments had been conducted were phased out. By the early autumn, at a farewell dinner for Hartmann, there were frank exchanges on what had gone wrong to disrupt what had been a mutually beneficial program. Hartmann was told that Russian officers would not have been sent to Germany anyway, because of anti-Soviet incidents there. But the Germans were not satisfied with that line, and bluntly questioned the Russians about what they saw as a pro-French tendency in Moscow. The Russians replied that there was nothing of substance in the renewed contacts with the French, and at any rate such a move could only have been expected, given the hostile anti-Soviet statements emerging from the new regime in Berlin. These could only be construed, the Russians said, as provocations, and therefore it was natural that the Soviet Union would seek to protect itself by making overtures to Poland and France.[16]

In reality, there was another reason for the Russians' seeking to distance themselves from the Germans after 1932. In the 1920s, the Red Army had been desperate to acquire modern arms, and Germany was the most convenient source. By the summer of 1933, that had changed. Whereas, at the beginning of 1931, the Red Army had only 300 MS-1 tanks and a few hundred BA-27 armored cars, by 1932 these numbers had increased to the point that the mechanized brigades set up in 1930 were now mechanized corps. The Stalin Academy of Mechanization and Motorization opened in 1932 to prepare commanders for this new wing of the Red Army.[17]

This mechanization drive in the Red Army brought considerable changes in the strategies of the Soviet High Command. Whereas in the past there had been continued emphasis on traditional methods involving the huge mass of infantry available to the Russians, now there was much greater diversification. To this trend, Tukhachevsky added his particular refinements.

By 1934, as illustrated by maneuvers held in previous years, the Russians seemed to be seeking to incorporate the new weaponry being produced through the industrialization program of the Five-Year Plans into the new military design. Thus, the old Russian mass offensive, relying principally on infantry and artillery for thrust and cavalry for mobility, now was adapted to include significant armored forces, both as independent units and in conjunction with the infantry. In addition, Tukhachevsky's pet creature, the paratroop unit, was brought into play to harass the enemy's rear and communications. This was part of the development of Soviet aviation, primarily as a kind of "air artillery," in Erickson's phrase. There was also a suggestion of the lessons learned in Germany; high-speed tank units were to be used for deep penetration of the enemy front.[18]

The Soviet munitions industry, with the help of the Germans, had progressed greatly. Some idea of its size can be gauged from the airplane plant at Fili, near Moscow, which by this time had 10,000 workers. But the rise of Hitler had evidently caused misgivings in the Soviet hierarchy, which seemed about to turn to the French for future weaponry assistance.

As Hartmann was leaving Russia in September 1933, the French air minister, Pierre Cot, was arriving for discussions. In later talks with the Germans, Tukhachevsky downplayed this contact, leaving the impression that the Russians had shown the French very little and had been chiefly interested in obtaining an insight into French aviation developments.

The French had noted a strangely cool attitude from Tukhachevsky. The French military attaché, Colonel Mendras, reported after one meeting:

> The welcome was correct, but cool. After a few minutes, Tukhachevsky let the conversation lapse. Colonel Mendras took his leave. It is not beside the point to note that Tukhachevsky. . . . former lieutenant in the Tsarist Guards and for a long time prisoner in Germany, had represented the

Red Army at the Reichswehr maneuvers, signing as well one of the instruments of the Russo-German collusion and . . . was known for violently anti-Polish feelings.[19]

During this diplomatic phase of his career, Tukhachevsky was still—perhaps even more vigorously—working strenuously for the mechanization of the Red Army. The rocket laboratory that he had helped to establish in Leningrad was already showing signs of success. On August 17, 1933, the first liquid-fueled rocket from the establishment was test-fired. The 44-pound projectile launched that summer day was the forerunner of the much larger ones that carried the Sputnik and Cosmos satellites into space decades later.[20]

But in another section of the aviation program, there had been a significant setback. Pyotr Ionovich Baranov, who had directed the Soviet air forces almost from the beginning, was killed in a plane crash when the aircraft failed to make an instrument landing. Baranov was another member of the higher echelons of the military who had served with Kirov, Frunze, and others in Turkestan, but in recent years he had been a close associate of Tukhachevsky in trying to develop a larger and better air force. His political connections as a member of the Central Control Commission and his rank as a candidate of the Central Committee had undoubtedly helped with the military's modernization plans.

Tukhachevsky was riding high. At the sixteenth anniversary celebration of the Bolshevik Revolution on November 7, 1933, he was the foremost representative of the Red Army during the ceremonies in Red Square. In front of Lenin's tomb, as Stalin, Kalinin, Molotov, and the other dignitaries watched, he took the salute from the massed units parading past. There was no doubt of his eminence. Tukhachevsky, nominally the number 2 man in the military, was officially substituting for Voroshilov, who had gone to Turkey for the tenth anniversary of Kemal Atatürk's Turkish Republic. But in actuality Tukhachevsky was now the operating head of the Red Army.[21] And it was a measure of his influence that the parade paid great attention to the new weapons —mechanized artillery, antiaircraft guns, radio cars, and new tanks—with which he was having the army equipped.

On the surface, the Stalin regime was growing stronger every day. This appearance was reinforced by the Seventeenth Congress of the Communist Party, held in Moscow from January 26 to early February 1934. This so-called Congress of Victors was, to the outsider, most notable for the bizarre adulation accorded the great feats of Stalin. Apparently leading the applause for the general secretary was Kirov.

But below the surface, it has now become clear, a large segment of the party was deeply antagonistic toward Stalin. And this opposition included—if it was not actually inspired by—several figures to whom Tukhachevsky was personally and politically close.

The elections for the Central Committee were to be held on the final day of the congress. The evening before, according to Anton-Ovseenko's detailed and authoritative account, some of the more prominent members of the opposition gathered at Ordzhonikidze's apartment to plot their strategy. Among those said to have been present were Kirov, Eykhe, Stanislav Kosior, and Grigory Petrovsky, all men with long and devoted service to the party. They urged Kirov to seek to replace Stalin as general secretary, but, apparently feeling that the attempt was futile, he demurred.[22]

Then came the election. When the ballots were counted, the officials were stunned to discover that almost a quarter of those taking part had cast votes against Stalin. According to Anton-Ovseenko, the actual number of such ballots was 292. By comparison, Kirov had collected just three such votes. When the apprehensive counters reported this development to Kaganovich, he is said to have ordered that 289 of the offending ballots be burned, leaving the same numbers for both Stalin and Kirov. The explanation for this discrepancy in the ballot is said to be based on a Khrushchev-era investigation into Stalin's crimes; when the ballots from the Seventeenth Congress were inspected, 289 fewer ballots were in the boxes than there had been delegates to the meeting.[23]

Khrushchev had a somewhat different recollection of the numbers involved, although he also made the point that there was serious opposition to Stalin. According to his memoirs, Stalin received endorsement for election to the Central Committee from all but six members of the congress. Khrushchev says that figure stuck in his mind because he got the same number of votes.[24]

The Russian historian Roy Medvedev offers a third, slightly different version. In this account, Stalin received the fewest votes of any candidate, and was elected only because the number of candidates was the same as the number of openings. Medvedev's version also includes the destruction of a large number of ballots and the final equalization of Kirov's and Stalin's totals.[25]

Like so many other stories from the Soviet Union, in the present circumstances there is no way of proving or disproving this story. Indeed, such a reputable authority as Adam Ulam casts doubt on the extent of the opposition.[26]

The opposition apparently was not so much to Stalin's goals as to his methods of achieving them and the associates he had chosen for that task. The Old Bolsheviks, such as Ordzhonikidze and Kosior, were said to be repelled by the sinister new group that included L. Z. Mekhlis, N. I. Yezhov, and G. G. Yagoda of the security organs, who were being promoted to high positions in the party. Doubtless, many of the veteran figures in the party recalled Lenin's so-called Testament, in which he bluntly criticized Stalin, and in particular suggested that he was not to be trusted with too much power. This group had already seen Stalin's destruction of Trotsky, Zinoviev, and others expelled from power in the late 1920s, and they may well have anticipated that Stalin could act just as easily against them. The recent second arrest of Ivan Smirnov, who had been working as head of the Gorki Automobile Factory, and the similar fate of Ivan Smilga were just two examples with which they were all familiar. Smirnov had been sentenced to ten years in prison; Smilga, to five.[27]

It would probably be a mistake to say that there was a pro-Stalin bloc and an anti-Stalin bloc in the upper reaches of the party, but from numerous sources it is known that on various specific issues and at various specific times, Kirov, Ordzhonikidze, and Valerian Kuibyshev had opposed Stalin. Sometimes they did it in conjunction. An example is the case of Martemyan N. Ryutin, the one-time director of the military journal *Krasnaya Zvezda*. He had been accused of treason for circulating a "platform" urging sweeping economic changes, rehabilitation of Bukharin and even of Trotsky, and restoration of democracy in the party. Stalin, claiming that the platform actually was a call for his assassination, had demanded the death penalty for Ryutin but had been opposed by most other members of the Politburo. Kirov, Ordzhonikidze, and Kuibyshev were in the majority against execution. Only Lazar Kaganovich is said to have sided completely with Stalin.[28]

Some substantiation for this opposition can be found in the Khrushchev-era history of the party, which talks about an alarming situation in the party at this time, and adds that some delegates "thought that the time had come to transfer Stalin from the post of General Secretary to some other job."[29]

But perhaps the most convincing evidence of the opposition at the Seventeenth Congress is provided by Khrushchev in his "secret speech." He reported that 98 of the 139 members and alternates elected to the Central Committee were subsequently arrested and shot. Even more chilling, of the 1,966 persons taking part in the congress, 1,108 were arrested in the purges of 1937–38.[30]

From all these accounts, although Kirov and Ordzhonikidze had been at odds on such matters as the diversion of scarce foodstuffs to Leningrad, at the congress they and Kuibyshev were active in at least discussing the removal of Stalin. Another prominent member of the group, according to Medvedev, was Vareikis, the poet-soldier who had rescued Tukhachevsky after he had been jailed by Muraviev. They agreed that Kirov should replace Stalin as general secretary.[31]

Because of his connections and friendship with many of the principals in the opposition, Tukhachevsky seems certain to have been aware of the machinations. But his actions at the 1934 congress were properly circumspect. In his report to the gathering, he paid the correct attention to the industrialization program that was the heart of the Five-Year Plans. But he also sounded a warning that industrialization must have a military purpose. "It is clear," he said, "that in the case of war the need for supplies of technical material, equipment, planes and tanks must increase hugely. . . . It is not enough to have a huge industrial base—it is necessary to be able to direct this, it is necessary to be able to move this from peaceful production to material for the front." He was politically adroit enough to couple this admonition with a reference to the preeminent role of the party in directing the industrialization plan and its military aspects.[32]

In the army itself, things seemed peaceful enough. Voroshilov remained the titular head of the military apparatus, with Tukhachevsky nominally chief of ordnance but in fact the principal operating officer of the Red Army. Yan Gamarnik held the parallel position as chief of the Political Administration. Yegorov was chief of the Red Army staff. Close Tukhachevsky associates were in most of the key commands. Innokenty A. Khalepsky, another veteran of the Kolchak battles, was head of mechanization and motorization. Feldman was chief of the Red Army administration, the quartermaster-general. Eideman was directing Osoviakhim, while Kork, Yakir, Uborevich, and Primakov commanded the strategic Moscow, Ukraine, Byelorussia, and Caucasus military districts. Shaposhnikov was on the sidelines as head of the Frunze Military Academy.

Under a statute promulgated on June 30, 1934, the structure of the military was reorganized. Voroshilov became the commissar for defense, but the basic power structure was not greatly affected. Through Voroshilov, Stalin still exercised political control over the military.

There seems to have been some tension in the military that led to the arrest of one high-ranking member of the Tukhachevsky circle, Primakov. Exactly what Primakov was supposedly guilty of has not come to light, but he was apparently reinstated and moved to the Leningrad Military District as deputy commander.[33]

In contrast with the inner turmoil of the political apparatus, the nation's foreign policy now took on a steady, conciliatory attitude. The Soviet Union joined the League of Nations, and strenuous efforts were made to establish friendly relations with that bastion of unredeemed capitalism, the United States. Maxim Litvinov traveled to Washington, where he was given an enthusiastic reception and made the appropriate engaging statements.

But soon Tukhachevsky, along with the rest of Russia, was to be shaken by one of the turning points of the middle Stalin years, the murder of his Leningrad colleague, Kirov. Prior to 1934, Kirov had been perceived as one of Stalin's close followers, even as one of his creations. But from the time of the Seventeenth Party Congress, he seems to have opposed Stalin on several key points. Medvedev cites as an instance a conference held during the summer on the subject of the machine tractor stations, which were used as much for political control as for increasing the agricultural output. Kirov supposedly spoke out at this conference, proposing that the stations be disbanded and that the rural soviets be restored. There were other instances in which the Leningrad secretary opposed Stalin, and in most cases he was supported by Valerian Kuibyshev and Ordzhonikidze. Tukhachevsky's friends were being very daring.[34]

Subsequent Soviet commentators, chief among them Khrushchev, have hinted that Stalin or his emissaries were directly involved in Kirov's assassination. There has been no proof that this was so, but the dictator certainly seized on the killing to launch the series of purges that were to climax in 1937 and 1938. Stalin seems to have had good cause—from his viewpoint—for eliminating Kirov. From many accounts, including that of Medvedev, Kirov had become the leader of the loose grouping inside and outside the Politburo that had begun to oppose Stalin openly, particularly in his attempts to remove some of the older party members from positions of influence. The Ryutin case was just one example. Another had involved A. P. Smirnov, Vladimir Tolmachev, and Nikolai Eismont, three Old Bolsheviks, who had merely discussed the replacement of Stalin. Eismont reportedly died in an accident, and the other two were executed.[35]

Kirov, moreover, was the head of the Leningrad party organization, and from that base had on several other occasions displayed an independence that could only have irritated Stalin. Finally, there was Kirov's undoubted popularity in the party and the nation, particularly the perception of his "Russianness," a factor that by all accounts would have aroused the jealousy of Stalin, whose Georgian accent made his origins all too apparent.

The immediate consequence of Kirov's murder, supposedly by a disgruntled party member, Leonid Nikolayev, was the launching of wide-scale terror. The newly rechristened NKVD swept into action, rounding up known members of the opposition and also arresting officials from within its own ranks. Their connection with the actual crime was often barely perceptible, or even completely invisible, but their trials were gradually expanded into a wholesale purge of those under any suspicion of opposition to Stalin.

Tukhachevsky and the army, however, seemed to be immune. In January 1935, at the Seventh Congress of Soviets, Tukhachevsky was able to announce that the Soviet government had decided to increase the Red Army by almost a third, to 900,000 men. There was no doubt in anyone's mind that this was necessary because of the events in Germany, and increasingly Tukhachevsky became the spokesman for the anti-Hitler attitude that seemed to be developing in Russia, a circumstance made fiercely ironic by the charges that were later made against him.[36]

On March 31, 1935, in an article in *Pravda,* Tukhachevsky summarized the military buildup in Germany since Hitler had come to power in January 1933. He added:

> It has been reported that in his conversation with [Lord] Simon [the British statesman], Hitler declared that in regard to the U.S.S.R., the situation "compels Germany to retain freedom of action in the future." . . . It is obvious that Hitler's imperialist plans are directed not only against the Soviet Union. That is merely a convenient screen for his plans for revenge in the west . . . and in the south.[37]

To the Germans, if not to the British and the French, this seemed to be an invitation to join a coalition against Germany's quest for access to oil and other raw materials. It became even more apparent to the Germans when, on May 2, 1935, a Franco-Soviet pact was agreed upon.

To the French, a partnership with the Red Army seemed strategically desirable. The French generals were having extreme difficulty in getting sufficient funds for the modernization and increase in effectiveness that they believed necessary. By comparison the Russians seemed able to get whatever matériel they wanted. One French general, after attending the 1935 field maneuvers of the Red Army, reported:

> The technique of the Red Army is on a particularly high level. . . . To achieve this level of armaments in three or four years demonstrates not only the success and power of Soviet industry, it also establishes the immense superiority of the Red Army over all the other European armies, which are often forced, and for a long time, to use old matériel. . . . The Red Army, at the present time, is probably one of the strongest armies in Europe, and this is a striking demonstration of the discipline with which the Soviet population consents to sacrifices required by National Defense.[38]

The workers and peasants of the Soviet Union might have offered a different view of those sacrifices.

But confidence in the Red Army command was undoubtedly high, and the command itself was apparently held in the highest regard by the political leadership. On November 20, 1935, under a decree that introduced new rank descriptions for the Red Army, Tukhachevsky was named one of the five marshals of the Soviet Union. The others given the same rank were Voroshilov, Budenny, Yegorov, and Blyukher.

During this period, Stalin's political warfare on actual and potential opponents was being ruthlessly intensified. Kirov's murder provided a convenient pretext. In January 1935, Zinoviev, Kamenev, and several other former opponents were tried and convicted of moral complicity in the Leningrad secretary's murder. Apparently because of opposition in the Politburo, their sentences were comparatively light. Zinoviev got ten years and Kamenev five, although later he was retried and the penalties equalized at ten years.[39]

This was the public side of the repression that was sweeping Russia. But there was a much more sinister and pervasive private aspect. Hundreds, if not thousands, of party and government officials suddenly found themselves under suspicion. The repression was accompanied by furious demands for increased production that reached a peak in September 1935 with the beginning of the Stakhanovite campaign. Supposedly during one heroic shift in a Donets pit, a miner named Stakhanov had hewed no less than 102 tons of coal, 13 times the normal amount. Immediately he became a model for similar feats in other mines, and a person to be emulated in the factories and on the farms. For the directors of mines and plants who were unable to instill the required fervor in their workers to reach these new goals, the results were terrifying. Visits from the NKVD soon followed, and then came arrest, deportation, or worse.

Victor Kravchenko describes the scene in his factory thus:

> The atmosphere.... became more oppressive every day. Kozlov, the party secretary, was "transferred" to the city of Krivoi Rog and soon we heard that he was under arrest. One administration official after another failed to show for work and their alleged "illness" proved permanent.

The rank-and-file workers at first took the view that these strange doings were no business of theirs. But now men and women close to them, comrades in their shops, workers like themselves, began to disappear. That was a different matter. The alarm became so pervasive that it cut deeply into production totals. The morale of the plant was badly shattered.[40]

Tukhachevsky could not have been unaware of this repression but, like the workers in Kravchenko's factory, he seems to have thought that such affairs were unlikely to affect the Red Army, now being hurriedly expanded to meet the all-too-apparent threat from Germany. And, apart from the Primakov affair, the army does seem to have escaped too much interference from the secret police.

Tukhachevsky's position, already weakened by the murder of Kirov, had undergone another change in January 1935 with the sudden death of his original patron, Valerian Kuibyshev. At the time, the official cause of death was reported as sclerosis of the heart, which seemed reasonable enough, given Kuibyshev's drinking habits. Even though Kuibyshev had openly differed with Stalin on recent occasions, he was still regarded in the party as belonging to the leader's intimate circle. Anton Antonov-Ovseenko recalled many years later that Kuibyshev was one of the few Politburo members who received visits from Stalin at his dacha, where they would relax, conversing over a bottle of wine.[41] Later, to suit Stalin's purposes, it was declared officially that Kuibyshev had been the victim of a medical murder ordered by Yagoda. (Stalin wanted to rid himself of Yagoda and other living links to his earlier crimes.)[42]

The result was the same, no matter who caused Kuibyshev's death. One more major figure opposed to Stalin's latest terror had been removed. And the removal further exposed Tukhachevsky. True, the marshal still had powerful friends, not the least of them Sergei Ordzhonikidze, although he, too, was increasingly estranged from Stalin.

And if there is one thing that was remarkable about Stalin, it was that his friendships were not forever. Kirov had been a friend and the closest of associates; Kuibyshev had been a friend and the most willing of Stalin's associates in the struggles against

Trotsky and Zinoviev. But Ordzhonikidze was something else. His association with Stalin dated to long before the revolution, to the time of the "expropriations" in the Caucasus. He was the man who had brought the "splendid Georgian" to Lenin's attention, and was largely responsible for Stalin's election to the Central Committee in 1912.

But these men also owed allegiance to the Communist Party, and they considered themselves to be just as much the heirs of Lenin as Stalin had come to see himself. Therefore, when they perceived what they believed were aberrations from Leninist norms, they objected. For, although they were ruthless men, quite capable of sacrificing life and liberty to the greater aims of the party, they were not quite so oblivious to human morality as was their leader. Thus, when Stalin had demanded the death penalty for Ryutin, they had objected. And when Stalin demanded new vengeance on Zinoviev and Kamenev, they objected once more. For Stalin there was only one solution: to remove them. And removed they were, whether solely by Stalin's dictate it is not possible to say with certainty.

At this time, however, Tukhachevsky was slightly apart from the maelstrom. Although he had become much more political over the years, accustomed to dealing through the party bureaucracy and given to making the appropriate party noises, he was not a political factor of consequence. His power, and by now it was considerable, rested principally on the army and the network of his friends throughout the military apparatus. That is not to say that the Tukhachevsky group was without political clout. Old revolutionaries such as Yakir, Gamarnik, and Uborevich, were just as much party men as they were military figures. Tukhachevsky himself was a member of the Central Committee and certainly privy to the Politburo's activities.

He frequently was the regime's public spokesman on military and foreign policy questions. Thus, his March 1935 article in *Pravda* was regarded as being official party line. And in January 1936, along with Maxim Litvinov, he was sent to London as head of the Russian delegation at the funeral of King George V. His journey to London has been the cause of some speculation, since it included an unexplained stopover in Berlin. In some versions, Tukhachevsky used this interval to renew acquaintances with the German military leaders but, especially in light of his recent articles and speeches, that seems unlikely. Although his reliability as a witness is less than might be desired, Hermann Goering soon afterward told his hosts on a visit to Poland that Hitler forbade the German military to receive the Russian marshal. Moreover, even if Tukhachevsky did meet some German officers, there is little doubt that the subjects of their conversations would soon have found their way into the files of the Gestapo.[43]

From Berlin, Tukhachevsky traveled to London, arriving on January 27. It was the London establishment's first opportunity to get a close-up view of the man generally regarded as the general who would lead Russia's forces in the war with Germany that many were already predicting. With his visit for the monarch's funeral as the official reason, Tukhachevsky took the opportunity for private talks with several important British officials, including Patrick Duff Cooper. Many of the other dignitaries at the funeral had similar talks, but as the *Manchester Guardian*'s diplomatic correspondent said, "Perhaps the most significant of all the talks that took place were those with the Russians." Both Britain and Russia were seeking a counterpoise to the Hitler threat. Ideology was taking a back seat.[44] Tukhachevsky seems to have been somewhat disappointed with London. In later conversation with an American diplomat, he recalled that the winter weather had made the British capital depressing.[45]

Tukhachevsky returned home by way of Paris, where he seems to have enjoyed himself much more. At that time, the French and the Russians were still in the process of sounding each other out on an alliance designed to contain the German threat. And despite whatever personal or ideological feelings they might have had about this Red general, the French went out of their way to entertain him and to show him something of France's military-industrial capabilities.

He arrived in Paris on February 10, accompanied by his wife and Putna. They were joined there by Uborevich. The next day, the three men were taken to French aircraft factories, and on February 12, Tukhachevsky inspected a French military aviation establishment at Chartres. The following day he made more of a typical tourist's trip, a visit to Fontainebleau. But on February 14, again with Putna and Uborevich, he was off to Le Havre to see the naval facilities. On February 15, in what must have been a strange confrontation, he went with Foreign Minister Flandin for an interview with Marshal Philippe Pétain. There was also the customary round of protocol visits. Tukhachevsky held conversations with Pietri, the minister of marine; Deat, the air minister; Maurin, the minister of war; and Flandin.[46]

But there were social aspects as well. General Maurice Gamelin had met Tukhachevsky in London, and it was primarily at his invitation that the Russian marshal had come to France. It was also Gamelin who hosted a dinner at which Tukhachevsky was reunited with some of the French who had been prisoners with him at Ingolstadt IX. It was a happy affair, and tongues seem to have been loosened to the point of a little indiscretion. Gamelin reports that he and Tukhachevsky talked at some length about German intentions, the Russian general repeating his frequent warnings about German imperialism and the danger that France faced from Hitler. In this vein he urged Gamelin to push strenuously for further armaments and teased the Frenchman somewhat. In response to Gamelin's reply to the urgings about rearming that he would do more, but that he did not control the purse strings, Tukhachevsky said: "There you are. That is the advantage of the Bolshevik regime. I get everything that I ask for." Gamelin, like many others, noted Tukhachevsky's inordinate curiosity about materials for France's latest tanks, and concluded: "He seemed very sure of himself and of his own importance."[47]

Another French observer noticed much the same situation at another function during the visit. The indefatigable journalist Genevieve Tabouis was present at a dinner in the Soviet Embassy during which Tukhachevsky became involved in an intense conversation with Rumanian Foreign Minister Titelescu, Herriot, Boncour, Soviet Ambassador Potemkin, and others. Mme. Tabouis had met Tukhachevsky on a visit to Moscow in company with Herriot, and had remarked at the time that he seemed a melancholy figure. Now the somber mien seemed to have vanished. She says: "He had just returned from a visit to Germany and he was heaping praise on the Nazis. Seated at my right, he said over and over again as he discussed an air pact between the Great Powers and Hitler's Germany: 'They are already invincible, Madame Tabouis!'" It was not the most discreet comment he might have made.[48]

Two days later, Tukhachevsky left Paris, and on February 19, he was back in Moscow. Not long after Tukhachevsky returned to the Soviet Union, there were signs that trouble was about to occur in Spain that might involve other European nations. On February 19, three days after an election, Manuel Azana formed a Spanish government that included Republicans, Socialists, and Communists. In April, President Alcala Zamora was removed for exceeding his powers. Azana was elected to succeed him on May 10, but this ascent of the left to supreme power infuriated the ultraconservatives in the Spanish military, and on July 18, following a revolt of the garrison at Melilla in Spanish Morocco, the Spanish Civil War began.

At first the Soviet Union was cautious about providing assistance to the embattled Spanish government, but in August, Stalin dispatched Antonov-Ovseenko and General J. K. Berzin, head of the Red Army intelligence, to supervise the aid being sent.[49] Officially, of course, the Soviet Union adhered to the policy of nonintervention proposed by the French, but Moscow had agreed on the condition that Germany and Italy did not aid the rebels. Berlin and Rome, of course, were already doing so.[50] The Russians supplied considerable matériel, including 700 or so tanks and a considerable number of planes. The number of personnel sent, however, was relatively small, probably between 500 and 600 at a time; the cadres were frequently rotated and included numerous bright young officers, such as Rodion Malinovsky.[51]

By several accounts, Tukhachevsky and Stalin quarreled over exactly what form the Russian aid to the Spanish government should take. In these versions, Tukhachevsky opposed sending overt aid because of the danger of exposing the Red Army's shortcomings, which he knew only too well, to the very people he did not want to see them. In the argument he stressed the point to Stalin that the Red Army was not ready for such a venture. Stalin is said to have responded sarcastically: "So everything you have done all these years, didn't it raise the army to the required level?"[52]

Tukhachevsky well knew the value of military propaganda, and the autumn maneuvers of the Red Army in 1936 gave him ample opportunity to indulge himself. Along with General Archibald Wavell and some other aides, the tank expert Sir Giffard Martel was in a British military delegation to those maneuvers, held near Minsk, in Uborevich's military district. Martel, who had once built a tank in his garage from junked auto parts, was impressed with the quality of the Soviet weaponry on display in the war games, though he felt the handling of the men and the machinery left no doubt that the Russians' officer corps was still in great need of education and instruction. He found Voroshilov pretty much of a nonentity, and Budenny merely a colorful relic. Yegorov was dismissed as a "figurehead." However, he was much impressed by Khalepsky, a kindred spirit, and Y. I. Alksnis.

Tukhachevsky, however, was the main focus of the visitors' interest. They quickly decided that he was the real brain of the Red Army, and were intrigued by his ideas on the use of tanks and other new weapons. Martel was especially interested in the work Tukhachevsky had done with paratroops, although by today's standards the Russian airborne forces were pitifully primitive. Martel says:

> In the afternoon we were taken to see . . . an infantry brigade dropped by parachute. . . . This was a most spectacular affair. The brigade commander did a "delayed" drop. That is to say, . . . he did not pull the rip cord until he was about halfway down. The battalion commanders did a semi-delayed drop and the remainder of the brigade dropped in the ordinary way, from a height of about 2,000 feet. In this way the brigade commander landed first, followed by the battalion commanders, and the men came last. The bulk of the men were carried on the wings of the aeroplanes, and were holding on to a rope to prevent themselves from being blown off. When they reached the right place they just slid off the wings and pulled their rip cords. They jumped into the air just as sea bathers might jump into the sea at a crowded seaside resort.

Despite the makeshift nature of their transport, the men had grown quite adept, and Martel reported surprisingly few injuries.[53]

Martel was much taken with Tukhachevsky, and was quick to note one of the Russian's notorious characteristics: he was forever trying to pump his military guests for information. He later wrote:

> By far the ablest officer whom we met was Marshal Tukhachevsky, who was deputy to Voroshilov. . . . He asked me to sit next to him at many of the parties and entertainments and we talked freely in French. At times it was rather amusing. On one occasion he wanted to find out about the nature of the . . . gun we were mounting on our tanks. He asked me for the muzzle velocity of our gun. It was a two-pounder gun and we had raised the muzzle velocity to a high figure. I replied to the Marshal by saying that I did not know the velocity in metres per second. He at once took a menu card and asked for the muzzle velocity in feet per second, saying that he could easily change this into metres. I did not want to tell him at once how high a muzzle velocity we had reached with this gun so I said casually that I thought it was about 2,000 feet per second. The Marshal made a few quick calculations and then said that he knew it was more than that and further that they had raised the velocity of their 37mm. gun — which corresponded to our gun — to over 2,400 feet per second. I at once replied that I now remembered that ours had about reached this figure also. In this sort of way we drew each other out and I certainly obtained a lot of detailed information in exchange for our general thoughts and ideas.[54]

French officers attending the same maneuvers were apparently less impressed with the Russians' capabilities. One French general returned home with a highly unfavorable report, all the more remarkable because the previous year, the French had been enthusiastic about what they had seen.[55]

Tukhachevsky's affability toward the British delegation did not betray any sign of anxiety about his position in the army or about his relationship with Voroshilov. But he could not have been ignorant of ominous signs close around him. Late in July, a top-secret letter had been circulated to all party committees about new Trotskyist plots and the need for vigilance against "wreckers." This was followed in August by the trial of Zinoviev, L. B. Kamenev, Sergei V. Mrachovsky, Ivan Smirnov, and other former party leaders for belonging to the "Trotsky-Zinovievite Center." Smirnov had been an intimate of Tukhachevsky's for years, and he knew Mrachovsky well from the period when the latter had won fame as a partisan commander in the Urals.

Both men, despite full use of NKVD "persuasions," and reportedly despite the personal intervention of Stalin, never broke completely. Their subsequent attempts to disavow their confessions in open court proved an embarrassment to the prosecution. But it did not save them from the death sentence.[56]

Even worse, from Tukhachevsky's view, about the same time two other of his subordinates were arrested: Dmitri Schmidt, who had recently worked in Yakir's Ukrainian Military District, and Vitovt Putna, Tukhachevsky's recent companion in London and Paris. No longer did the army seem immune. Schmidt was a rough-and-ready character who on one celebrated occasion in 1927, when he had sided with the opposition, had threatened to "lop off" Stalin's ears during an argument. He had been a party member since 1915 and had won renown as a cavalry commander in the Ukraine during the Civil War. It was typical of him that he had once shot, though not fatally, an officer who had insulted his wife.[57] Nothing is known definitely about his trial, if there was one, but it seems that he was shot soon after his arrest, thus becoming the first victim of what was to be Stalin's gruesome purge of the Red Army. Putna survived for some time, although nothing is known of what happened to him in the ensuing ten months.

In addition, about this time another of Tukhachevsky's friends, the composer Shostakovich, seemed to be heading for serious difficulties with the regime. Early in 1936 his opera *Lady Macbeth of Mtsensk District* (completed in 1932) was playing simultaneously at three theaters in Moscow. Until then, although there had been some critical reviews, generally the opera had received overwhelmingly favorable responses. But now an ominous editorial had appeared in *Pravda* under the headline "Chaos, Not Music." Shostakovich was accused of formalism, naturalism, and, somewhat contradictorily, breaking with reality. Tukhachevsky had been greatly taken with the work, and is reported to have told one friend: "This tragedy will become the first classic Soviet opera. One cannot grasp all its strengths at one hearing." But now the marshal's opinion seemed to be of little help in the face of what was obviously a deepening campaign against Shostakovich.

The composer, however, turned to Tukhachevsky for advice. He later recalled what happened.

Back at that time, in 1936, I was called to Moscow for a show whipping. Like the sergeant's widow, I had to declare to the whole world that I had whipped myself. I was completely destroyed. It was a blow that wiped out my past. And my future.

To whom could I turn for advice? To whom could I go? I went to Marshal Tukhachevsky. He had recently returned from his triumphant visit to London and Paris. *Pravda* wrote about him every day. And I was a leper, people were afraid to come up to me. I was shunned. Tukhachevsky agreed to see me. We locked ourselves in his office. He turned off his phones. We sat in silence. And then we started talking very softly. I spoke softly because . . . my grief and despair wouldn't let me speak in my normal voice. Tukhachevsky spoke softly because he feared prying ears. . . . Tukhachevsky knew Stalin incomparably better than I. He knew that Stalin pursued a man to the end. In those days it looked as though that would happen to me. A second article in *Pravda*, destroying my ballet this time, confirmed my worst fears.

Tukhachevsky promised to do what he could. He spoke carefully. I could see him controlling himself when the talk turned to Stalin.[58]

Another version of the same incident has been provided by one of the composer's friends. He says he met Shostakovich

> . . . crushed and distraught at Tukhachevsky's apartment. You should have seen how sympathetically Tukhachevsky treated him! They went off together into his study for a long while. I don't know what they talked about, but when Shostakovich came out he was a new man. He went determinedly over to the piano and started to improvise. Tukhachevsky was all ears. He didn't shift his gaze from his friend: He had faith in Shostakovich, and could make him have faith in himself.[59]

The Shostakovich episode seems to have been part of a much wider Stalin campaign that included a continuing drive to finally get rid of Bukharin, Rykov, and some other Old Bolshevik leaders. Since Putna's name had been mentioned during the Zinoviev trial, there also seemed to be an indication that the Red Army would be involved.

But Stalin was not yet an absolute dictator. There is considerable evidence that his plans for widening the purge had met strenuous opposition in the Central Committee and in the Politburo. According to one report, at the autumn plenum of the committee, a wide majority had voted against Stalin's plans. But, significantly, this opposition to Stalin was passive, in that it evidently was not followed by active organization to replace him — if that were possible, given his control over the NKVD and the other organs of repression. There is little doubt that Tukhachevsky, Yakir, and the other military leaders on the committee would have opposed anything that would have added to Russia's internal instability when they all too obviously were facing the possibility of war with Germany in the near future. They were already preoccupied with the difficulties of mobilizing their forces in the face of continued difficulties with Russia's still unreliable transportation systems. They certainly did not want any situation that would disrupt the huge peasant mass on which they had to rely for the bulk of their soldiers.[60]

The military leaders would seem to have had further reasons for opposing Stalin at this time. According to a German diplomatic report dated September 28, 1936, Stalin and Yagoda (he was replaced on Stalin's orders on September 26) had planned to use Putna as the center of a new show trial of "Trotskyists" in the army, but the plan had been thwarted by the Central Committee. Even so, there was no doubt that Tukhachevsky, because of his friendship with Putna, was again in trouble. One report suggests that Tukhachevsky would have been a target at such a trial, since in a "confession" Putna had implicated him as a British spy.[61] The Germans, however, believed that the decision not to proceed with Putna's trial was a victory for Tukhachevsky, and this seems to have been borne out by events. Tukhachevsky continued to be an important public figure.

There was no doubt of Tukhachevsky's continuing popularity in the army and in the party. At the Eighth (Extraordinary) Congress of Soviets held late in 1936, the military was able to recite an impressive list of advances. During the congress, V. V. Khripin, the deputy air chief, could boast of the progress in numbers and quality of the air force. V. M. Orlov, of the navy, reported that Soviet submarine strength had multiplied seven times. But the whole recital seemed to center on Tukhachevsky. In the Great Palace of the Kremlin, where the congress was held, the entire crowd rose in a storm of applause when he mounted the platform. They also noted approvingly that, unlike many of the new party speakers, his address was given extemporaneously, in the "old heroic style."[62]

But behind the facade, the contest between Stalin and the NKVD—which itself was undergoing a massive "cleansing"—on the one hand, and the military on the other hand, was apparently being waged relentlessly. And in this internecine struggle, Tukhachevsky's "indiscretions" earlier in the year seemed to grow in importance.

At this stage of the affair there entered a controversial figure among the Russian émigrés in Paris, General Nikolai Skoblin. He had been a relatively minor figure in the Civil War, but by 1936 seems to have become a double agent, working both for the NKVD and for Richard Heydrich's SD. Whatever his motives, about this time he is said to have passed to Heydrich a report that the Red Army commanders, chief among them Tukhachevsky, were plotting a coup in the Soviet Union. Moreover, they were said to be in collusion with the leading figures in the German military, a natural enough supposition, since Tukhachevsky and the other top Russian officers were still on amicable terms with the Germans with whom they had worked for more than a decade. The report must have doubly gratified the devious Heydrich, for it not only gave him a pretext to move against the military figures in Berlin with whom Hitler was having trouble, but also must have seemed a way to weaken the Soviet military at its very heart.

The timing of this report is far from certain, but it must have occurred either late in 1936 or early in 1937. German military records that seem to be related to the incident mention that starting in February 1937, German army officials—not the SD—were seeking documents pertaining to "Leutnant Tuchatschewski."

In roughly the same period the Czechs were beginning to become involved. The French statesman Paul Reynaud says that somewhere at the end of 1936, he received from the Czechoslovak leader Eduard Benes a message given to Reynaud's son, who had been visiting Prague. The gist of the message was to be careful in dealing with the Soviet military command, and in particular to watch out for Tukhachevsky. Benes implied that Tukhachevsky and his colleagues had reached some arrangement with the German military command.[63]

In his memoirs, Benes links Tukhachevsky with Rykov, suggesting that the marshal was involved in a plot going beyond the purely military sphere that most others have suggested. But he offers no evidence for this, and from the context it would seem that his timing of the plot was somewhat later than that offered by Reynaud. At the time, Benes was seeking allies wherever he could find them, to offset the all-too-apparent threat from Hitler. He passed the news to Reynaud, to Léon Blum, and, if the British leader's memory is accurate, to Winston Churchill. But, most important, he passed the word to Stalin. Benes gives this rationale: "If the attempt to disrupt the Soviet Union had succeeded, the whole situation in Europe would have been transformed, but Stalin prevented that just in time. . . ."[64]

Word of the possibility of a coup against Stalin was widely current in Europe, and even in the United States, at this time. The most surprising thing about many of the reports, and one reason why they were probably discounted, was that in many of them Voroshilov was pictured as the central opposition figure.

The blurring of the time element in these accounts makes it difficult to trace exactly where the talk of the plot originated. In many versions written when German documents became available after World War II, Heydrich is credited with originating the whole scheme. There is no doubt that compromising the German High Command in a plot with the Red Army would have been useful to Hitler for his own political purposes, but now the weight of the evidence suggests that the affair started in Moscow, not Berlin.

From signs such as the arrest of Putna and others, it seems almost certain that Stalin was preparing to move against Tukhachevsky long before the earliest possible date for the start of the Heydrich scheme. Even the first public mention of Tukhachevsky's name in compromising circumstances in Moscow would seem to predate the German adventure. This mention occurred during the trial of Pyatakov, Radek, and others that began in early 1937, just as the Germans had apparently started to gather their material. As Erickson notes, preparations for such a prominent showpiece of Stalinist terror must have been in progress long before Heydrich's dossier was being collected, and that as part of the preparation, Stalin's men must already have accumulated material on the marshal.[65]

When Heydrich's material, including fabricated correspondence between the Russian and German generals did reach Stalin, it was no doubt still useful to him, even after the arrest, and possibly the execution, of the Red generals. It may have provided sufficient "proof" to convince those, such as Blyukher and Alksnis, who were eventually to condemn Tukhachevsky and his colleagues.

But there is little doubt that at least some incriminating material had come earlier from poor Vitovt Putna, Tukhachevsky's comrade and fellow Semyenovsky Guardsman. In one version of these events, as we have already seen, Putna had implicated Tukhachevsky in a "confession" as a spy for Britain. This is said to have become known to the marshal, who characteristically took the matter directly to Stalin. In the subsequent interview, Tukhachevsky is supposed to have demanded that he be allowed to confront Putna and challenge his statements. Stalin is said to have responded almost cavalierly, tut-tutting about the inefficiency of the NKVD. "I am persuaded," he is quoted as saying, "that he has told fables about you. This is also part of the schemes of the enemy; to throw suspicion on the men most devoted to us. But I advise you in waiting for the atmosphere to clear, to find a post in one of our military districts, perhaps on the Volga."[66]

The account has the air of truth. It fits neatly with Stalin's behavior in several similar cases where he lulled an adversary into complacence while preparing to trap him later, at the dictator's convenience.

The Radek-Pyatakov trial, which opened on January 23, 1937, was a threat to Tukhachevsky from yet another direction. Pyatakov was Ordzhonikidze's deputy in the Commissariat for Heavy Industry, where, in the course of his duties, he had been on the closest terms with Tukhachevsky. Moreover, through Pyatakov, Stalin seemed to be striking at Ordzhonikidze and the other veteran party officials who had opposed him on the purges. To strike at Ordzhonikidze meant to strike at Tukhachevsky, because the Georgian commissar was now the marshal's only remaining political supporter of consequence. Moreover, about this time Ordzhonikidze's older brother, Papulia, was under arrest. There could be no doubt where this train of events was heading. It was aimed at the core of the party leadership, or at least at the part of it that had stood in Stalin's way the previous year, and at the military command structure.

On the second day of the trial, the prosecutor, Andrei Vishinsky, was questioning Radek:

> Vishinsky: Accused Radek, in your testimony you said "In 1935 . . . in January . . . Vitaly Putna came to me with a request from Tukhachevsky. . . . " I want to know in what connection you mention Tukhachevsky's name?
> Radek: Tukhachevsky had been commissioned by the government with some task for which he could not find the necessary material. He rang me up and asked if I had this material. I had it and he accordingly sent Putna, with whom he had to discharge this commission, to get this material from me. Of course, Tukhachevsky had no idea either of Putna's role or of my criminal role. . . .

After a short time, Vishinsky returned to the subject.

> Vishinsky: So Putna came to see you, having been sent by Tukhachevsky on official business having no bearing whatsoever on your affairs since he, Tukhachevsky, had no relations with them whatsoever.
> Radek: Tukhachevsky never had any relations with them.

After another interval, the same subject arose.

> Vishinsky: Do I understand you correctly that Putna had dealings with the members of your Trotskyite underground organization, and that your reference to Tukhachevsky was made in connection with the fact that Putna was on official business on Tukhachevsky's orders?
> Radek: I confirm that, and I say that I never had and could not have any dealings with Tukhachevsky connected with counter-revolutionary activities, because I knew Tukhachevsky's attitude to the party and the Government to be that of an absolutely devoted man.

To most Russians it seemed that Radek did protest too much.

The mention of the army commander's name in the trial of people like Radek and Pyatakov, who in Stalinist Russia were already believed guilty when they were brought to trial, was enough to suggest that before long Tukhachevsky himself would stand in the dock. Vishinsky's superficial effort to clear the marshal fooled no one.[67]

At the same time there began a series of command changes in the army that further weakened Tukhachevsky's position. It almost seemed that Stalin was depriving him of the base of support represented in the commanders of the various military districts, men who could have supported their favorite marshal in any showdown with Stalin.

One key change was the replacement of Vekhlichev as Gamarnik's deputy in the political administration of the Moscow Military District by Lev Aronstam, who had previously been with Blyukher in the Far East. In addition, Primakov was officially removed from his post as deputy commander of the Leningrad Military District. With these moves Stalin let it be known that he was acting against two of the nation's marshals.

During this period, Ordzhonikidze was apparently trying to intervene on behalf of his beleaguered deputy, Pyatakov. Mistakenly, he seemed to be convinced that Pyatakov's life would be spared. When the verdicts were announced at 3 A.M. on January 30, Pyatakov was one of those sentenced to death. The cooperative Radek got off with a comparatively light ten-year sentence.

Ordzhonikidze was understandably furious at the double cross. He and Stalin reportedly had been estranged even before the Pyatakov trial. There is one report that the commissar for heavy industry, on discovering that the NKVD had arrested one of his subordinates, immediately called Stalin on a private, direct line and shouted into the phone: "Koba, why do you let the NKVD arrest my men without informing me?" After Stalin answered, Ordzhonikidze continued: "I demand that this authoritarianism cease! I am still a member of the Politburo! I am going to raise hell, Koba, if it's the last thing I do before I die."[68]

But even with Pyatakov's execution, Ordzhonikidze did not

seem to realize that Stalin was not merely ignoring his old Georgian comrade; he was aiming directly at him and, through him, at Tukhachevsky and the military leadership.

The campaign against Ordzhonikidze was particularly vicious. His brother had recently been arrested, and eventually was shot. Medvedev reports that a copy of the interrogation, with its patently false confession, was sent to Ordzhonikidze. In addition, many of his subordinates had fallen prey to the NKVD. Stalin is said to have forwarded their "confessions," too, but not before appending a note saying "Comrade Sergo, look what they're writing about you."[69]

Ordzhonikidze remained defiant. But after the next incident he must finally have realized what was up, even though he continued futilely to oppose Stalin. The police arrived at his apartment with a search warrant. After some difficulty, he managed to get through to Stalin, who coolly told him: "It is the sort of organ that is even liable to search my place. That is nothing extraordinary. . . ."[70]

Then, on February 17, Ordzhonikidze had a meeting with Stalin that went on for hours. He then left for the Commissariat of Heavy Industry, where he remained until 2 A.M. From there he returned home, where he had another telephone conversation with Stalin. By 5:30 in the afternoon he was dead. His wife telephoned Stalin, who quickly arrived to take over the formalities. It was a bizarre scene that was more like a political strategy session than a time of grief. The official announcement said that Ordzhonikidze had died of a heart attack, plus kidney and asthmatic problems. This seemed reasonable enough, because the dead commissar had been in poor health for some time. But almost immediately rumors began to circulate that more than a simple illness and overwork were involved. Soon it became an accepted fact that a distraught Ordzhonikidze had committed suicide, although there were also persistent rumors that Stalin had had him murdered.[71]

Two days later, Ordzhonikidze's body was cremated, and on February 20, the funeral was held. It was a great Stalinist spectacle. The General Secretary was there to carry his old comrade's ashes to their last resting place in Red Square. Nikita Khrushchev was one of the eulogists, taking the opportunity to lambaste the "wreckers," who in sabotaging industry had broken Ordzhonikidze's heart. Tukhachevsky was another of the prominent mourners.

A few days later, Tukhachevsky wrote a lachrymose eulogy for his friend in the military journal, *Krasnaya Zvezda*. He recalled his first meetings with Ordzhonikidze in the troubled days of the fighting against Denikin in 1919. He even remembered the first meeting with Voroshilov and Budenny and the First Cavalry. He went on: "Conditions were very difficult. It was spring. We were in a hurry to restore serious washouts. Communications were interrupted incessantly. It required a colossal effort to restore the work of the front amid conditions of sneak attacks and harassment by the enemy. Comrade Ordzhonikidze worked day and night and his Communist spirit infected both the leaders and the Red Army masses."[72]

The death of such a veteran party figure did not derail Stalin's plans for the purges. If anything, it hastened them, for Ordzhonikidze's opposition had been removed. Not that there were not some obstacles to his plans in the party leadership that gathered in Moscow in the last week of February for a meeting of the Central Committee. By this time, the purge swept through the political apparatus not only in Moscow but throughout the entire country. Moreover, it began to be felt in the military, especially in the group involved in Spain.

While the repression was beginning to increase in the Soviet Union, Heydrich's plans were gaining momentum in Germany. This did not provide Stalin, Yezhov, and Georgi Malenkov, who was now involved in the purges, with the basic material they needed to compromise Tukhachevsky, but it probably did give them, at the right time, a convenient additional weapon for later victims. By April, the earliest date when the Heydrich forgeries of the correspondence supposedly incriminating Tukhachevsky, von Seeckt, other German officers, and Trotsky was in the NKVD's hands, the latter had almost certainly obtained enough "incriminating" material from Putna, possibly from Primakov, and perhaps from Radek, whose German friend Ernst Niekisch, had been arrested by the Gestapo on March 22.

In April the Soviet Army journal, *Krasnaya Zvezda*, published an article that was sharply critical of Kork. The campaign was now moving up the ladder and dangerously close to Tukhachevsky.⁷³ There is evidence that Malenkov's role in this political agitation in the army brought him into conflict not only with Tukhachevsky, Yakir, and the senior military commanders but also with Gamarnik and the purely political officers. But from the beginning, Malenkov was essentially Stalin's surrogate, and his influence was decisive. And the conflict was not purely political; to a considerable extent it was also social. The higher-ranking military personnel, like their leader Tukhachevsky, tended to be well-educated men from middle-class backgrounds. The new political workers who were injected into the military structure tended to be largely unlettered and uncultured men from the humblest backgrounds. They were all too ready to find fault with the "aristocratic" officers.

Stalin and his drinking crony Voroshilov were worried about another trend that they discerned in various sections of the military: the growing political links between some of the more politically astute commanders, such as Yakir and Uborevich, and the local political apparatuses in the Ukraine and Byelorussia. They gave Yakir and Uborevich—and of course Tukhachevsky—a potential political base that could be dangerous. It was apparently to destroy this link that Malenkov set to work. His tactic was to unsettle the military apparatus in those key areas. Hurried transfers of military political officers were ordered. Overnight the garrison political workers were ordered to new posts not less than 300 kilometers from their previous bases. The families of the transferred officers were ordered to stay behind, apparently to add to the disruption. Then the transfer orders were rescinded, further heightening the upheaval. The whole military apparatus, especially its political wing, was in turmoil. According to one account, an unexpected side effect was tension between Gamarnik, on the one hand, and Tukhachevsky and Yakir, on the other. Gamarnik seems to have been politically isolated not only from Stalin and Malenkov but also from his long-time associates Tukhachevsky and Yakir. He was left a complete outsider early in 1937, and this may have led to his suicide. Later, of course, Malenkov was to dominate the military-political apparatus, and therefore he must have been a key figure in the bloodshed that swept through the Soviet officer cadres.⁷⁴

Tukhachevsky was definitely on the defensive, but outwardly spirits seemed to remain high among the Red Army commanders. On March 23, 1937, the United States ambassador, Joseph E. Davies, gave a lavish dinner party at the embassy to return the hospitality shown him and his staff on previous occasions. After cocktails, about 60 people sat down for the meal. Voroshilov sat to the right of Mrs. Davies, and Tukhachevsky sat to her left. Ambassador Davies later remembered that Tukhachevsky conversed with the Davies' daughter Marjorie about Marxism and women's rights in the Soviet Union and the United States. Later there were toasts of friendship and a polite, if propagandistic, speech by Voroshilov.[75]

Elbridge Durbrow, an American diplomat, was present at the dinner. He had met Tukhachevsky at several previous embassy functions, and he later recalled that he and the marshal chatted amiably in French. On learning that the young American had recently returned from London, Tukhachevsky asked if anything had been done to spruce up the British capital for the coming coronation, which he was to attend. The marshal then commented that during his previous visit the fog and the rain had depressed him.[76]

About this time, George Kennan, another member of the United States Embassy staff, was working on a report on "difficulties" that seemed to have arisen in higher Soviet military circles. After checking with other embassies, it became apparent that quite a few high-ranking Red Army officers seemed to have disappeared from their usual places. Tukhachevsky's statement about his planned trip to London would seem to have excluded him from those in trouble, however.[77]

Soon after came the annual rite of spring in Moscow, the May Day parade in Red Square. Tukhachevsky was present, but he was not the ebullient Tukhachevsky who had shouted hurrahs at the marching units and their commanders. Instead, although he was the first of the high-ranking officers to arrive at the reviewing stand, he came alone and stood to one side. Yegorov arrived soon after, but did not salute or otherwise acknowledge the presence of his fellow marshal. Gamarnik joined them, without speaking. And when the military section of the parade had finished filing through the great cobblestoned square, Tukhachevsky left before the civilian groups entered. Hands in his pockets, he walked morosely off the stand, across the square, and out of sight.

There still had been no public action against him. The latest issue of the magazine *Bolshevik* contained his long article commenting on the 1936 Field Service Regulations, of which he had been the prime author. The article is especially interesting, not only for its timing but also for several ideas it contains. It seemed to represent a deep change in Tukhachevsky's military thinking, away from his previous ideas about the primacy of maneuverability. It dealt extensively with the use of tanks and argued that they alone could not win wars. Like infantry, Tukhachevsky said, they must rely on massive support from the artillery, and could be successful only if completely integrated with all the other branches of the military. Significantly, the marshal criticized Voroshilov for proclaiming that the superior morale of the Soviet forces alone would be enough to ensure victory. That idea, he said, was merely "self-deception" that would lead to unnecessary losses of lives and equipment.[78]

On May 3, Tukhachevsky's documents were sent to the British Embassy so that he could attend the coronation of King George VI. He had been nominated to the Soviet delegation in April, but on May 4, the British were suddenly informed that the marshal had taken ill and would be unable to go. V. M. Orlov, the navy commander, was named to replace him.

An American diplomat was told by the British ambassador that he had received a rather mysterious call from Tukhachevsky, thanking him for the visa to enter Britain but saying that, regretfully, on doctor's orders he had had to cancel the trip. The British envoy commented to the American that Tukhachevsky made quite a point of coughing and hacking, and did all he could to sound as if he really did have a severe cold.[79]

But the implication to foreign diplomats was unambiguous; there was no doubt that Tukhachevsky was in serious trouble.

10
BEHEADING THE MILITARY

THE CAMPAIGN AGAINST THE MILITARY had long been in preparation under the direction of Yezhov and Malenkov, who since 1935 had been head of ORPO, the security agency charged with keeping watch on the highest officials of the Communist party, including those in the military.[1]

But even so the country at large was hardly ready for the shock that came with the announcement on May 11 of a shift in military commands. Some of the changes looked innocuous enough; Yakir, for example, was transferred from Kiev to Leningrad. There were some surprises; however; Shaposhnikov was recalled from Leningrad to replace Yegorov as chief of the General Staff. And there was a major shock: Tukhachevsky had been demoted to command the unimportant Pri-Volga Military District.

The net effect of the changes was to create further turmoil and confusion in the upper echelons of the military and a sense of foreboding in the party and the citizenry.

Some of Tukhachevsky's stunned colleagues gathered at his dacha just outside Moscow. It was a curious group, by all accounts. They had gathered almost for a wake, to offer their condolences to the leader as he left for his "exile" in the hinterland. Tukhachevsky was in sardonic mood. Recalling his recent visit to London, he said:

> The characteristic trait of His Majesty's British army is that its chief does not have to see an agent of Scotland Yard; and as for shoemakers[2] they admit them only to the waiting room, and not without a party card. The English do not speak openly of their patriotism, for to them it seems natural to be uniquely English. There is not there, in England, the line of the "right, authentic or general," there are only English politics, that a lord or a worker, Conservative or Laborite, an officer or a common soldier shows equal zeal to serve.
>
> For sure, the British soldier is a complete ignoramus about things concerning the history of the party and the production indices, but on the other hand, he knows the topography of the world as well as the layout of his own home.
>
> Over there, the King is full of honors, but he has no personal power. For the officer's career, two qualities are required: courage and knowledge.[3]

It must have been a gloomy meeting. The fellow officers of those in attendance were being rounded up. No one knew who would be the next to fall prey to the NKVD. Khalepsky had been removed from his tank command and switched to the Posts and Telegraphs Commissariat, which for several others had been a way station to oblivion. And on May 18, Kork, the head of the Frunze Military Academy and one of Tukhachevsky's long-time associates, was arrested.

About this time Tukhachevsky is reported to have taken up his new command on the Volga. As he left for the new post, Tukhachevsky was showing his anxiety. So much so that the chauffeur, Ivan Fedorovich Kudryavtsov, who had been with him since 1919, asked what was troubling him. The marshal answered that his enemies had been circulating "cock and bull" stories about him. Kudryavtsov suggested: "Write to Stalin." The marshal replied that he had already sent a letter to Stalin. There was no word about a reply. Kudryavtsov took Tukhachevsky and his wife to Moscow's Kazan Station, from which he was to leave for the city now called Kuibyshev. Tukhachevsky promised to call when he was settled. There was no call.

When Tukhachevsky arrived in Kuibyshev, one of those who met him was Yevgeny Vasilevich Shilov. To him, Tukhachevsky seemed quite calm. Shilov had the impression that the marshal had been promised a speedy return to Moscow. Shilov later said that he was led to believe that the second trip to London had been canceled because there was said to be a plot against the marshal's life as he passed through Warsaw on his way to Britain. Shilov had his doubts that this could have occurred, since Tukhachevsky undoubtedly would have traveled with a military escort.

Soon after he reached Kuibyshev, Tukhachevsky went to a meeting of the political staff of the military district. This was apparently one of many such gatherings being held at that time in all the military districts, since Yakir and Uborevich have been reported at similar gatherings in the middle of May. Someone who saw Tukhachevsky at that time noticed that in the last few months, the marshal had turned quite gray. He was showing signs of strain and fatigue, but he spoke clearly and precisely about problems of military training and impending work. He was obviously expecting to be allowed to work as usual in his new command. One of the last people who met him there was an officer named Vishki. He describes the incident:

> After a conference with the command staff, Mikhail Nikolaevich asked to me to stay behind and when everyone else had gone offered me the post as head of the command staff. The offer was flattering but I said candidly that I preferred for the time being to remain as a divisional commander.
> Mikhail Nikolaevich treated me with understanding and, it seemed, was ready to leave. But at this time, suddenly, he received a telephone call from Moscow and I was unwittingly a witness to a very somber scene.
> It did not escape my notice that, speaking with Moscow, Tukhachevsky was growing exceedingly worried. Hanging up the receiver, he was silent for a few minutes. Then he confessed that he had received bad news: the arrest of the head of the command staff operation, Feldman.

"What an immense provocation!" said Mikhail Nikolaevich painfully.

This was the end of our interview.

Tukhachevsky did not return from the meeting. Anxiously his wife waited for word from him. Finally she was given the news by a thoroughly shaken Dybenko, the man whom Tukhachevsky was to succeed in the command. The marshal had been arrested.[4] The arrest was not made public.

Now the purge of the military swung wide. On May 29, Uborevich was arrested and Yona Yakir was summoned from Kiev for an urgent meeting in Moscow. He was arrested en route.

Years later, Yakir's son described his father's departure for Moscow. On the three previous days the general had been attending a party conference in Kiev, and he was glad to get back to his family at their dacha outside the Ukrainian capital. When he arrived home, his son was studying algebra in preparation for an upcoming exam. The father was helping the boy with some of the problems when they were interrupted by a telephone call from Moscow. It was Voroshilov, summoning him to a conference. Yakir asked if it was urgent enough for him to take a plane, but Voroshilov said no, take the train. The next day, the Yakir family saw the general off from the cavernous Kiev station. Tenderly the father embraced his son, telling him to be a "little man." The boy and his mother heard nothing from Yakir for ten days. On the eleventh they were staggered to read in a newspaper that he had been executed along with Tukhachevsky, Uborevich, and the others for treason. Their own arrests followed soon after.[5]

On May 31, Yan Gamarnik, the jovial, full-bearded head of the Red Army's Political Administration, committed suicide.[6] Even more than the arrests, this publicly signaled the end of Tukhachevsky, for the marshal and Gamarnik had formed a partnership that worked to create an army where political affairs were parallel, not superior, to actual military duties.

By June 3, Eideman was being referred to in the Soviet press as the former head of Osoviakhim.

Amid this turmoil, an extraordinary session of the Military Soviet of the Defense Commissariat was held in Moscow. It was one of the most bizarre and terrifying episodes in the whole of Stalin's reign of terror. Altogether, about 120 commanders and military commissars were summoned to the meeting. As they entered, the participants was searched and their sidearms were taken. Each was given a blue folder of the depositions concerning the treason supposedly committed by Tukhachevsky and his fellow accused.

Stalin presided over the meetings flanked by Voroshilov and Yezhov. A parade of speakers abused the accused generals, and as they spoke, fresh blue folders were brought in by police employees, containing new depositions by officers more recently arrested. After examining the new material, Yezhov would whisper to Stalin, who would nod slightly. With that, another officer would be escorted from the hall, provoking a fresh stream of vituperation from those remaining in the hall. Somehow a list was drawn up of those swearing vengeance on the "traitors" and loyalty to Stalin. When it was complete, Stalin perused it.

According to one account, he studied it for a while and then said: "I don't see Comrades Bulin and Slavin on this list." Those two Old Bolsheviks could not bring themselves to denounce the men who had been their comrades for so many years. Their fate was sealed.

Dybenko, who had first won prominence as a revolutionary sailor in the Baltic Fleet, rose to peak. He was furious. "That Gamarnik!" he shouted. "He pretended to be as pure as Jesus Christ. Never had an extra stick of furniture in his house. . . . We've been saying all along these bluebloods were sticking together. Wouldn't give us a chance to move up."[7]

On June 9, Tukhachevsky, Yakir, and Uborevich were formally relieved of their commands. But it was not until June 11, in *Pravda*, that the news of all these events was broken to the Russian people. The newspaper that day announced that the investigation of the case of Tukhachevsky, Yakir, Eideman, Kork, Primakov, and Putna had been concluded. It was now to be transferred to a special military tribunal of the Soviet Supreme Court. V. V. Ulrikh, the pudgy, venomous bully who had presided over numerous earlier special trials, would head the tribunal. The other members of the court were reported to be Alksnis, Belov, Blyukher, Budenny, Dybenko, Goryachev, Kashirin, and Shaposhnikov. Whether this was the actual composition of the court is highly uncertain, for, from various accounts, it seems that at least some of those named were either themselves in custody or otherwise absent. Dybenko's role is especially uncertain, for several sources suggest he was in custody, even when testifying at the trial. But as important a source as Ilya Ehrenberg tends to confirm that Belov was indeed one of the judges.

In his *Memoirs*, Ehrenberg wrote:

> I remember a terrible day at Meyerhold's. We were sitting peacefully looking through an illustrated monograph on Renoir, when a friend of Meyerhold, the Corps Commander I. P. Belov, arrived. He was very worked up and, without paying any attention to our presence, began to describe the trial of Tukhachevsky and other high-ranking officers. Belov was a member of the Military Collegium of the Supreme court. "They were sitting like that—facing us. Uborevich looked me in the eyes. . . . —And tomorrow I'll be put in the same place!"[8]

The following day, Voroshilov issued an order of the day announcing that the tribunal had found the accused guilty and had condemned them to death for treason. They were supposed to have had contact with powers unfriendly to the Soviet Union, to have been spies for those powers, to have committed sabotage against the very army in which they served, and to have plotted the restoration of capitalism in the Soviet Union. All were supposed to have confessed.

An air of unreality hangs over the proceedings, even almost five decades later. Some people, among them those familiar with the inner workings of Stalinist Russia, have declared that there was no trial, that the accused were shot separately, and that the joint announcement of their deaths was a Stalinist subterfuge to cover up a fait accompli. Others, including the surviving families of some of the victims, insist that there was indeed a trial, however much a travesty of justice it was.

To many of these survivors, the role of Voroshilov is especially villainous. They see him as willingly sacrificing the very men on whom he had depended to organize the military, something that was quite beyond his limited abilities, to save his own skin. In recent years, it has become clear that Voroshilov not only passively condoned the repression of his colleagues but also actively assisted in its being carried out. For example, Yakir wrote to Stalin reiterating his innocence and his continued loyalty: "Every word I say is honest. I die with words of love on my lips for the party and the country, with boundless faith in the victory of Communism."

Stalin scribbled on the letter, "A scoundrel and a prostitute." Molotov endorsed the label. Voroshilov added: "A completely precise description." But Lazar Kaganovich went further: "For this traitor, bastard and [obscenity] there is only one punishment—execution."[9]

To the end, however, Yakir continued to place his faith in Stalin. Just before he was shot, he shouted: "Long live Comrade Stalin!"[10]

The cynical role of Budenny is also notorious.

There is, for example, a widely current anecdote about the crafty old cavalryman. He is supposed to have met one of his former subordinates, who in some alarm said: "Semyon, look what's happening! They're taking everybody, one after another." Budenny answered: "Don't worry, they won't touch us. They're only taking the smart ones."[11]

The trial was apparently conducted in an air of disbelief on the part of the defendants. At one point Tukhachevsky is supposed to have protested: "Have you been dreaming all this?"[12]

These soldiers could not, even in their extreme predicament, believe that all their loyal service would count for nothing. To the end they seemed to think that this trial was some monstrous aberration to be blamed on ugly little Yezhov, something that was occurring without Stalin's knowledge or approval. Yakir, for example, is said to have demanded in court that Stalin be summoned to set matters right, whereupon he was reprimanded by Primakov. "Hey Yona. I thought you had brains. Who do you think planned this farce?"[13]

In one reconstruction of the trial, purportedly from the account of an eyewitness, the accused were divided into two groups immediately after being arrested. The ones who were believed to be resistant to "scientific methods of investigation" were held separately. These were Tukhachevsky, Yakir, Primakov, and Kork. The others—Putna, who had already been in custody for almost a year; Uborevich; Feldman; and Eideman—were treated much more harshly.

According to this version of the proceedings:

> The appearance of Eideman, Uborevich, Putna and Feldman was very strange. Outwardly, they seemed not so bad, but they were somehow strangely apathetic in speech and action, and the unnatural coolness with which they admitted all charges sank them and their friends. In contrast was the appearance of Tukhachevsky, Yakir, Primakov and Kork, who were at first stunned and confused with the evident betrayal by their accused friends. But later, embittered, they were harsh and rough themselves, Ulrikh frequently cut them off and threatened to remove them from the room.
>
> "Who is the judge here?" he is said to have interrupted Tukhachevsky. "Don't you butt in. . . . Don't you know that you are prisoners? The tribunal isn't interested in what you think about Uborevich and Putna, our interest is in your crimes against the party and the Soviet people, of which they convict you and all like-minded associates."

Yakir is then supposed to have shouted: "They are insane. We don't know what deal you have made with them. . . ."

Eideman was then asked by the prosecutor if he felt unwell or insane. He is said to have answered, staring blanky at the prosecutor: "No, I am fine and feel quite well." Uborevich and Putna gave similar subdued answers.

Tukhachevsky and Yakir stared at each other. Primakov merely shrugged his shoulders.

In this version of the trial, one of the key witnesses against the marshal and his fellow accused was their old comrade Pavel Dybenko. Officially he was also a member of the tribunal, but since serious doubts have been raised about the presence of other supposed judges, it is quite possible Dybenko was also a prisoner by this time. His testimony against Tukhachevsky and Primakov is said to have been especially damaging. Kork apparently could not believe what he was hearing, and is said to have shouted: "Dybenko! Do you remember August the third?" Kork went on to explain that on that date, Primakov saved Dybenko's life.

The presiding judge, Ulrikh, ruled that the question was irrelevant, and ordered that the hearing proceed. Dybenko was stumped. He is said to have pursed his lips and repeated to himself: "The third of August? . . . . the third of August. . . . ?"

"Comrade Dybenko," interrupted the prosecutor, "if you feel unwell, the tribunal will question you later. Now you must go outside."

The witness lowered his head and made his way to the door. After a short time, those present in the courtroom heard thunderous voices and heavy sounds in the corridor. Dybenko was dragged back into the chamber, where, although he seemed terrified, he looked straight at the accused and said to them: "Comrades, don't believe them. Don't believe me, what I say. . . ." He was then seized again and dragged from the chamber. Dybenko was still shouting, "Comrades! Comrades!" For a while the commotion continued in the corridor, and then Dybenko screamed a long, painful curse.

Amid this turmoil, Ulrikh called a 20-minute recess in the proceedings. During the break an agitated Voroshilov tried to find out what had happened to Dybenko, but was rebuffed. "He is tidying himself up," the prosecutor told the defense commissar. "It's not unusual. . . . It was necessary, he was a bit drunk, but then he was getting soft. . . . all these veterans of the Civil War. . . . many wounds. . . . a doctor is with him now. Let Dybenko calm down. He is resting."

After the interruption, Dybenko reappeared on the witness stand, very pale but looking better. Ulrikh addressed him: "It seems you wish to say something more to the court, Comrade Dybenko."

"Yes. Please excuse me, but I felt nervous for some reason. Please excuse my profound, shocking refusal to speak to the court."

"Then you wish to notify the court that that would explain your outburst 'Don't believe them.'"

Dybenko said limply, "Yes, that's it."

After two or three questions about his military service and his wounds, Ulrikh let Dybenko go.

Despite the apparent hopelessness of their situation, Tukhachevsky, Yakir, Primakov, and Kork are said to have been defiant to the end. The Marshal is reported to have said in his final statement:

> Throughout all my work and life was the mistake that, above all, I trusted the Soviet Government and party and honestly

served them—I counted on the leadership. I do not intend to beg for indulgence because no sensible comrade could respect this trial, based on falsifications fit only for a third-rate detective story. You call this a trial—but I tell you, that you, and not we, are guilty.

And, sooner or later, as a result of this low-down effort you will receive retribution from fate. You all know me. When you sit here in this dock, or behind bars, where tomorrow I must stand. . . ."

The attendants interrupted Tukhachevsky, and with great effort silenced him. But in reply to one final question about his last wishes, after the guilty verdict had been rendered, Tukhachevsky burst out again: "I wish you would tell Joseph Djugashvili—Stalin—that he, not I, is the enemy of the people and the Red Army, that he is a criminal such as the whole world has not seen. . . ."

"Stop this shameless outburst, you capitalist stooge," ordered Ulrikh.[14]

Despite this display of anger, Tukhachevsky seems to have been resigned to his fate. He had spent several weeks in prison before his execution, and presumably was tortured. When he did not break, Stalin is said to have sent underlings with personal messages urging him to confess. Instead, Tukhachevsky spent his last days working on a book on strategy, emphasizing the danger posed to the Soviet Union by the ambitions of Hitler's Germany. General Todorsky, during the relative "thaw" of the Khrushchev years, read the 300-page manuscript and quotes one prescient fragment: "Fascist Germany will attack the Soviet Union in the spring of 1941 with up to 200 mobile divisions." Hitler did indeed launch "Operation Barbarossa" in 1941, and he committed 180 divisions to the attack.[15]

Stalin did not wait long after the trial was over before the sentences were carried out. The details of the executions are hazy, however. Usual practice would have had them shot individually in the cellars of the NKVD building. But in several accounts, this custom was not followed with Tukhachevsky and the others. Instead, they were taken to the courtyard of the building, where Marshal Blyukher was forced to command the firing squad. Ivan Serov, later the head of military intelligence, is said to have been a member of the detail. As the fatal shots rang out, trucks parked nearby were revved up to make sufficient noise to drown out the shots.[16]

But Stalin and the NKVD, were not finished. Vengeance was taken against most of Tukhachevsky's family and many of his acquaintances. By the dictator's personal order, the marshal's wife, Nina, and his two brothers, Aleksandr and Nikolai, were executed soon afterward. Three sisters and his aged mother were deported to prison camps, where one sister, Sofia, and his mother died. All had refused to denounce their brother. Even the marshal's 12-year-old daughter, Svetlana, as soon as she was of legal age, was carted off to the camps along with the surviving children of the other generals.[17]

Even the court that had doomed the marshal and the other generals did not escape. It seems likely that both Alksnis and Dybenko were already in custody when they were supposed to have been sitting in judgment on their fellow officers; Alksnis was executed in 1940, and Dybenko in July 1938. Blyukher continued to serve in the Far East for some months but was shot in September 1938. Kashirin simply vanished. Goryachev died of natural causes. Even Yezhov fell into disfavor. It is almost certain that soon after the Tukhachevsky trial, Beria and Malenkov persuaded Stalin to have him arrested. In some accounts he committed suicide; in others he was shot. Belov survived long enough to serve in World War II, as did Shaposhnikov. Budenny outlasted them all, an almost comic figure in his final years.

Even women rumored to have been involved with Marshal Tukhachevsky were arrested and sent into exile. And when an Old Bolshevik, N. N. Kulyabko, who had been one of those who had originally recommended Tukhachevsky for membership in the party in 1918, wrote a letter protesting his friend's arrest, he was quickly taken into custody.[18]

Yosif Vareikis, the man who had saved Tukhachevsky from Muraviev in the early days of the Civil War, is said to have questioned the arrest of Tukhachevsky. At the time he was serving in Blyukher's Far East command, and is said to have telephoned Stalin to register his protest. Stalin is supposed to have shouted into the phone: "That's none of your business. Don't interfere in what doesn't concern you. The NKVD knows what it is doing. Only an enemy would defend Tukhachevsky." He then slammed down the receiver. In September, Vareikis was summoned to Moscow on official business. On October 9, he was arrested just outside Moscow. Four days later he was shot.[19]

A sorrowful Dmitri Shostakovich recalled that terrible time as it affected Tukhachevsky's old friend, Zhilayev.

> He had a large picture of Tukhachevsky in his room, and after the announcement that Tukhachevsky had been shot as a traitor to the nation, Zhilayev did not take the picture down. I don't know if I can explain how heroic a deed that was. How did people behave then? As soon as the next poor soul was declared an enemy of the people, everyone destroyed everything connected with that person. If the enemy of the people wrote books, they threw away his books, if they had letters from him, they burned the letters. The mind can't grasp the number of letters and papers burned in that period, no war could clean out domestic archives like that. And naturally, photographs flew into the flames first, because if some one informed on you, reported that you had a picture of an enemy of the people, it meant certain death.
> Zhilayev wasn't afraid. When they came for him, Tukhachevsky's prominently hung portrait amazed even the executioners. "What? It's still up?" they said. Zhilayev replied: "The time will come when they will erect a monument to him."[20]

Eventually they did.

11
POST MORTEM

THEY WERE MODEST MONUMENTS. A plaque on the house where he had lived in Moscow. A street bearing his name in Simbirsk. A memorial in the house where he had lived as commander of the Western Military District in Smolensk. It is perhaps no accident that they were put in place when Tukhachevsky's one-time subordinate, Georgi Zhukov, was a power in the Soviet Union.[1]

At the start of July 1957, Zhukov traveled to Leningrad for the celebration of Navy Day. It was at this time that Khrushchev was embroiled in his struggle for supremacy with the so-called Anti-Party Group: Molotov, Kaganovich, Malenkov, and their sympathizers. Zhukov got an enthusiastic reception in Leningrad, and in his speech on July 5, he urged that the whole question of Stalin's purges be reopened. There was no doubt that what Zhukov had in mind was the exoneration of the military leaders, including Tukhachevsky. That would have suited Krushchev too, except for one thing. Zhukov was apparently willing to let the blame fall where it might in the political apparatus. On the other hand, although Krushchev certainly had less to do with the military purges—indeed, one general's family believes that it was through Khrushchev's intervention that some of their relatives survived the purges—completely unfettered investigation of that period could lead to his own downfall. Zhukov had gone too far. By the end of 1957, he was out of office.[2]

But even with Zhukov gone, the rehabilitation of Tukhachevsky continued, albeit gradually. His name, which had been fit only for public execration—if it was mentioned at all—returned to good repute in the Soviet Union after almost a quarter of a century. His legacy in purely military matters, however, had long been evident in others ways.

During his term as commander of the Leningrad Military District, one of Tukhachevsky's preoccupations had been to strengthen the defenses around the old capital. It was therefore no accident that during World War II, the one place where the German advances was stalled almost from the beginning was in that area. In the mid-1930s, Tukhachevsky had urged the construction of similar defenses along the entire western frontier area of the Soviet Union, a line of fortifications ironically labelled the Stalin Line. Some work was done to carry out his suggestion, but unfortunately for the legions who lost their lives as a result of the catastrophe that followed the German invasion in 1941, the work was never completed; and the Germans were able to penetrate deep into the Russian heartland with relatively little difficulty. There is little doubt that if Tukhachevsky had survived, that would not have been the case. He saw only too clearly, and publicly proclaimed that Hitler meant to invade Russia. If his warnings had been heeded, it is not unreasonable to conclude that the war could have been shortened, perhaps by as much as two years, the time that it took Zhukov to drive the Germans back across the Soviet border.

Likewise, the emphasis he had placed on the development of efficient air transport was shown to advantage in the Soviet Union's massive resupply of Syrian forces during the 1973 Middle East war with Israel. It also enabled the Russians to supply the Ethiopian forces in the war with Somalia a few years later.

In a similar fashion, it provided the means for the swift Soviet intervention in Afghanistan when Russian interests there were threatened in the early 1980s. These great movements of men and matériel were far removed from the early experiments in the 1920s, when tanks were strapped to the fuselages of primitive planes in Leningrad, but the connection was no less real. Similarly, Tukhachevsky's sponsorship of the early rocket experiments in Leningrad quickly led to the development of Katyusha weapons that first scored so heavily against German tanks in World War II and then to the newer weapons that in the 1980s are such a prominent part of the Soviet arsenal. Indeed, the whole Soviet space program, from Sputnik to the Cosmos and Salyut vehicles, can be said to have originated under Tukhachevsky's guidance. In tactics, too, the marshal's influence has continued to be felt.

Most notable of Tukhachevsky's disciples was Zhukov, dating from their first meeting in the campaign against Antonov. The great battle of Kursk in 1943 was where this was most notably shown. It was probably the biggest single battle of the war and also one of the greatest tank battles of all time, with more than 6,000 tanks and 2 million troops deployed by both sides. Zhukov followed a strategy of which Tukhachevsky would have approved. He knew from intelligence sources that the Germans were planning a large-scale offensive, and he prepared very thoroughly to repel it. As Tukhachevsky had always ordained, the tank forces were not to be used in isolation. They were to be heavily reinforced by the artillery and infantry units. Moreover, they were to be concentrated so that a devastating counterpunch could be delivered as soon as the direction of the German attack could be determined. Mobility was also a key component of Zhukov's plans. The artillery particularly was converted to motorized traction, enabling it to be shifted quickly as the battle developed. The outcome was devastating for Hitler's forces. The Germans lost almost 500,000 men to the sledgehammer blow of Zhukov's armor. The victory added one more irony to the Tukhachevsky story, because it was from Kursk in 1919 that the disconsolate young general had written to Trotsky, begging for an active assignment. But, more important, it displayed the soundness of the marshal's beliefs: the need for coordination of all arms of the military—tanks, artillery, infantry, and air support; the need for concentration of reserves for a decisive and punishing counterthrust into the enemy's weak point.[3]

Tukhachevsky left the military another legacy. In all his years as the guiding spirit of the Red Army, he had sought most to transform it from the tsarist mélange of an often incompetent and disinterested officer class in which promotion was based on connections, and a huge mass of recruits with questionable motivation, into a cohesive army proud of its traditions and its abilities. Under Zhukov, the ultimate professional soldier, that dream came closer to realization. And in the 1980s, although the Russian military is undergoing the same stresses as the rest of Soviet society, Tukhachevsky's ideal is still emphasized.

In political matters, too, the precedent set by Tukhachevsky at Kronstadt and Tambov has been followed by the Soviet authorities in the years since World War II. As Tukhachevsky created it and forged it, the Red Army has been an instrument for repressing counterrevolution or dissidence. The only differences between Kronstadt and Budapest are those of location, time, and weight of numbers.

By the time the great battle of Kursk was fought, Tukhachevsky had been dead for six years, but the military—or at least some of those who survived—had not forgotten his teachings. In fact, he had become a sort of Scarlet Pimpernel for some of them. They refused to believe that Stalin could have been so stupid as to liquidate the man these loyal soldiers regarded as the military genius of the Soviet Union.

For this reason, there are several tales insisting that Tukhachevsky had not been shot in the summer of 1937, but was being held in isolation where his expertise could be called on in moments of crisis. There were several precedents for this belief, among them that of the noted aircraft designer A. N. Tupolev. Such a story was related to a Western newspaper correspondent by a Russian officer during the 1960s. The Russian said that during the war he had run afoul of the secret police and was being escorted through the Lubyanka for interrogation. As was customary, when he came upon another prisoner being escorted in the opposite direction, he was thrust with his face toward the wall while the other prisoner passed. This would prevent recognition and the transmission of messages. On this occasion the officer was thrust with his face directly in front of a peephole of a cell door, and as he stood there, he peeked into the room; to his amazement, he saw, calmly writing at a table, none other than Tukhachevsky. Impossible as it may have been, the officer swore that he was not mistaken.[4]

This Pimpernel factor is evident in other, typical Russian stories that are a mixture of sardonic humor and brutal realism. One such tale, recounted by a woman related to one of Tukhachevsky's colleagues who died with him in June 1937, involves a special camp for the kin of those who perished in the military purge. After the execution of her relative, the woman was transported to a labor camp in Siberia. Life there was hard for the women, but they developed a camaradarie that enabled them to cope with the miseries of their lives. One day, during a break in their labors, they were chatting about lovers they had had. One after another they recounted the attributes of men in their lives, what great lovers they had been. Finally, one older woman said with disdain:

"Ach, what do you girls know about lovers? I knew the greatest lover of them all, Marshal Tukhachevsky. Now there was a real man! He was the greatest lover of them all!"

She went on to describe the marshal's prowess in the most adulatory fashion while the others giggled. But what the old woman did not know was that, as so often was the case, among her listeners was a political stooge who promptly carried the story to the camp authorities. Thereupon the old woman was summoned before the camp commandant and placed on trial. Four years were added to her sentence for speaking favorably of an enemy of the people.[5]

Over the years some of the mystery about Tukhachevsky's final months has been lifted. But on the fundamental question of why Stalin was provoked to destroy the cream of the nation's military establishment, no substantial information has been offered. In the West, Stalin is often pictured as a latter-day Ivan the Terrible: paranoid, striking blindly at those to whom he had taken a personal dislike in the most bloodthirsty fashion. To some degree, that must have been true. But even though Stalin, from all accounts, was jealous of Tukhachevsky, that alone could hardly account for the gigantic scale of the military purge that was initiated following Tukhachevsky's death.

From the revelations about the 1934 Seventeenth Party Congress, it is obvious that there was indeed substantial opposition to Stalin in the party, and even more in the military. Significantly, the key figures in this opposition were close associates of Tukhachevsky. And even more significantly, one by one, they had all been removed violently between 1934 and May 1937. Kirov's murder was the first act in the ghoulish progression. Then came Valerian Kuibyshev's sudden death. Then Ordzhonikidze's suicide.

At the same time, there were numerous rumors about military plots against Stalin's rule and even about an attempt on his life. The Russian émigré centers abroad, particularly Paris, were full of such stories. But it is interesting that in most of these stories the central character was not Tukhachevsky but the titular head of the Soviet military establishment, Klementi Voroshilov.

But in some of them Tukhachevsky's name was raised. Edward Carr, for example, mentions an account that appeared in the German military journal *Deutsche Wehr* in October 1938. According to the account, Tukhachevsky had been plotting a coup against Stalin as far back as 1935 and it was designed to occur in May 1937. Supposedly it was betrayed by the émigré general Nikolai Skoblin.[6]

Some of these stories doubtless were fueled by the purge trials taking place at the time in the Soviet Union. For example, at the trial of Bukharin, Rykov, Yagoda, and 18 others, which started on March 2, 1938, Bukharin implicated Tukhachevsky. During his testimony he discussed the Bonapartist threat in the Soviet Union. Bukharin said that he was "thinking particularly of Tukhachevsky. . . . In my conversations I always called Tukhachevsky a 'potential little Napoleon,' and you know how Napoleon dealt with so-called ideologists."[7]

However, there is no strong evidence to support the plot thesis, although it is apparent that Tukhachevsky was in a strong position to initiate such an adventure as late as the final months of 1936 and the beginning of 1937. Politically, he was aligned with some of the most influential leaders of the party, Ordzhonikidze and Kuibyshev. The military leadership was dominated by kindred spirits, Uborevich, Yakir, Primakov, and Blyukher. Many of these military men, especially Yakir, were also eminent party figures who had devoted their youth to the revolution. Had Tukhachevsky been so inclined, it seems highly likely that they would have supported any attempt he might make to overthrow Stalin. Like Tukhachevsky, many of them had traveled widely outside Russia. They knew the full danger that Hitler's Germany posed to their homeland, and they were anxious to strengthen the defenses of the Soviet Union against a German attack and resentful that Stalin did not seem to share their beliefs. Tukhachevsky was openly their leader, and as such he was possibly the one man in Russia who could have filled Stalin's place. But one by one, the props of this possible coup were chopped away. The death of Ordzhonikidze certainly doomed it for all time.

Since the Khrushchev years, Tukhachevsky's position as an eminent figure in Soviet history has been carefully restored. Several cautiously tailored biographies have been produced, and a collection of memoirs by his friends and relatives has been published. Excerpts from the marshal's voluminous writings were reissued. In the Brezhnev era, the number of these books and articles declined. But unofficially there continued to be small pockets of bitterness about the fate of the marshal and his colleagues. In Moscow, in the early-1980s, two high school officials were accused of holding illegal gatherings dedicated to the memory of Tukhachevsky and Yakir.[8] But even in the Brezhnev period, occasional items in the press referred not only to Tukhachevsky's military achievements but also to some that apparently sought to enhance his political legitimacy.

Perhaps the most surprising of such articles was an obviously carefully coordinated sequence that appeared in February 1983 to mark the ninetieth anniversary of the marshal's birth. Under almost identical headlines about "leadership skill" these pieces appeared in *Pravda, Izvestia, Krasnaya Zvezda, Sovetskaya Rossiya*, and the other leading publications of the Soviet Union. They all stressed Tukhachevsky's career as a precocious hero of the Civil War. But, perhaps even more significant, they also recalled that it was he who quashed the dangerous counterrevolutions at Kronstadt and in Tambov. And they all recalled Tukhachevsky's epic battle with the bourgeois conservatives of Poland and his warnings against the German military threat.

Despite all this, to the great mass of Russians today, only Tukhachevsky's death stands out. When his name is mentioned in conversations with ordinary Russians, the usual response is "Oh yes, he was one of the generals that Stalin shot."

Others remembered him in a more intimate way. Among

them, of course, was Shostakovich. In his old age, the famous composer said that he often thought of his friend. "I wonder who plays the violins that Tukhachevsky made," he wrote, "if they survived at all, that is. I have a feeling that the violins emit a pathetic sound."[9]

NOTES

CHAPTER 1

1. Dmitri Shostakovich, *Testimony* (New York: Harper and Row, 1979), p. 99.
2. Lidia Nord, *Marshal M. N. Tukhachevsky* (Paris: Lev, 1978), p. 64.

CHAPTER 2

1. Nicolas Ikonnikov. *La noblesse de Russie*. 2d. ed. Paris: Nicolas Ikonnikov, 1962. Erich Wollenberg, *The Red Army* (London: Secker and Warburg, 1938), p. 59.
2. L. V. Nikulin, *Tukhachevsky* (Moscow: Voennoe Izdatelstvo Ministerstva Oboroni SSSR, 1964), p. 12.
3. The Tukhachevsky children appear to have been Olga, Nadia, Sofia, Marie, Aleksandr, Nikolai, Jr., Igor, Mikhail, and one other daughter.
4. Nikulin, *Tukhachevsky*, p. 13.
5. Ibid., p. 14.
6. Dmitri Shostakovich, *Testimony* (New York: Harper and Row, 1979), p. 121.
7. Roman Goul, *Toukhatchevsky, maréchal rouge* (Paris: Société Française d'Editions Libraries et Techniques, 1935), p. 8.
8. Nikulin, *Tukhachevsky*, p. 19.
9. Ibid., p. 18.
10. Ibid., p. 20.
11. Goul, *Toukhatchevsky, maréchal rouge*, p. 13.
12. Ibid., p. 11.
13. Nikulin, *Tukhachevsky*, p. 30.
14. Ibid.
15. R. H. Bruce Lockhart, *British Agent* (New York and London: G. P. Putnam's Sons, 1933), p. 103.
16. Bernard Pares, *A History of Russia* (New York: Knopf, 1944), p. 458.

17. Michel Berchin and Eliahu Ben-Horin, *The Red Army* (New York: W. W. Norton, 1942), p. 111.
18. Goul, *Toukhatchevsky, maréchal rouge*, p. 22.
19. Nikulin, *Tukhachevsky*, p. 30.
20. Ibid., p. 33.
21. Ibid.; Goul, *Toukhatchevsky, maréchal rouge*, p. 31.
22. Nikulin, *Tukhachevsky*, p. 36; N. I. Koritsky et al., *Marshal Tukhachevsky* (Moscow: Voennoe Izadatelstvo Ministerstva Oboroni SSSR, 1965), p. 14.
23. Nikulin, *Tukhachevsky*, p. 36.
24. Goul, *Toukhatchevsky, maréchal rouge*, p. 37.
25. Ibid.; Nikulin, *Tukhachevsky*, pp. 34–35.
26. Goul, *Toukhatchevsky, maréchal rouge*, pp. 33ff.
27. A. J. Evans, *The Escaping Club* (London: John Lane-Bodley Head, 1921), p. 61.
28. David Schoenbrun, *The Three Lives of Charles de Gaulle* (New York: Atheneum, 1966), pp. 37–38.
29. Pierre Fervacque, *Le chef de l'armée rouge — Mikhail Tukhachevsky* (Paris: Bibliothèque Charpentier, 1928), p. 50.
30. Ibid., p. 65.
31. Albert Parry, letter to the *New York Times*, June 9, 1973.
32. William Hand, *History Observed. Raymond Robins' Own Story* (New York: Harper and Brothers, 1920) p. 46.
33. Jean Lacouture, *De Gaulle* (New York: Avon, 1968), pp. 25–29.
34. Goul, *Toukhatchevsky, maréchal rouge*, pp. 58–59.
35. Nikulin, *Tukhachevsky*, p. 38. Exactly how Tukhachevsky got back to Russia is uncertain. It seems likely that first he crossed the Swiss frontier, but what happened after that, until he reached Russia, is a mystery.

CHAPTER 3

1. Mikhail Tukhachevsky, *Krasnaya Zvezda* (1935), no. 14:
2. Richard Goldhurst, *The Midnight War* (New York: McGraw-Hill, 1978), p. 151.
3. Lidia Nord, *Marshal M. N. Tukhachevsky* (Paris: Lev, 1978), pp. 30–31; N. I. Koritsky et al., *Marshal Tukhachevsky*. Moscow: Voennoe Izdatelstvo Ministerstva Oboroni SSSR, 1965), pp. 28–29.
4. Michel Garder, *A History of the Soviet Army* (New York: Frederick A. Praeger, 1966), p. 85.
5. Dmitri Shostakovich, *Testimony* (New York: Harper and Row, 1979), p. 104.
6. Roman Goul, *Toukhatchevsky, maréchal rouge* (Paris: Société Française d'Editions Libraires et Techniques, 1935), p. 82.
7. Ibid., p. 80.
8. B. N. Chistov and M. A. Zhokhov, *Poslanets partii*, (Moscow: Voennoe Izdatelstvo Ministerstva Oboroni SSSR, 1980) pp. 62–63.

9. Ibid., p. 65.

10. Mikhail Tukhachevsky, *Izbrannie proizvedennya*, I (Moscow: Voennoe Izdatelstvo Ministerstva Oboroni SSSR, 1964), p. 79.

11. Ibid., p. 80.

12. Goul, *Toukhatchevsky, maréchal rouge*, pp. 89ff.; Tukhachevsky, *Izbrannie proizvedennya*, p. 80; Dennis Wheatley, *Red Eagle* (London: Hutchison, 1937), pp. 179–180.

13. David Footman, *Civil War in Russia* (Westport, Conn.: Greenwood Press, 1975), p. 99.

14. John Bradley, *Allied Intervention in Russia* (New York: Basic Books, 1968), p. 101; Peter Fleming, *The Fate of Admiral Kolchak* (London: Rupert Hart-Davis, 1963), p. 88; Victor Serge, *Year One of the Russian Revolution*, p. 281; D. D. Fedorovich, *General V. O. Kappel*, (Melbourne: Izdannye Russkogo Doma V. Melbourne, 1967) (New York: Stein and Day, 1967) pp. 37–39.

15. Leon Trotsky, *Stalin*, p. 299.

16. Chistov and Zhokov, *Poslanets partii*, p. 120.

17. Ibid., p. 73.

18. Ibid., pp. 118–119.

19. Ibid., p. 120; Fedorovich, *General V. O. Kappel*, pp. 33–41.

20. Erich Wollenberg, *The Red Army* (London: Secker and Warburg, 1938), p. 92.

21. Goul, *Toukhatchevsky, maréchal rouge*, pp. 102ff.; Wheatley, *Red Eagle*, p. 190.

22. Roland Gaucher, *Opposition in the U.S.S.R.* (New York: Funk and Wagnalls, 1969), p. 19.

23. Ibid., p. 23.

24. Serge, *Year One*, pp. 288–89.

25. Bradley, *Allied Intervention in Russia*, p. 146.

26. Ibid., p. 150; Louis Fischer, *The Life of Lenin* (New York: Harper Colophon Books, 1964), p. 342.

27. Goul, *Toukhatchevsky, maréchal rouge*, p. 111.

28. Trotsky, *Stalin*, pp. 292ff.

29. Louis Aragon, *A History of the U.S.S.R. from Lenin to Khrushchev* (New York: David McKay, 1964), p. 232.

30. Footman, *Civil War in Russia*, p. 86; Fleming, *The Fate of Admiral Kolchak*, p. 158; Bradley, *Allied Intervention in Russia*, pp. 88–89.

31. Trotsky, *Stalin*, p. 311.

32. Aragon, *A History of the U.S.S.R.*, p. 133.

33. Bradley, *Allied Intervention in Russia*, pp. 114ff.

34. George Stewart, *The White Armies of Russia* (New York: Macmillan, 1933), p. 271.

35. Ibid., p. 273.

36. Ibid., p. 274.

37. L. V. Nikulin, *Tukhachevsky* (Moscow: Voennoe Izdatelstvo Ministerstva Oboroni SSSR, 1964), p. 72.

38. Ibid., p. 71.
39. Ibid., pp. 70–71.
40. Ibid., p. 73.
41. Wollenberg, *The Red Army*, p. 96.
42. Goul, *Toukhatchevsky, maréchal rouge*, p. 117.
43. Gen. A. I. Todorsky, *Marshal Tukhachevsky*, (Moscow: Izdatelstvo Politicheskoi Literaturi, 1963) p. 52.
44. Fleming, *The Fate of Admiral Kolchak*, p. 150.
45. Wheatley, *Red Eagle*, p. 216.
46. Tukhachevsky, *Krasnaya Zvezda* (1935), no. 14:
47. A. Samoylo, *Dve zhizni*, (Moscow: Voennoe Izdatelstvo Ministerstva Oboroni SSSR, 1958) pp. 250ff, gives the other side of the story.
48. Todorsky, *Marshal Tukhachevsky*, p. 53.
49. Nikulin, *Tukhachevsky*, p. 75.
50. Tukhachevsky, *Krasnaya Zvezda* (1935) no. 14.
51. Trotsky, *Stalin*, p. 312.
52. Ibid., p. 313.
53. Todorsky, *Marshal Tukhachevsky*, p. 54.
54. Tukhachevsky, *Krasnaya zvezda* (1935), no. 14:
55. Goul, *Toukhatchevsky, maréchal rouge*, p. 129.
56. Todorsky, *Marshal Tukhachevsky*, p. 54.
57. Ibid., p. 55; Goul, *Toukhatchevsky, maréchal rouge*, p. 131.
58. John Erickson, *The Soviet High Command* (London: St. Martin's Press, 1962), p. 782.
59. Tukhachevsky, *Krasnaya Zvezda* (1935), no. 14:
60. Ibid.
61. L. M. Spirin, *Razgrom Kolchaka* (Moscow: Voennoe Izdatelstvo Ministerstva Oboroni SSSR, 1969) p. 111.
62. Stewart, *The White Armies of Russia*, p. 284.
63. Goul, *Toukhatchevsky, maréchal rouge*, p. 120.
64. William S. Graves, *America's Siberian Adventure* (New York: Jonathan Cape and Harrison Smith, 1931), p. 306.
65. Stewart, *The White Armies of Russia*, p. 134.
66. Ibid., p. 287.
67. Fleming, *The Fate of Admiral Kolchak*, p. 159.
68. Tukhachevsky, *Krasnaya Zvezda* (1935), no. 14:
69. Trotsky, *Stalin*, p. 325.
70. Fleming, *The Fate of Admiral Kolchak*, p. 216.
71. Ibid., p. 157.
72. Todorsky, *Marshal Tukhachevsky*, p. 57.

CHAPTER 4

1. Dimitry V. Lehovich, *White Against Red: The Life of General Anton Denikin* (New York: Norton, 1974), pp. 25–26.
2. Lehovich, chs. V–XIV.

3. George Stewart, *The White Armies of Russia* (New York: Macmillan, 1933), p. 179.
4. Leon Trotsky, *Stalin*, p. 313.
5. Lehovich, p. 356.
6. Trotsky, *Stalin*, pp. 314ff.
7. Roman Goul, *Toukhatchevsky, maréchal rouge*, (Paris: Société Française d'Editions Libraires et Techniques, 1935), p. 145.
8. Trotsky, *Stalin*, pp. 326–27.
9. L. V. Nikulin, *Tukhachevsky* (Moscow: Voennoe Izdatelstvo Ministerstva Oboroni SSSR, 1964), p. 96.
10. Edgar O'Ballance, *The Red Army* (London: Faber, 1964), p. 67.
11. Roy Medvedev, *Khrushchev* (Garden City, N.Y.: Anchor Press/Doubleday, 1983), p. 7.
12. Lehovich, p. 353
13. Ibid., p. 375.
14. Ibid., p. 338.
15. Nikulin, *Tukhachevsky*, p. 99; John Erickson, *The Soviet High Command* (London: St. Martin's Press, 1962), p. 71; A. I. Denikin, *The White Army* (London: Jonathan Cape, 1930), p. 342.
16. Nikulin, *Tukhachevsky*, p. 99.
17. Gen. A. I. Todorsky, *Marshal Tukhachevsky* (Moscow: Izdatelstvo Politicheskoi Literaturi, 1963), p. 70.
18. Ibid., p. 50.
19. *Istoria Grazhdanskoi Voiny v S.S.S.R.*, IV (Moscow: Gosudarstvennoe Izdatelstvo Politicheskoi Literaturi, 1959), p. 296; Trotsky, *Stalin*, p. 281.
20. Denikin, *The White Army*, p. 342.
21. Trotsky, *Stalin*, p. 326.
22. Nikulin, *Tukhachevsky*, p. 102.
23. Ibid., p. 103.
24. John Ernest Hodgson, *With Denikin's Forces* (London: Lincoln Williams, Temple Bar Publishing, 1932), p. 153.
25. Denikin, *The White Army*, p. 344.
26. Semyon M. Budenny, *Proidennii put*, (Moscow: Voennoe Izdatelstvo Ministerstva Oboroni SSSR, 1958) pp. 434–36.
27. Lehovich, p. 381.
28. Ibid., pp. 386–87.
29. Denikin, *The White Army*, p. 355.
30. Todorsky, *Marshal Tukhachevsky*, p. 62.

CHAPTER 5

1. Viscount D'Abernon, *The Eighteenth Decisive Battle of the World* (London: Hodder and Stoughton, 1931).
2. Robert Machray, *Poland 1914–1931* (London: George Allen and Unwin, 1932), p. 36.

3. Joseph Pilsudski, *Memories of a Polish Revolutionary and Statesman*. (London: Faber, 1931) p. 16.
4. Ibid., p. 14.
5. Ibid., p. 25; Machray, *Poland 1914–1931*, pp. 37–38.
6. Machray, *Poland 1914–1931*, p. 40.
7. Ibid., p. 63.
8. Ibid., p. 81.
9. Louis Fischer, *The Soviets in World Affairs* (Princeton, N.J.: Princeton University Press, 1951), pp. 168–169.
10. Ibid., p. 170.
11. Ibid., pp. 170–71.
12. Roman Goul, *Toukhatchevsky* (Paris: Société Français d'Editions Libraries et Techniques, 1935), p. 158.
13. Leon Trotsky, *Stalin*, p. 328.
14. Adam Ulam, *Stalin, the Man and His Era* (New York: Viking, 1973), p. 186.
15. Gen. A. I. Todorsky, *Marshal Tukhachevsky* (Moscow: Izdatelstvo Policheskoi Literaturi, 1963), p. 61.
16. John Erickson, *The Soviet High Command* (London: St. Martin's Press, 1962), p. 89.
17. Goul, *Toukhatchevsky*, pp. 162–63.
18. Mikhail Tukhachevsky, in *L'année 1920* (Paris: La Renaissance du Livre, 1929), p. 207.
19. N. F. Kuzmin, *Krushenie posledogo pokhoda antanti* (Moscow: Gosudarstvennoe Izdatelstvo Politicheskoi Literaturi, 1958), p. 119.
20. Ibid., p. 120.
21. Ibid., p. 122.
22. Ibid., p. 123.
23. Ibid., p. 124; Joseph Pilsudski, *L'année 1920* (Paris: La Renaissance du Livre, 1929), p. 32.
24. Kuzmin, *Krushenie posledogo pokhoda antanti*, p. 126.
25. Tukhachevsky, *L'année 1920*, p. 241.
26. Erickson, *The Soviet High Command*, pp. 88–89.
27. Ibid., p. 86.
28. Ibid., p. 93.
29. Ibid., p. 92.
30. Kuzmin, *Krushenie Posledogo Pokhada Antanti*, p. 198.
31. Goul, *Toukhatchevsky*, p. 178.
32. Victor Serge, *Memoirs of a Revolutionary* (London: Oxford University Press, 1963), p. 198.
33. Erickson, *The Soviet High Command*, p. 94.
34. Kuzmin, *Krushenie posledogo pokhada antanti*, pp. 257–258.
35. Isaac Deutscher, *The Prophet Armed* (New York: Vintage Books, 1959), p. 467; Serge, *Memoirs of a Revolutionary*, pp. 108–09.
36. Pilsudski, *L'année 1920* , pp. 113–15.
37. Ibid., p. 113.
38. Ibid., p. 120.

39. *New York Times*, August 4, 1920.
40. Tukhachevsky, *L'année 1920*, p. 244.
41. Viscount D'Abernon, *The Eighteenth Decisive Battle of the World*, p. 38.
42. Ibid., p. 118.
43. Ibid., p. 62.
44. Jean Lacouture, *De Gaulle* (New York: Avon, 1968), p. 31.
45. Brian Crozier, *De Gaulle* (New York: Charles Scribner's Sons, 1973), p. 35.
46. Viscount D'Abernon, *The Eighteenth Decisive Battle of the World*, p. 40.
47. Ibid., p. 64.
48. Kuzmin, *Krushenie posledogo pokhada antanti*, pp. 224ff; Fischer, *The Soviets in World Affairs*, p. 194.
49. Pilsudski, *L'année 1920*, p. 147.
50. Ibid., pp. 147-48.
51. Ibid., p. 149.
52. Ibid., p. 112.
53. Ibid., p. 150.
54. Ibid., p. 152.
55. Tukhachevsky, *L'année 1920*, pp. 250-51.
56. Pilsudski, *L'année 1920*, p. 152.
57. Ibid., p. 200.
58. Tukhachevsky, *L'année 1920*, pp. 240-41.
59. Kuzmin, *Krushenie posledogo pokhada antanti*, p. 265.
60. Ibid., p. 266; quoting V. K. Triandafilov, in *Voina i Revolutsiya*, vol. 2, 1925, pp. 21-51.
61. Kuzmin, *Krushenie posledogo pokhada antanti*, p. 267; quoting A. I. Yegorov, *Lvov-Warsaw*, p. 7.
62. Erickson, *The Soviet High Command*, p. 99.

CHAPTER 6

1. Paul Avrich, *Kronstadt 1921* (Princeton, N.J.: Princeton University Press, 1970), p. 23.
2. Ida Mett, *La commune de Cronstadt* (Paris: Spartacus, 1937), p. 29.
3. Avrich, *Kronstadt 1921*, p. 43.
4. Mett, *La commune de Cronstadt*, p. 26.
5. Avrich, *Kronstadt 1921*, pp. 73-74.
6. Ibid., p. 78; Roland Gaucher, *Opposition in the U.S.S.R.* (New York: Funk and Wagnalls, 1969), p. 33.
7. M. I. Vassiliev was a veteran Bolshevik who had served as Lenin's special emissary to the Black Sea fleet in 1905.
8. Mett, *La commune de Cronstadt*, p. 42, quoting *Kronstadt Izvestia*, March 5, 1921.
9. Quoted in Dimitri Fedotoff-White, *The Growth of the Red Army*,

(Princeton, N.J.: Princeton University Press, 1944), p. 149.

10. Alexander Berkman, *The Russian Tragedy* (Montreal: Black Rose Books, 1976), p. 82.

11. Avrich, *Kronstadt 1921*, p. 138; Fedotoff-White, *The Growth of the Red Army*, p. 156.

12. Berkman, *The Russian Tragedy*, p. 83.

13. Emma Goldman, *Living My Life* (New York: Alfred A. Knopf, 1931), p. 879.

14. Berkman, *The Russian Tragedy*, p. 98.

15. Voline, *La révolution inconnue* (Paris: Les Amis de Voline, 1947), p. 492.

16. L. V. Nikulin, *Tukhachevsky* (Moscow: Voennoe Izdatelstvo Ministerstva Oboroni SSSR, 1964), pp. 136–37.

17. Ida Mett, *La commune de Cronstadt* (Paris: Spartacus, 1937), p. 51.

18. Nikulin, *Tukhachevsky*, pp. 136–37.

19. Voline, *La révolution inconnue*, pp. 492ff.

20. Ibid., pp. 457–58.

21. Mett, *La commune de Cronstadt*, pp. 51–52; Victor Serge, *Memoirs of a Revolutionary* (London: Oxford University Press, 1963), p. 131; Fedotoff-White, *Growth of the Red Army*, p. 153.

22. Avrich, *Kronstadt 1921*, p. 202.

23. Mett, *La commune de Cronstadt*, p. 53.

24. Gaucher, *Opposition in the U.S.S.R.*, pp. 38–39.

25. Petrichenko was repatriated to Russia in 1945 and shot. Serge, *Memoirs of a Revolutionary*, p. 132.

26. Goldman, *Living My Life*, p. 886. Fedotoff-White, *Growth of the Red Army*, p. 56, suggests there were executions by hundreds.

27. Mett, *La commune de Cronstadt*, p. 87.

28. Serge, *Memoirs of a Revolutionary*, p. 129.

29. Gen. A. I. Todorsky, *Marshal Tukhachevsky* (Moscow: Izdatelstvo Politicheskoi Literaturi, 1963), p. 71.

30. Leon Trotsky, *The Trotsky Papers*, II (The Hague and Paris: Mouton, 1971), pp. 461–62.

31. Ibid., pp. 485–87.

32. Mikhail Lidin, "Antonovschina" (New York: Columbia University, Butler Library, Russian Archive), p. 38.

33. Mikhail Lidin, *Memoirs* (New York: Columbia University, Butler Library, Russian Archive), pp. 1–2.

34. Michel Heller and Alexander Nekrich, *L'utopie au pouvoir* (Paris: Calmann-Levy, 1982), p. 87.

35. Trotsky, *Trotsky Papers*, II, p. 481.

36. Mikhail N. Tukhachevsky, *Voina i revolyutsiya* (June 1926), no. 6: 3–6.

37. Todorsky, *Marshal Tukhachevsky*, pp. 72–73.

38. Lidin, *Memoirs*, pp. 20–21.

39. Trotsky, *Trotsky Papers*, II, p. 481.

40. I. P. Donkov, *Antonovschina: Zamisli i deistvitelnost* (Moscow: Izdatelstvo Politicheskoi Literaturnoi, 1977), pp. 90–92, P. I. Aleksandrov et al., *Komandarm Uborevich* (Moscow: Voennoe Izdatelstva Ministerstva Oboroni SSSR, 1964), p. 104.

41. Donkov, *Antonovschina*, p. 93.

42. Georgi K. Zhukov, *Vospominaniya i razmish Leniya* (Moscow: Izdatelstvo Agentstva Pechati Novosti, 1969), p. 66.

43. Trotsky, *Trotsky Papers*, II, p. 483.

44. Seth Singleton, "The Tambov Revolt," *Slavic Review* 25 (Sept. 1966): 497–512.

45. Donkov, *Antonovschina*, p. 99; Trotsky, *Trotsky Papers*, II, pp. 470–471.

46. Trotsky, *Trotsky Papers*, II, p. 403.

47. Otto Preston Chaney, Jr., *Zhukov* (Newton Abbott: David and Charles, 1972), p. 13.

48. Robert Payne, *The Life and Death of Lenin* (New York: Simon and Schuster, 1964), p. 556.

CHAPTER 7

1. Erich Wollenberg, *The Red Army* (London: Secker and Warburg, 1938), pp. 171–73; Raymond L. Garthoff, *Soviet Military Doctrine* (Glencoe, Ill.: The Free Press, 1953), p. 42.

2. John Erickson, *The Soviet High Command* (London: St. Martin's Press, 1962), p. 785.

3. Dimitri Fedotoff-White, *The Growth of the Red Army* (Princteon, N.J.: Princeton University Press, 1944), p. 188.

4. Marshal S. Buryuzov, in N. I. Koritsky et al., *Marshal Tukhachevsky* (Moscow: Voennoe Izdatelstvo Ministerstva Oboroni SSSR, 1965), p. 26.

5. Erickson, *The Soviet High Command*, p. 114.

6. Alexander Barmine, *One Who Survived*, (New York: Putnam's, 1945), pp. 109–10.

7. M. V. Frunze, *Izbrannie proizvedeniya* (Moscow: Voennoe Izdatelstvo Ministerstva Oboroni SSSR, 1965), pp. 57–84.

8. Fedotoff-White, *The Growth of the Red Army*, pp. 172–73.

9. Erickson, *The Soviet High Command*, pp. 133–34.

10. Ibid., p. 155.

11. G. W. F. Hallgarten, "General Hans von Seeckt and Russia, 1920–1922" *Journal of Modern History*, vol. XXXI, no. 1, 1949, p. 33. Hans W. Gatzke, "Russo-German Military Collaboration During the Weimar Republic." *American Historical Review*, 1958, vol. LXIII, no. 3, p. 571.

12. Edward Hallet Carr, *German-Soviet Relations Between the Two World Wars* (Baltimore: Johns Hopkins Press, 1951), p. 59.

13. Otto Preston Chaney, Jr., *Zhukov* (Newton Abbott: David and Charles, 1972), p. 14.

14. Gen. A. I. Todorsky, *Marshal Tukhachevsky* (Moscow: Izdatelstvo Politicheskoi Literaturi, 1963), p. 8.
15. Leon Trotsky, *Stalin*, (New York: Stein and Day, 1967), pp. 366–67.
16. Ibid., pp. 367–68.
17. Ibid., p. 371.
18. *New York Times*, November 28, 1924.
19. *Sovetskaya Rossiya*, April 4, 1982, *Polkovodets-Agitator*, p. 4.
20. Lidia Nord, *Marshal M. N. Tukhachevsky* (Paris: Lev, 1978), pp. 8–9.
21. Ibid., pp. 30–37.
22. Erickson, *The Soviet High Command*, p. 183.
23. Walter Goerlitz, *History of the German General Staff 1657–1945* (New York: Praeger, 1953), p. 232.
24. Erickson, *The Soviet High Command*, p. 198.
25. Trotsky, *Stalin*, p. 341; Boris Bajanov, *Stalin, der Rote Diktator* (Berlin: Verlag der Paul Aretz, 1931), pp. 73–74.
26. *New York Times*, November 20, 1925.
27. Dmitri Shostakovich, *Testimony* (New York: Harper & Row, 1979), p. 182.

CHAPTER 8

1. Lidia Nord, *Marshal M. N. Tukhachevsky* (Paris: Lev, 1978), pp. 7–15, 99.
2. Dmitri Shostakovich, *Testimony* (New York: Harper & Row, 1979), pp. 96–97.
3. Dmitri and Ludmilla Sollertinsky, *Pages from the Life of Dmitri Shostakovich* (New York: Harcourt, Brace Jovanovich, 1980), p. 77.
4. Shostakovich, *Testimony*, p. 99.
5. Nord, *Marshal M. N. Tukhachevsky*, p. 64.
6. Erich Wollenberg, *The Red Army* (London: Secker and Warburg, 1938), pp. 190–91.
7. *Christian Science Monitor*, January 28, 1927.
8. Y. P. Petrov, *Partiinoe stroitelstvo v Sovetskoi armii i flote* (Moscow: Voennoe Izdatelstvo Ministerstva Oboroni SSSR, 1964), pp. 268–71.
9. Nord, *Marshal M. N. Tukhachevsky*, p. 64.
10. John Erickson, *The Soviet High Command* (London: St. Martin's Press, 1962), p. 266; Anton Antonov-Ovseenko, *The Times of Stalin*, (New York: Harper & Row, 1980) p. 183, says that Tukhachevsky asked to be relieved of his command.
11. Erickson, *The Soviet High Command*, p. 296.
12. Shostakovich, *Testimony*, pp. 101–02.
13. Ibid., p. 102.
14. N. I. Koritsky et al., *Marshal Tukhachevsky* (Moscow: Voennoe Izdatelstvo Ministerstva Oboroni SSSR, 1965), pp. 193–94.
15. Ibid., p. 195.

16. Gen A. I. Todorsky, *Marshal Tukhachevsky* (Moscow: Izdatelstvo Politicheskoi Literaturi, 1963), pp. 83–84.
17. Koritsky et al., *Marshal Tukhachevsky*, pp. 196–97.
18. Erickson, *The Soviet High Command*, p. 266.
19. Wollenberg, *The Red Army*, p. 191.
20. Erickson, *The Soviet High Command*, pp. 241ff.
21. *New York Times*, November 18, 1926.
22. *New York Times*, November 18, 1932.
23. S. V. Krasnikov, *S. M. Kirov v Leningrade* (Leningrad: Lenizdat, 1966), p. 87.
24. Koritsky et al., *Marshal Tukhachevsky*, p. 198.
25. Ibid.
26. Nord, *Marshal M. N. Tukhachevsky*, pp. 84–87; Antonov-Ovseenko, *The Times of Stalin*, p. 184.
27. Wollenberg, *The Red Army*, p. 193.
28. Koritsky et al., *Marshal Tukhachevsky*, pp. 199–202.
29. Todorsky, *Marshal Tukhachevsky*, p. 84.
30. Koritsky et al., *Marshal Tukhachevsky*, p. 212.
31. Edgar O'Ballance *The Red Army*, (London: Faber, 1964), p. 115.
32. Artur Just, *The Red Army* (London: Figurehead, 1936), pp. 34–35.
33. Erickson, *The Soviet High Command*, pp. 308–09.
34. L. V. Nikulin, *Tukhachevsky* (Voennoe Izdatelstvo, Ministerstva Oboroni SSSR, 1964), p. 117.

CHAPTER 9

1. Adam Ulam, *Stalin* (New York: Viking, 1973), p. 342.
2. Ibid., p. 344.
3. Ibid., p. 332; Raphael R. Abramovich, *The Soviet Revolution* (New York: International Universities Press, 1962), pp. 337–48.
4. Ulam, *Stalin*, p. 352.
5. Robert Conquest, *The Great Terror* (New York: Macmillan, 1968), p. 533; John Dornberg, *Brezhnev: The Masks of Power* (New York: Basic Books, 1974), pp. 59ff.
6. Isaac Deutscher, *The Prophet Armed* (New York: Vintage Books, 1959), pp. 296–97.
7. Jean-Baptiste Duroselle, *Les relations germano-soviétiques de 1933 à 1939* (Paris: Librairie Armand Colin, 1954) p. 10.
8. Georges Castellan, in Duroselle, *Les relations germano-soviétiques*, p. 247.
9. Ibid., p. 248.
10. Ibid., p. 192.
11. Erich von Manstein, *Aus einem Soldatenleben* (Bonn: Athenaum, 1958), p. 143; Heinz Höhne, *Canaris* (Garden City, N.Y.: Doubleday, 1979), p. 256.
12. Manstein, *Aus einem Soldatenleben*, p. 141.

13. John Erickson, *The Soviet High Command* (London: St. Martin's Press, 1962), p. 343.
14. L. V. Nikulin, *Tukhachevsky* (Moscow: Voennoe Izdatelstvo Ministerstva Oboroni SSSR, 1964), p. 176.
15. Erickson, *The Soviet High Command*, p. 345.
16. Ibid., p. 348.
17. Ibid., p. 350.
18. Ibid., p. 351.
19. Castellan, p. 254, note.
20. *New York Times*, November 24, 1969.
21. *New York Times*, November 8, 1933.
22. Anton Antonov-Ovseenko, *The Time of Stalin* (New York: Harper & Row, 1980), pp. 79–80.
23. Ibid., pp. 80–81.
24. Nikita Khrushchev, *Khrushchev Remembers* (Boston: Little, Brown, 1970), pp. 48–49.
25. Roy A. Medvedev, *Let History Judge* (New York: Alfred A. Knopf, 1972), pp. 156–57.
26. Ulam, *Stalin*, pp. 370ff.
27. Conquest, *The Great Terror*, p. 30.
28. Ibid., p. 28; Antonov-Ovseenko, *The Time of Stalin*, pp. 111–12; Abramovich, *The Soviet Revolution*, p. 355.
29. Roy Medvedev, *Let History Judge*, pp. 155–56; Khrushchev, *Khrushchev Remembers*, pp. 61–62; Conquest, *The Great Terror*, p. 37.
30. Khrushchev, *Khrushchev Remembers*, p. 573.
31. Medvedev, *Let History Judge*, pp. 154–56.
32. Nikulin, *Tukhachevsky*, p. 177.
33. W. G. Krivitsky, *In Stalin's Secret Service* (New York and London: Harper and Brothers, 1939), p. 131.
34. Medvedev, *Let History Judge*, p. 157.
35. Antonov-Ovseenko *The Time of Stalin*, p. 79; Medvedev, *Let History Judge*, p. 155.
36. Castellan, p. 256.
37. Jane Degas, *Soviet Documents on Foreign Policy* (London: Oxford University Press, 1953), pp. 124–26.
38. Paul-Marie de La Gorce, *The French Army* (New York: George Braziller, 1963), p. 258; and *La république et son armée* (Paris: Librairie Artheme Fayard, 1963), p. 331, quoting Gamelin.
39. Ulam, *Stalin*, p. 383.
40. Victor Kravchenko, *I Chose Freedom* (New York: Charles Scribner's Sons, 1946), pp. 211–12.
41. Antonov-Ovseenko, *The Time of Stalin*, p. 120.
42. Ulam, *Stalin*, p. 481.
43. Erickson, *The Soviet High Command*, pp. 411–12.
44. *Manchester Guardian*, February 1, 1936.
45. Hon. Elbridge Durbrow, letter to the author.

46. Castellan, p. 224.
47. Gen. M. J. Gamelin, *Servir*, II (Paris: Librairie Plon, 1946), pp. 195–96.
48. Genevieve Tabouis, *They Called Me Cassandra* (New York: Charles Scribner's Sons, 1942), p. 257.
49. Conquest, *The Great Terror*, p. 230.
50. George Kennan, *Russia and the West Under Lenin and Stalin* (Boston: Little, Brown, 1960), pp. 308ff.
51. Erickson, *The Soviet High Command*, p. 430.
52. Lidia Nord, *Marshal M. N. Tukhachevsky* (Paris: Lev, 1978), p. 124.
53. Sir Giffard Martel, *An Outspoken Soldier* (London: Sifton Praed, 1949), p. 139.
54. Ibid., p. 145.
55. La Gorce, *The French Army*, p. 265; Paul Reynaud, *Au coeur de la mêlée* (Paris: Flammarion, 1951), p. 96.
56. Erickson, *The Soviet High Command*, p. 425.
57. Conquest, *The Great Terror*, p. 209.
58. Dmitri Shostakovich, *Testimony* (New York: Harper and Row, 1979), pp. 98–99.
59. Dmitri and Ludmilla Sollertinsky, *Pages from the Life of Dmitri Shostakovich* (New York: Harcourt, Brace Jovanovich, 1980), p. 78.
60. Alexandre Ouralov, *Staline au pouvoir* (Paris: Les Iles d'Or, 1951), pp. 42ff.
61. Ibid., p. 46.
62. Alexander Barmine, *One Who Survived* (New York: G. P. Putnam's Sons, 1945), p. 221.
63. Paul Reynaud, *Au coeur de la mêlée*, pp. 96–97.
64. Eduard Benes, *Memoirs* (Boston: Houghton Mifflin, 1954), p. 47 note.
65. Erickson, *The Soviet High Command*, p. 436.
66. Ouralov, *Staline au pouvoir*, p. 46.
67. Nathan Leites and Elsa Bernault, *Ritual of Liquidation* (Glencoe, Ill.: The Free Press, 1954), p. 210.
68. Kravchenko, *I Chose Freedom*, p. 239.
69. Medvedev, *Let History Judge*, p. 193.
70. Conquest, *The Great Terror*, p. 187.
71. Ibid., p. 189.
72. Gen. A. I. Todorsky, *Marshal Tukhachevsky* (Moscow: Izdatelstvo Politicheskoi Literaturi, 1963), pp. 60–61.
73. Erickson, *The Soviet High Command*, pp. 458–59.
74. M. Ereli, "Partiia Bolshevikov v Sovetskoi armii," (Columbia University, Butler Library, Research Project—USSR), pp. 29–30, 57–58, 68–73.
75. Joseph E. Davies, *Mission to Moscow* (New York: Simon and Schuster, 1941), pp. 132–34.
76. Durbrow.

77. Ibid.
78. Erickson, *The Soviet High Command*, pp. 458–59.
79. Durbrow.

CHAPTER 10

1. Robert Frazier, *Malenkov* (New York: Lion Books, 1953), p. 39; Martin Ebon, *Malenkov, Stalin's Successor* (New York: McGraw-Hill, 1953), p. 33.
2. A reference to Stalin's father's trade.
3. Alexandre Ouralov, *Staline du pouvoir* (Paris: Les Iles d'Or, 1951), p. 45.
4. L. V. Nikulin, *Tukhachevsky* (Moscow: Voennoe Izdatelstvo Ministerstva Oboroni SSSR, 1964), pp. 189–90.
5. P. I. Yakir and Y. A. Geller, *Komandarm Yakir* (Moscow: Voennoe Izdatelstvo Ministerstva Oboroni SSSR, 1963), pp. 229–40.
6. Roman Goul, *Les maitres de la Tcheka* (Paris: Editions de France, 1938), p. 230, says that Gamarnik was shot resisting arrest.
7. Anton Antonov-Ovseenko, *The Time of Stalin* (New York: Harper & Row, 1980), p. 183.
8. Ilya Ehrenberg, *Memoirs: 1921–1941* (Cleveland: World Publishing, 1955), p. 427.
9. Roy Medvedev, *Let History Judge* (New York: Alfred A. Knopf, 1972), p. 345.
10. Antonov-Ovseenko, *The Time of Stalin*, p. 186.
11. Ibid., p. 183.
12. Robert Conquest, *The Great Terror* (New York: Macmillan, 1968), p. 223.
13. Antonov-Ovseenko, *The Time of Stalin*, p. 186.
14. Lidia Nord, *Marshal Tukhachevsky* (Paris: Lev, 1978), pp. 136–41.
15. Gen. A. I. Todorsky, *Marshal Tukhachevsky* (Moscow: Izdatelstvo Politicheskoi Literaturi, 1963), p. 90; Antonov-Ovseenko, *The Time of Stalin* (New York: Harper & Row, 1980) pp. 186–87.
16. Conquest, *The Great Terror*, p. 224; Goul, *Les maitres de la Tcheka*, pp. 233ff.
17. Nikulin, *Tukhachevsky*, p. 191; Alexander Solzhenitsyn, *The Gulag Archipeligo*, III (New York: Harper & Row, 1976), p. 88.
18. *Sovetskaya Rossiya*, April 4, 1982, Polkovodets Agitator, p. 4; Medvedev, *Let History Judge*, p. 400.
19. Conquest, *The Great Terror*, pp. 246–47.
20. Dmitri Shostakovich, *Testimony* (New York: Harper and Row, 1979), p. 121.

CHAPTER 11

1. Gen. A. I. Todorsky, *Marshal Tukhachevsky* (Moscow: Izdatelstvo Politicheskoi Literaturi, 1963), p. 92.
2. Carl A. Linden, *Khrushchev and the Soviet Leadership 1957–61* (Baltimore: Johns Hopkins Press, 1966), pp. 48, 53; Wolfgang Leonhard, *The Kremlin Since Stalin* (New York: Frederick A. Praeger, 1962), p. 256.
3. Marshal Georgi K. Zhukov, *Marshal Zhukov's Greatest Battles*, pp. 197ff.
4. Raymond H. Anderson, conversation with author.
5. From a conversation in Moscow.
6. Edward Hallett Carr, *German–Soviet Relations Between the Two World Wars* (Baltimore: Johns Hopkins Press, 1951), p. 120.
7. George Katkov, *The Trial of Bukharin* (New York: Stein and Day, 1969), p. 205.
8. Michel Heller and Aleksandr Nekrich, *L'utopie au pouvoir* (Paris: Calmann-Levy, 1982), p. 508.
9. Dmitri Shostakovich, *Testimony* (New York: Harper & Row, 1979), pp. 104–05.

BIBLIOGRAPHY

Abramovich, Raphael R. *The Soviet Revolution 1917–1939*. New York: International Universities Press, 1962.
Aleksandrov, P. I., et al. *Komandarm Uborevich, Reminiscences of Friends and Companions in Arms*. Moscow: Voennoe Izdatelstvo Ministerstva Oboroni SSSR, 1964.
Alexandrov, Victor. *The Tukhachevsky Affair*. Translated by John Hewish. Englewood Cliffs, N.J.: Prentice-Hall, 1964.
Andic, Hellmut. *Rule of Terror, Russia Under Lenin and Stalin*. Translated by Alexander Lieven. New York: Holt, Rinehart and Winston, 1969.
Antonov-Ovseynko, Anton. *The Time of Stalin*. Translated by George Saunders. New York: Harper & Row, 1980.
Anweiler, Oskar. *The Soviets: The Russian Workers, Peasants and Soldiers Councils, 1905–1921*. Translated by Ruth Hein. New York: Pantheon Books, 1974.
Aragon, Louis. *A History of the U.S.S.R. from Lenin to Khrushchev*. Translated by Patrick O'Brian. New York: David McKay, 1964.
Ashcroft, Edward. *De Gaulle*. London: Odhams Press, 1962.
Avrich, Paul. *Kronstadt 1921*. Princeton, N.J.: Princeton University Press, 1970.
Bajanov, Boris. *Bajanov révèle Staline, souvenirs d'un ancien secretaire de Staline*. Paris: Gallimard, 1979.
_____. *Stalin, der Rote Diktator*. Berlin: Verlag der Paul Aretz, 1931.
Balabanoff, Angelica. *Impressions of Lenin*. Translated by Isotta Cesari. Ann Arbor: University of Michigan Press, 1964.
_____. *My Life as a Rebel*. London: Hamish Hamilton, 1938.
Barmine, Alexander. *One Who Survived*. New York: G. P. Putnam's Sons, 1945.
_____. *Memoirs of a Soviet Diplomat*. Translated by Gerard Hopkins. London: Lovat Dickson, 1938.
Barres, Philippe. *Charles de Gaulle*. Garden City, N.Y.: Doubleday, Doran, 1941.
Basseches, Nikolaus. *Stalin*. Translated by E. W. Dickes. New York: E. P. Dutton, 1952.
Benes, Eduard. *Memoirs of Dr. Eduard Benes from Munich to New War and*

New Victory. Translated by Godfrey Lias. Boston: Houghton Mifflin, 1954.

Berchin, Michel, and Eliahu Ben-Horin. *The Red Army.* New York: W. W. Norton, 1942.

Berkman, Alexander. *The Russian Tragedy.* Montreal: Black Rose Books, 1976.

Bey, Essad. *Staline.* Translated by Andhrée Vaillant and Jean R. Kuckenberg. Paris: Gallimard, 1931.

Blackstock, Paul W. *The Secret Road to World War Two.* Chicago: Quadrangle Books, 1969.

Blagonravov, A. A., et al. *Iz istorii raketoi tekhniki.* Moscow: Izdatelstvo Nauka, 1964.

Bonheur, Gaston. *Charles de Gaulle.* Paris: Gallimard, 1958.

Bradley, John. *Allied Intervention in Russia.* New York: Basic Books, 1968.

Brissard, André. *Histoire du service secret nazi.* Paris: Plon, 1972.

Brown, Anthony Cave, and Charles B. MacDonald. *On a Field of Red.* New York: G. P. Putnam's Sons, 1981.

Bruce Lockhart, R. H. *British Agent.* New York and London: G. P. Putnam's Sons, 1933.

Bryant, Louise. *Mirrors of Moscow.* New York: Thomas Seltzer, 1923.

Brzezinski, Zbigniew K. *The Permanent Purge. Politics in Soviet Totalitarianism.* Cambridge, Mass.: Harvard University Press, 1956.

Budenny, S. M. *Proidennii Put.* Moscow: Voennoe Izdatelstvo Ministerstva Oboroni SSSR, 1958.

Carr, Edward Hallett. *German-Soviet Relations Between the Two World Wars, 1919-1939.* Baltimore: Johns Hopkins Press, 1951.

Carroll, E. Malcolm. *Soviet Communism and Western Opinion 1919-1921.* Chapel Hill: University of North Carolina Press, 1965.

Cecil, Robert. *Hitler's Decision to Invade Russia 1941.* New York: David McKay, 1976.

Chamberlin, William Henry. *The Russian Revolution 1917-1921.* New York: Macmillan, 1935.

Chaney, Otto Preston, Jr. *Zhukov.* Newton Abbott: David and Charles, 1972.

Chernov, Victor. *The Great Russian Revolution.* Translated and abridged by Philip E. Mosely. New Haven: Yale University Press, 1936.

Chistov, B. I. and Zhokhov, M. A. *Poslants Partii.* Moscow: Voennoe Izdatelstvo Ministerstva Oboroni SSSR, 1980.

Ciliga, A. *Au pays du grand mensonge.* 5th edition. Paris: Gallimard, 1938.

Clark, Stanley. *The Man Who Is France.* New York: Dodd, Mead, 1960.

Conquest, Robert. *The Great Terror.* New York: Macmillan, 1968.

Crawley, Aidan. *De Gaulle.* London: Collins, 1969.

Crozier, Brian. *De Gaulle.* New York: Charles Scribner's Sons, 1973.

D'Abernon, Viscount. *The Eighteenth Decisive Battle of the World, Warsaw 1920.* London: Hodder and Stoughton, 1931.

_____. *The Diary of an Ambassador. Versailles to Rapallo 1920-22.* Garden City, N.Y.: Doubleday, Doran, 1929.

Danilov, Gen. Yuri. "The Red Army." *Foreign Affairs* 7, no. 1 (1928).
Davies, Joseph E. *Mission to Moscow*. New York: Simon and Schuster, 1941.
Degras, Jane. *Soviet Documents on Foreign Policy*. London: Oxford University Press, 1953.
Deniken, A. I. *The White Army*. Translated by Catherine Zvegintzov. London: Jonathan Cape, 1930.
Deutscher, Isaac. *The Prophet Armed. The Prophet Unarmed. The Prophet Outcast*. New York: Vintage Books, 1959.
Dinayevsky, Aleksandr. *Po sledam gaya*. Erevan: Izdatelstvo Ayastan, 1966.
Donkov, I. P. *Antonovshchina: Zamisli i deistvitelnost*. Moscow: Izdatelstvo Politicheskoi Literaturi, 1977.
Dornberg, John. *Brezhnev, The Masks of Power*. New York: Basic Books, 1974.
Duroselle, Jean-Baptiste, with Georges Castellan, Raoul Girardot, and Jacques Grunewald. *Les relations germano-soviétiques de 1933 à 1939*. Paris: Librairie Armand Colin, 1954.
Dziewanowski, M. K. *Joseph Pilsudski. A European Federalist 1918–1922*. Stanford, Calif.: Hoover Institution Press, 1969.
Earle, Edward Mead, ed., with Gordon A. Craig and Felix Gilbert. *Makers of Modern Strategy, Military Thought from Machiavelli to Hitler*. Princeton, N.J.: Princeton University Press, 1943.
Eastman, Max. *Since Lenin Died*. New York: Boni and Liveright, 1925.
Ebon, Martin. *Malenkov, Stalin's Successor*. New York: McGraw-Hill, 1953.
Ehrenburg, Ilya. *Memoirs: 1921–1941*. Cleveland: World Publishing, 1955.
Ereli, M. "Partiia Bolshevikov v sovetskoi armii." Columbia University: Butler Library, Research Project-USSR.
Erickson, John. *The Soviet High Command*. London: St. Martin's Press, 1962.
Evans, A. J. *The Escaping Club*. London: John Lane-Bodley Head, 1921.
Fainsod, Merle. *How Russia is Ruled*. Cambridge, Mass.: Harvard University Press, 1962.
Fedorovich, A. A. *General V. O. Kappel*. Melbourne: Izdaniye Russkogo Doma Melbourne, 1967.
Fedotoff White, Dimitri. *The Growth of the Red Army*. Princeton, N.J.: Princeton University Press, 1944.
_____. *Survival Through War and Revolution in Russia*. Philadelphia: University of Pennsylvania Press, 1939.
Fervacque, Pierre. *Le chef de l'armee rouge—Mikail Toukatchewski*. Paris: Bibliothèque Charpentier, 1928.
Fischer, Louis. *The Soviets in World Affairs*. Princeton, N.J.: Princeton University Press, 1951.
_____. *The Life of Lenin*. New York: Harper Colophon Books, 1964.
Fleming, Peter. *The Fate of Admiral Kolchak*. London: Rupert Hart-Davis, 1963.
Footman, David. *Civil War in Russia*. Westport, Conn.: Greenwood Press, 1975.
Frank, Pierre. *Renaissance du Bolchevisme en U.R.S.S. Memoires d'un*

Bolchevik-Leniniste. Paris: Francois Maspero, 1970.
Frazier, Robert. *Malenkov*. New York: Lion Books, 1953.
Freund, Gerald. *Unholy Alliance*. New York: Harcourt, Brace, 1957.
Frunze, M. V. *Izbrannie proizvedeniya*. Moscow: Voennoe izdatelstvo Ministerstva Oboroni SSSR, 1965.
Furmanov, Dmitry. *Chapayev*. Moscow: Foreign Languages Publishing House, 1923.
Gai, G. D. *Na Varshavy!* Gosudarstvennoe izdatelstvo. Moscow—Leningrad: Otdel Voennoi Literaturi, 1928.
―――. *Pervii udar po Kolchaku*. Leningrad: Izdanie Voennoi Tipografii. 1926.
Gamelin, Gen. M. J. *Servir*. 3 vols. Paris: Librairie Plon, 1946.
Garder, Michel. *A History of the Soviet Army*. New York: Frederick A. Praeger, 1966.
Garthoff, Raymond L. *Soviet Military Doctrine*. Glencoe, Ill.: The Free Press, 1953.
Gatzke, Hans W. *Russo-German Military Collaboration During the Weimar Republic*. American Historical Review, 1958, vol. LXIII, no. 3.
Gaucher, Roland. *Opposition in the U.S.S.R.* Translated by Charles Lam Markmann. New York: Funk and Wagnalls, 1969.
Goerlitz, Walter. *History of the German General Staff 1657–1945*. Translated by Brian Battershaw. New York: Praeger, 1953.
Goldman, Emma. *Living My Life*. New York: Alfred A. Knopf, 1931.
Gordon, Harold J., Jr. *The Reichswehr and the German Republic 1919–1926*. Princeton, N.J.: Princeton University Press, 1957.
Gorbatov, A. V. *Years off My Life*. Translated by Gordon Clough and Anthony Cash. New York: W. W. Norton, 1965.
Goul, Roman. *Les maitres de la Tcheka. Histoire de la terreur en URSS (1917–1938)*. Paris: Editions de France, 1938.
―――. *Toukhatchevsky, maréchal rouge*. Translated by J. Civel. Paris: Société Francaise d'Editions Libraires et Techniques, 1935.
Graves, William S. *America's Siberian Adventure*. New York: Jonathan Cape and Harrison Smith, 1931.
Grey, Ian. *Stalin, Man of History*. Garden City, N.Y.: Doubleday, 1979.
Grey, Marina, and Jean Bourdier. *Les armées blanches*. Paris: Editions Stock, 1968.
Hallgarten, G. W. F. *General Hans von Seeckt and Russia, 1920–1922*. Journal of Modern History, vol. XXXI, no. 1. 1949.
Hard, William. *Russia Observed. Raymond Robins' Own Story*. New York: Arno Press and New York Times, 1971.
Harriman, W. Averell. *America and Russia in a Changing World. A Half Century of Personal Observation*. Garden City, N.Y.: Doubleday, 1971.
Heller, Michel, and Aleksandr Nekrich. *L'utopie au pouvoir. Histoire de l'U.R.S.S. de 1917 à nos jours*. Paris: Calmann-Levy, 1982.
Herriot, Edouard. *Eastward from Paris*. London: Victor Gollancz, 1934.
Hilger, Gustav, and Alfred G. Meyer. *The Incompatible Allies. A Memoir-*

History of German-Soviet Relations 1918–1941. New York: Macmillan, 1953.
Hingley, Ronald. *The Russian Secret Police*. London: Hutchison, 1970.
Hodgson, John Ernest. *With Denikin's Forces*. London: Lincoln Wiliams, Temple Bar Publishing, 1932.
Hoettl, Wilhelm. *The Secret Front. The Story of Nazi Political Espionage*. Translated by R. H. Stevens. London: Weidenfeld and Nicolson, 1953.
Höhne, Heinz. *Canaris*. Translated by J. Maxwell Brownjohn. Garden City, N.Y.: Doubleday, 1979.
Hyde, H. Montgomery. *Stalin: The History of a Dictator*. New York: Farrar, Straus and Giroux, 1972.
Istoria grazhdanskoi voiny v SSSR. IV. Moscow: Gosudarstvenoe Izdatelstvo Politicheskoi Literaturi, 1959.
Ikonnikov, Nicolas. *La noblesse de Russie*. 2d. ed. Paris: Nicolas Ikonnikov, 1962.
Janin, Gen. Maurice. *Ma mission en Sibérie 1918–1920*. Paris: Payot, 1933.
Just, Artur W. *The Red Army*. Translated by N. M. Potter. London: Figurehead, 1936.
Katkov, George. *The Trial of Bukharin*. New York: Stein and Day, 1969.
Kennan, George. *Russia and the West Under Lenin and Stalin*. Boston: Little, Brown, 1960.
———. *The Decision to Intervene*. London: Faber and Faber, 1958.
———. *Russia Leaves the War*. Princeton, N.J.: Princeton University Press, 1956.
Kerensky, Alexander F. *The Catastrophe*. New York: D. Appleton, 1927.
Khrushchev, Nikita S. *Khrushchev Remembers*. Translated and edited by Strobe Talbot. Boston: Little, Brown, 1970.
Kilmarx, Robert A. *A History of Soviet Air Power*. London: Faber and Faber, 1962.
Knox, Maj. Gen. Sir Alfred. *With the Russian Army 1914–1917*. London: Hutchison, 1921.
Kochan, Lionel. *Russia and the Weimar Republic*. Cambridge: Bowes and Bowes, 1954.
Koritsky, N. I., S. M. Melnik-Tukhachevskaya, and B. N. Chistov. *Marshal Tukhachevsky*. Moscow: Voennoe Izdatelstvo Ministerstva Oboroni SSSR, 1965.
Krasnikov, S. V. *S. M. Kirov v Leningrade*. Leningrad: Lenizdat, 1966.
———. *Sergei Mironovich Kirov, zhizn i deyatelnost*. Moscow: Izdatelstvo Politicheskoi Literaturi, 1964.
Kravchenko, Victor. *I Chose Freedom*. New York: Charles Scribner's Sons, 1946.
Krivitsky, W. G. *In Stalin's Secret Service*. New York and London: Harper and Brothers, 1939.
Krupskaya, N. K. *Reminiscences of Lenin*. Translated by Bernard Isaacs. Moscow: Foreign Languages Publishing House, 1959.
Kuzmin, N. F. *Krushenie posledogo pokhoda antanti*. Moscow: Gosudar-

stvennoe Izdatelstvo Politicheskoi Literaturi, 1958.
Lacouture, Jean. *De Gaulle*. Translated by Francis K. Price. New York: Avon, 1968.
La Gorce, Paul-Marie de. *The French Army*. Translated by Kenneth Douglas. New York: George Braziller, 1963.
_____. *La République et son armée*. Paris: Librairie Artheme Fayard, 1963.
Lee, Asher. *The Soviet Air Force*. New York: John Day, 1962.
_____. *The Soviet Air and Rocket Forces*. New York: Frederick A. Praeger, 1959.
Leites, Nathan, and Elsa Bernault. *Ritual of Liquidation. The Case of the Moscow Show Trials*. Glencoe, Ill.: The Free Press, 1954.
Lenin, V. I. *O voine armii i voennoi nauke*. Moscow: Voennoe Izdatelstvo Ministerstva Oboroni SSSR, 1958.
Leonhard, Wolfgang. *The Kremlin Since Stalin*. Translated by Elizabeth Wiskemann and Marian Jackson. New York: Frederick A. Praeger, 1962.
Liddell Hart, B. H. *Europe in Arms*. London: Faber and Faber, 1937.
_____, ed. *The Soviet Army*. London: Weidenfeld and Nicholson, 1965.
Lidin, Mikhail (Fomichev, M.) "Antonovschina." New York: Columbia University, Butler Library, Russian Archive.
_____. "Antonovschina iz vospominanii Antonovtsa." New York: Columbia University, Butler Library, Russian Archive.
Linden, Carl A. *Khrushchev and the Soviet Leadership 1957–61*. Baltimore: Johns Hopkins Press, 1966.
Lyons, Eugene. *Assignment in Utopia*. New York: Harcourt, Brace, 1937.
Machray, Robert. *Poland 1914–1931*. London: George Allen and Unwin, 1932.
Mackintosh, J. M. *Juggernaut. A History of the Soviet Armed Forces*. New York: Macmillan, 1967.
_____. *Strategy and Tactics of Soviet Foreign Policy*. London: Oxford University Press, 1962.
Makhine, Col. Theodore H. *L'armée rouge. La puissance militaire de l'URSS*. Paris: Payot, 1938.
Mandelstam, Nadezhda. *Memoirs*. New York: Chekhov, 1970.
Manstein, Erich von. *Aus einem Soldatenleben*. Bonn: Athenaum, 1958.
Martel, Lieut.-Gen. Sir Giffard. *An Outspoken Soldier*. London: Sifton Praed, 1949.
Medvedev, Roy. *Khrushchev*. Translated by Brian Pearce. Garden City, N.Y.: Anchor Press/Doubleday, 1983.
_____. *Let History Judge*. Translated by Colleen Taylor. New York: Alfred A. Knopf, 1972.
Mehring, Walter. *Timoshenko, Marshal of the Red Army*. New York: Albert Unger, 1942.
Messenger, Charles. *The Blitzkrieg Story*. New York: Charles Scribner's Sons, 1976.
Mett, Ida. *La commune de Cronstadt*. Paris: Spartacus, 1949.

Miliukov, Paul. *History of Russia*. Translated by Charles Lam Markmann. New York: Funk and Wagnalls, 1969.
Moorehead, Alan. *The Russian Revolution*. New York: Harper and Row, 1958.
Morizet, André. *Chez Lenine et Trotski*. Paris: La Renaissance du Livre, 1922.
Nikulin, L. V. *Tukhachevsky*. Moscow: Voennoe Izdatelstvo Ministerstva Oboroni SSSR, 1964.
Nord, Lidia. *Marshal M. N. Tukhachevsky*. Paris: Lev, 1978.
Orlov, Alexander. *The Secret History of Stalin's Crimes*. New York: Random House, 1953.
Ouralov, Alexandre. *Staline au pouvoir*. Translated by Jacques Fondeur. Paris: Les Iles d'Or, 1951.
Pasternak, Boris. *I Remember. Sketch for an Autobiography*. New York: Pantheon, 1959.
Parry, Albert. *Russian Cavalcade*. New York: Washburn, 1944.
Payne, Robert. *The Rise and Fall of Stalin*. New York: Avon Books, 1966.
———. *The Life and Death of Lenin*. New York: Simon and Schuster, 1964.
Petrov, Vladimir, and Evdakia Petrov. *Empire of Fear*. London: Andre Deutsch, 1956.
Petrov-Skitaletz, E. *The Kronstadt Thesis*. Translated by John F. O'Connor. New York: Robert Speller and Sons, 1964.
Pulsudski, Joseph. *The Memories of a Polish Revolutionary and Statesman*. Translated and edited by D. R. Gillie. London: Faber and Faber, 1931.
———. *L'année 1920*. Translated by Charles Jeze and J.-A. Tesler. Paris: La Renaissance du Livre, 1929.
Pitra, Rudolf. *Z Penzy du Ufy*. Prague: Knihovna Pamatiiku Odboje, 1922.
Putna, Vitovt. *K Visle i Obratno*. Moscow: Voenii Vestnik, 1927.
Radkey, Oliver Henry. *The Sickle Under the Hammer*. New York: Columbia University Press, 1963.
Rakovsky, Leontin. *Mikhail Tukhachevski*. Leningrad: Lenizdat, 1967.
Rauch, Georg von. *A History of Soviet Russia*. Translated by Peter and Annette Jacobsohn. New York and London: Frederick A. Praeger, 1964.
Reissner, Larissa. *Svyazhsk. From Leon Trotsky, the Man and His Work*. New York: Merit Publishers, 1969.
Reynaud, Paul. *Au coeur de la Mêlée*. Paris: Flammarion, 1951.
Rizhinov, A. "Polkovodets Agitator." In *Sovetskaya Rossiya* (April 4, 1982), no. 78 p. 4.
Ruslanov, P. "Marshal Zhukov." In *The Russian Review* 15, no. 2 (April 1956) and no. 3 (July 1956).
Samoylo, A. A. *Dve Zhizni*. Moscow: Voennoe Izdatelstvo Ministerstva Oboroni SSSR, 1955.
Savostyanov, V., and P. Egorov. *Komandarm Pervogo Ranga*. Moscow: Izdatelstvo Policheskoi Literaturi, 1966.
Schapiro, Leonard. *The Communist Party of the Soviet Union*. 2nd edition. London: Eyre and Spottiswoode, 1970.

———. *The Origin of the Communist Autocracy*. London: G. Bell and Sons, 1955.
Schellenberg, Walter. *The Labyrinth*. Translated by Allan Bullock. New York: Harper and Brothers, 1956.
Schoenbrun, David. *The Three Lives of Charles de Gaulle*. New York: Atheneum, 1966.
Seaton, Albert. *Stalin as Military Commander*. New York: Praeger, 1976.
Seeckt, Hans von. *The Future of the German Empire. Criticisms and Postulates*. Translated by Oakley Williams. London: Thornton Butterworth, 1930.
Segal, Ronald. *Leon Trotsky*. New York: Pantheon, 1979.
Serge, Victor. *Memoirs of a Revolutionary 1901–1941*. Translated and edited by Peter Sedgwick. London: Oxford University Press, 1963.
———. *Vie et mort de Trotsky*. Paris: Amiot Dumont, 1951.
———. *Year One of the Russian Revolution*. Translated by Peter Sedgwick. New York: Holt, Rinehart and Winston, 1972.
Sheridan, Clare. *Mayfair to Moscow. Clare Sheridan's Diary*. New York: Boni and Liveright, 1921.
Shostakovich, Dmitri. *Testimony*. As related to and edited by Solomon Volkov. Translated by Antonia W. Bouis. New York: Harper and Row, 1979.
Shub, David. *Lenin*. Garden City, N.Y.: Doubleday, 1948.
Singleton, Seth. "The Tambov Revolt." *Slavic Review* 25 (September 1966): 497–512.
Sofinov, P. G. *Ocherku istorii VChK (1917–22)*. Moscow: Gosudarstvennoe Izdatelstvo Politicheskoi Literaturi, 1960.
Sollertinsky, Dmitri, and Ludmilla Sollertinsky. *Pages from the Life of Dmitri Shostakovich*. Translated by Graham Hobbs and Charles Midgley. New York: Harcourt, Brace, Jovanovich, 1980.
Solzhenitsyn, Aleksandr J. *The Gulag Archipelago, Three*. Translated by Harry Willetts. New York: Harper & Row, 1976.
Souvarine, Boris. *Stalin. A Critical Survey of Bolshevism*. New York: Longmans, Green, 1939.
Spirin, L. M. *Razgrom Kolchaka*. Moscow: Voennoe Izdatelstvo Ministerstva Oboroni SSSR, 1969.
Strong, Anna Louise. *The Stalin Era*. New York: Mainstream Publishers, 1956.
Steffens, Lincoln. *The Autobiography of Lincoln Steffens*. New York: Harcourt, Brace, 1931.
Stewart, George. *The White Armies of Russia*. New York: Macmillan, 1933.
Tabouis, Genevieve. *They Called Me Cassandra*. New York: Charles Scribner's Sons, 1942.
Tansky, Michel. *Joukov, le maréchal d'acer*. Paris: Robert Laffont, 1956.
Thayer, Charles W. *Bears in the Caviar*. Philadelphia and New York: J. B. Lippincott, 1951.
Thyssen, Fritz. *I Paid Hitler*. Translated by Cesar Saerchinger. New York

and Toronto: Farrar and Rinehart, 1941.
Todorsky, Gen. A. I. *Marshal Tukhachevsky*. Moscow: Izdatelstvo Politcheskoi Literaturi, 1963.
Trifonov, I. Y. *Klassi i klassovaya borba v SSSR v Nachale Nyena (1921–23)*. Leningrad: Izdatelstvo Leningradskogo Universtiteta, 1964.
Trotsky, Leon. *The Trotsky Papers*. 2 vols. Edited and annotated by Jan M. Meijer. The Hague and Paris: Mouton, 1971.
―――. *Stalin*. Translated by Charles Malamuth. New York: Stein and Day, 1967.
―――. *My Life. An Attempt at an Autobiography*. With an introduction by Joseph Hansen. New York: Pathfinder Press, 1970.
―――. *Military Writings*. New York: Merit Publishers, 1969.
Tukhachevsky, Mikhail N. *Izbrannie proizvedennya*. Moscow: Voennoe Izdatelstvo Ministerstva Oboroni SSSR, 1964.
―――. *Sentinel of Peace*. New York: International Publishers, 1936.
―――. In *Voina i revolyutsiya* (June 1926), no. 6:.
Ulam, Adam. *Stalin, the Man and His Era*. New York: Viking, 1973.
Vernadsky, George. *A History of Russia*. New Haven and London: Yale University Press, 1961.
Voline (Vsevolod M. Eichenbaum). *La révolution inconnue (1917–1921)*. Paris: Les Amis de Voline, 1947.
Weissberg, Alex. *Conspiracy of Silence*. Translated by Edward Fitzgerald. Preface by Arthur Koestler. London: Hamish Hamilton, 1952.
Werner, Max (A. M. Shifrin). *The Military Strengths of the Powers*. Translated by Edward Fitzgerald. London: Victor Gollancz, 1939.
Werth, Alexander. *De Gaulle. A Political Biography*. New York: Simon and Schuster, 1966.
Wheatley, Dennis. *Red Eagle. The Story of the Russian Revolution*. London: Hutchison, 1937.
Wolin, Simon, and Robert M. Slusser. *The Soviet Secret Police*. New York: Frederick A. Praeger, 1957.
Wollenberg, Erich. *The Red Army*. Translated by Claud W. Sykes. London: Secker and Warburg, 1938.
Woroszylski, Wiktor. *The Life of Mayakovsky*. Translated by Boleslaw Taborski. New York: The Orion Press, 1970.
Wrangel, Gen. Baron Peter N. *Always with Honor*. New York: Robert Speller and Sons, 1957.
Yakir, P. I., and Y. A. Geller, *Komandarm Yakir. Vospominaniya druzei i soratnikov*. Moscow: Voennoe Izdatelstvo Ministerstva Oboroni SSSR, 1963.
Zetkin, Klara. *Reminiscences of Lenin*. London: Modern Books, 1929.
Zhukov, G. K. *Vospominaniya i razmish Leniya*. Moscow: Izdatelstvo Agentstva Pechati Novosti, 1969.

MAPS

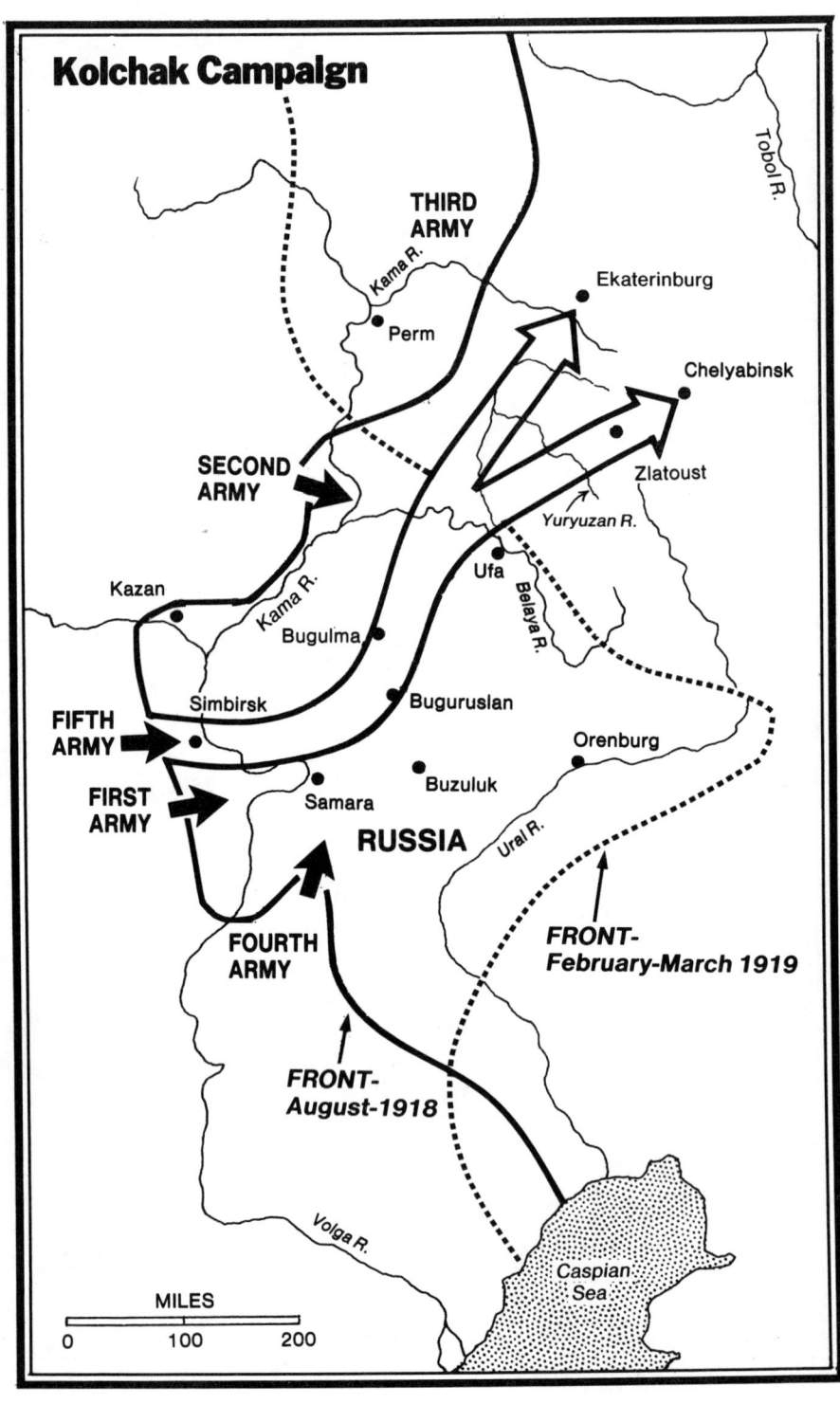

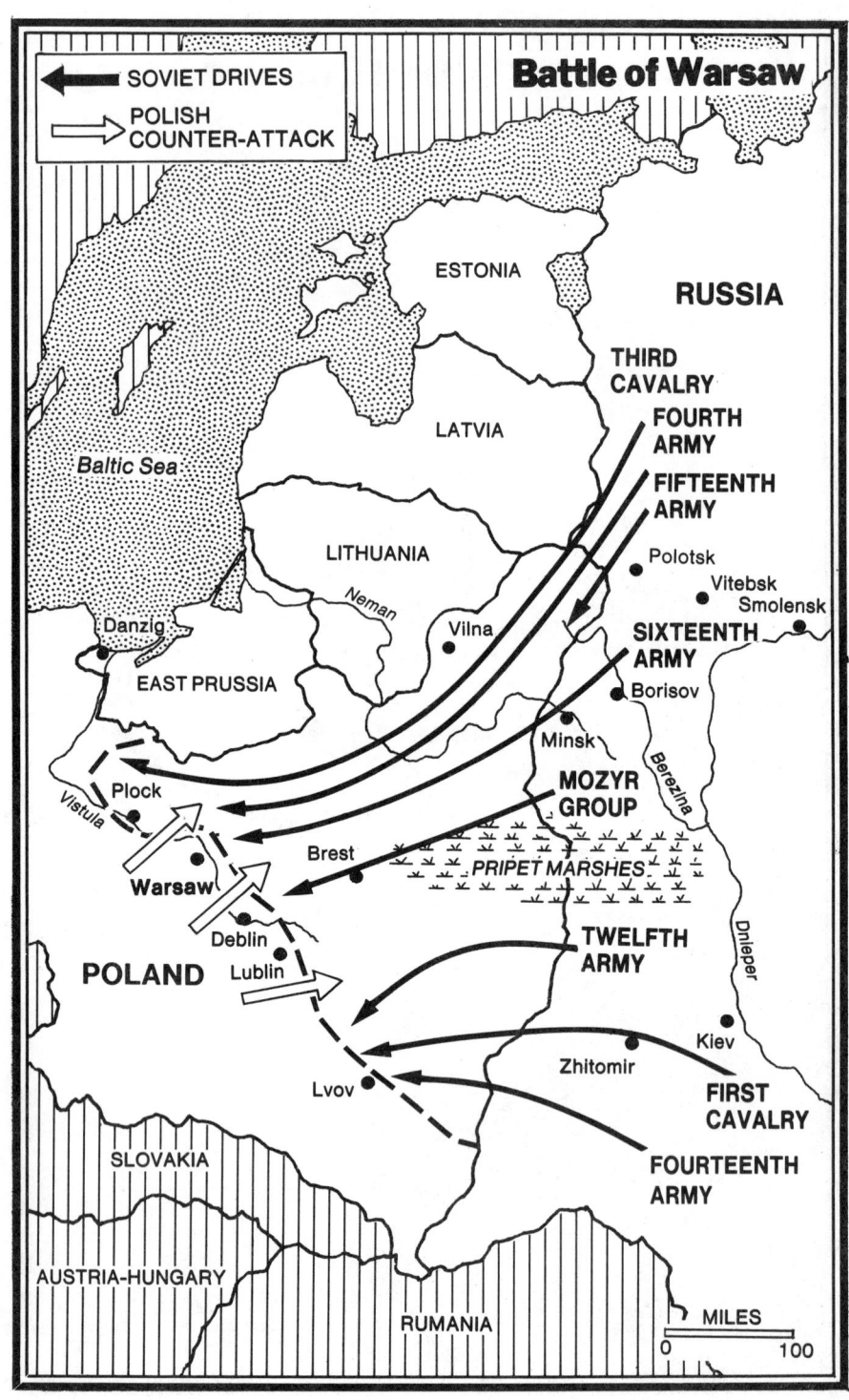

INDEX

Alekseyev (White commander), 60
Alexander II, 81
Alexandra, Tsarina, 12
Alexandrovsky Academy, 10, 11, 27, 60, 179
Alksnis, Y. I., 205, 225, 231
Antonov, A. S., 132, 133, 134, 139; proclamation to military, 136; death, 140
Antonov-Ovseenko, V. A., 132, 138, 204
Anzelovich, N. M., 114
Aronstam, Lev, 214
Astoria Hotel, 121, 123
Atbassar, massacre, 40
Avrov, Dmitri N., 114, 122, 124
Azana, Manuel, 204
Badstauer, 16, 17
Baranov, P. I., 192
Barmine, Alexander, 153
Bataisk, 69, 70, 72; is occupied, 75
Bedni, Demian, 33
Bekauri, V. I., 182
Belov, I. P., 225, 231
Benes, Eduard, 210–11
Berezina River, 94
Beria, Lavrenti, 231
Berkman, Aleksandr, 126
Berlin, Treaty of, 170
Berzin, Gen. J. K., 204
Beskov, 16
Blomberg, Field Marshal Wehrner von, 172, 177, 188
Blum, Léon, 211
Blyukher, Marshal V. K., 111, 177, 199, 214, 225, 230, 231, 238
Bockelberg, Lt. Gen. Alfred von, 189

Boncour, French minister, 203
Brest-Litovsk, Treaty of, 25
Brezhnev, Leonid I., 239
British, intervention by, 28, 62, 74
Brusilov, Gen. A. A., 60; son's lynching, 37
Bryshkov, Yuri, 167
Bubnov, A. S., 125, 159
Budenny, Marshal Semyon, 4, 58, 67, 68–69, 70, 71, 72, 73, 75–76, 86, 89, 91, 94, 96, 99, 107, 109, 159, 188, 199, 204, 216, 225, 227, 231
Bukharin, Nikolai, 157, 238
Bulin, A. S., 225

Cadets, First Catherinian, 10
Chemical warfare tests, 189
Chernolizky, Tatiana, 165
Chernov, Viktor M., 120, 133
Chiang Kai-shek, 160, 170
Chicherin, Georgi V., 83, 84
Chita, massacre, 54
Churchill, Winston, 211
Clausewitz, 10
Clemenceau, 37
Congress, Eighth Party, 38, 148
Congress, Ninth Party, 148
Congress, Tenth Party, 125, 152
Congress, Eleventh Party, 154
Congress, Twelfth Party, 157
Congress, Seventeenth Party, 192, 238
Congress of Soviets, Seventh, 197
Congress of Soviets, Eighth, 209
Conquest, Robert, 186
Constituent Assembly, 133, 137
Cot, Pierre, 191

Czech Legion, 26; uprising, 27, 36, 39, 50, 54

Davies, Joseph E., 218
D'Abernon, Lord, 95, 101, 102, 103
Deat, French minister, 203
de Gaulle, Charles, 2; meets Tukhachevsky, 20; in Poland, 102
Denikin, Gen. A. I., 1, 26, 35, 36, 75, 78, 82, 168, 216; background, 59–61; commands Volunteer Army, 61; forces at and near Orel, 63, 65, 69, 71, 72; feud with Wrangel, 74, 77
d'Esperey, Gen. Franchet, 37
Domizhirov, Gen., 52
Don cossacks, 53, 65, 69, 73
Duff Cooper, Patrick, 202
Dumenko, B. M., 71
Durbrow, Elbridge, 218
Dybenko, Pavel E., 125, 129, 224, 225, 228–29, 231
Dzerzhinsky, Feliz, 38, 62, 86, 87, 105, 119, 135

Ehrenberg, Ilya, 226
Eideman, Robert P., 57, 160, 168, 169, 184, 196, 224, 225, 227, 228
Eismont, Nikolai, 197
Evans, Flt. Lt. A. J., 18
Evdomikov, Grigory, 157
Eykhe, Genrikh K., 52, 57, 66, 193

Fabritsius, Yan, 125, 181
Fedko, Ivan, 125, 135, 179, 180
Feldman, Boris M., 31, 57, 160, 175, 179, 180, 187, 196, 228
Fervacque, Pierre, 21, 22
Fischer, Louis, 83
Five Year Plans, 185, 195
Flandin, French minister, 203
Franco-Soviet pact, 198
Frederick the Great, 18
Frunze Military Academy, 196
Frunze, Mikhail V., 39–40, 43, 45, 57, 71, 152; presents program for army reform, 153–54, 155, 159, 160–62; death of, 163, 168, 192
Fuller, J. F. C., 2

Gai, G. D., 34, 35, 43, 57, 75, 94, 103, 106, 108

Gajda, Gen. Rudolf, 39, 40, 41, 45; his Immortals defect, 53; dismissed by Kolchak, 54
Gamarnik, Yan, 196, 201, 214, 217, 224, 225
Gamelin, Gen. Maurice, 203
Gatovsky, 152
Gazodynamichesky Laboratory, 183
George V, 201
George VI, 219
German-Russian military cooperation, 162, 169, 187
Gestapo, 209, 216
Ginsberg, Grigori, 167
Gittis, V. M., 87
Gladovsky, Arseny, 174
Goering, Hermann, 202
Goldman, Emma, 121, 126, 130, 131
Goryachev, Y. I., 225, 231
Grabski, Stanislas, 93, 95
Grigoriev, Ataman, 37
Gusev, S. E., 42, 46, 64, 132, 152, 158

Haller, Joseph, 84, 102
Hartmann, Otto, 189, 190
Hasse, Gen. Otto, 156
Herriot, Edouard, 203
Heydrich, Richard, 210, 211, 211–12
Hitler, 80, 189, 211, 234
Hoffman, Lt. Col. Max, 14

Ignatiev, Marucia (see Tukhachevsky, Marucia), 203
Indris, 7
Ingolstadt IX, 18, 203
Ironside, Maj. Gen. William, 41, 45

Janin, Gen. P., 40

Kaganovich, Lazar, 193, 195, 227, 233
Kalinin, Mikhail, 117, 118, 121, 192
Kalmykov, 53
Kamenev, L. B., 156, 158, 168, 178, 199, 201, 206
Kamenev, Sergei S., 39, 42, 45, 47, 51, 64, 65, 87, 90, 91, 94, 96, 97, 109, 122, 151, 159, 161; quarrel with Vatsetis, 48
Kaplan, Dora (Fanny), 35

Kappel, Gen. V. O., 39, 50, 57
Kapp-Luttwitz putsch, 93
Karelian Peninsula, 176
Kashirin, N. D., 225, 231
Katyusha rockets, 2, 183, 235
Kazansky, E. S., 127
Kennan, George, 218
Kerensky, Alexander, 21, 60, 121, 133
Khalepsky, I. A., 196, 205, 222
Khanzhin, Gen., 39, 41, 42, 43, 44, 50
Khrupin, V. V., 209
Khrushchev, Nikita S., 4, 44, 68, 178, 193, 195, 215, 234, 239; "secret speech," 5, 195
Khvesin, T. S., 92
Kirov, Sergei M., 4, 168, 176, 178, 179, 192; at Seventeenth Party Congress, 193–94, 195; murder, 196–97 199, 200
Kobozev, P. A., 33
Kolchak, Adm. A. V., 1, 26, 36, 39, 40, 44, 48, 54, 55, 61, 82, 119, 154, 160, 196; execution, 56, 75; slogan, 61
Kon, Felix, 105
Kork, A. I., 87, 88, 90, 160, 169, 187, 196, 216, 222, 225, 227, 229
Kornilov, Gen. L. G., 21, 26, 60
Kosiov, Stanislav, 193, 194
Kostring, Col., German attaché, 189
Kotlin Island, 115–16, 125
Kotovsky, G. I., 135
Kozlovsky, Aleksandr N., 120, 125, 130
Kravchenko, Victor, 199
Kronstadt, 2, 116, 117, 118, 121, 123, 132, 133, 134, 136, 152, 157, 236, 239; capture of, 127–30
Kudryavtsov, I. F., 222–23
Kuibyshev, Nikolai, 27, 160
Kuibyshev, Valerian, 4, 27, 29, 155, 161, 178, 194, 197; death, 200, 238
Kulyabko, N. N., 231
Kun, Bela, 38, 65
Kuropatkin, Gen. Aleksei N., 10
Kursk, Battle of, 235
Kutepov, Gen. A. P., 63
Kutyakov, I. S., 91
Kuzmin, N. N., 114, 117, 118

Land and Liberty, Movement, 133
Lashevich, Mikhail, 46, 48, 64, 114, 124, 157
Lazarevich, V. S., 94
Lebedev, P. P., 156, 158
Lenin, V. I., 1–2, 5, 21, 33, 34, 37, 51, 86, 90, 95, 98; on Polish campaign, 110, 112, 117, 119, 121, 132, 152, 157; meets Tukhachevsky, 27; seeks news from Tambov, 140; death and funeral, 158; Testament, 194
Liddell Mart, Basil, 2
Litvinov, Maxim, 201
Lloyd George, 37, 95
Lunacharsky, Anatoli, 220
Lvov, 36, 107, 108, 109

Makhno, Nestor, 64, 71, 111, 135, 140
Malenkov, Georgi, 216, 217, 221, 231, 233
Malinovsky, Rodion, 57, 204
Mamontov, Gen. E. M., 62, 64–65, 70; raid in Tambov, 62, 135
Manchuria crisis, 177
Manstein, Gen. Erich von, 188, 189
Markhlevsky, Julian, 83, 86, 105
Martel, Sir Giffard, 204–05
Maurin, Louis Felix, 203
Medvedev, Rov, 193, 195
Mekhlis, L. Z., 194
Melnikov (Red commander), 37
Mendras, Col., Franch attaché, 191
Mensheviks, 115
Mett, Ida, 116, 131
Meyerhold, V. E., 166, 167, 226
Mezheninov, S. A., 43, 91
Mikeledze, V. I., 71
Mirbach, Count Wilhelm von, 28
Mironov, Philip, 111
Molotov, V. M., 132, 155, 192, 227, 233
Moltke, Helmuth von, 10
Mozyr Group, 87, 92, 104
Mrachovsky, S. V., 206
Muraviev, Mikhail A., 28, 29, 30, 30–31, 231; death, 31
Mussolini, Benito, 155

Napoleon, 10, 155

Nicholas, Grand Duke, 12
Nicholas II, 12, 21; assassination, 28
Niekisch, Ernst, 216
Nieman River, 94
Nikolayev, Leonid, 197
NKVD, 197, 209, 210, 214, 215, 216, 222, 230, 231
Novorossisk, 77, 78

Oborin, Lev, 167
Ol'derroge, Vladimir A., 51, 52, 55
Oranienbaum, 124; mutiny at, 120, 127
Ordzhonikidze, Papulia, 157
Ordzhonikidze, Sergei, 4, 73, 76, 157, 159, 168, 178, 193, 194, 195, 197, 200, 212–13, 214–15; quarrel with Stalin and death, 215, 238; funeral and Tukhachevsky's eulogy, 215–16
Orel, 63
Orenburg Cossacks, 47
Orlov, V. M., 209
Osoviakhim, 170, 184, 224

Pacelli, Msgr. Eugenio, 20
Pahlevi, Riza, 112
Paratroops, 2, 181, 184, 191, 205
Pauka, I. K., 92
Pavlov, Aleksandr V., 50
Pavlov, Gen. (White general), 75
Penza, 9, 23, 140
Pétain, Marshal Philippe, 203
Peter and Paul Fortress, 123
Peter the Great, 11, 115
Petlura, Semyon V., 35, 61, 67, 76, 84
Petrichenko, Stepan M., 118, 119, 120, 130
Petrovsky, Grigory, 193
Pietri, French minister, 203
Pilsudski, Marshal Joseph, 2, 65, 80–82, 84, 85, 89, 92–93, 94, 97, 103; on Tukhachevsky's advance, 98–99; counterattacks near Warsaw, 105–07,
Pogroms, 84
Poland, Russo-Polish War, 79–110; armistice with, 111
Popov, P. K., 75
Potemkin, Russian ambassador, 203
Povolzhe, Republic of, 31

Primakov, V. M., 168, 196, 225, 227, 229, 238
Pripet Marshes, 90, 94
Putna, Vitovt K., 35, 42, 57, 125, 127, 160, 187, 202, 207, 209, 211, 212, 213, 225, 227, 228
Pyatakov, G. L., 211, 212, 214

Radek, Karl, 86, 156, 211, 212–13, 214, 216
Rakovsky, Christian G., 87
Rapallo, Treaty of, 156, 170, 187
Raskolnikov, F. F., 32
Rasputin, Gregory, 12
Ratti, Msgr. Achille, 103
Rennenkampf, Gen. P. K., 14
Reynaud, Paul, 210, 211
Ridz-Smigly, Gen., 84
Rimsky-Korsakov (White general), 57
Robins, Raymond, 22
Robotnik, 81
Rockets, 192, 235
Rubinstein, Nikolai, 8
Rugen Island, 15
Russo-Japanese War, 9, 14
Rykov, A. I., 208, 238
Ryutin, M. N., 194, 201

Samoylo, Gen. Aleksandr A., 45, 46, 48
Samsonov, Gen. A. V., 14
Sayres (U.S. official), 53
Schleicher, Maj. Kurt von, 156, 187
Schmidt, Dmitri, 207
Scriabin, Aleksandr N., 9
Sedyakin, Aleksandr, 125, 127, 187
Seeckt, Hans von, 93, 156, 216
Selchow, von, 156
Semyonov, Grigor, M., 53–54
Semyenovsky Guards, 11, 13, 179, 212
Sergeyev, Y. N., 87, 94
Serov, Ivan, 230
Shaposhnikov, B. M., 109, 161, 172, 175, 177, 196, 221, 225, 231; *Brain of the Army*, 171
Shilling, Gen. N. N., 76
Shilov, Y. V., 223
Shorin, V. I., 43, 70–71
Shostakovich, D. D., 9; on friendship with Tukhachevsky, 4, 166–67, 173, 207–08, 232, 239

Index / 279

Shvarts, N. N., 160
Sikorski, Gen. Wladyslaw, 107, 108
Simbirsk, 29, 33, 34, 233
Simon, Lord, 198
Singhelyev (Red commander), 37
Skhuro, Gen., 63
Sklyansky, Ephraim, 86, 132, 139, 158, 159
Skoblin, Gen. Nikolai, 210, 238
Skulski, Leopold, 93
Slaven, P. A., 33, 36
Slavin, I. Y., 225
Sletov (Social Revolutionary), 133
Smilga, Ivan, 48, 64, 87, 108, 194
Smirnov, A. P., 197
Smirnov, Ivan, 55, 194, 206
Smolensk, 233
Snesarev, A. Y., 184
Socialist Revolutionary Party, 28, 35, 115, 120, 133
Sokolnikov, Grigori Y., 72
Sollogub, N. V., 88, 89, 90, 94
Sosnkowski, Gen., 105
Spanish Civil War, 204
Spiridonova, Maria, 133
Stakhanov (Russian miner), 199
Stalin, J. V., 1, 4, 5, 38, 39, 63, 67, 72, 85, 86, 90, 94, 109, 152, 157, 161, 162, 163, 164, 168, 172, 178, 180, 184, 186-87, 192-93, 208; opposition to, 195, 196, 204, 207, 211, 212, 214, 215, 216, 217; and military purge, 225-31
Stalin Academy of Mechanization, 190
Stalin Line, 234, 237
Suklominov, Gen. Vladimir, 12
Suvorov, Gen., 10, 73
Svechin, Maj. Gen. A. A., 152, 154, 184
Sverdlov, Yakov M., 38
Szattamary, Eugene, 99ff, 101

Tabouis, Genevieve, 203
Taganrog, 65, 69, 76
Tambov, 2, 62, 65, 132, 133, 137, 140, 152, 236, 239
Tanaka, Gen. Giichi, 177
Timareva, Anna, 56
Timoshenko, Marshal Semyon K., 68, 104
Tipolt, Aleksandr, 122-23

Tobol River, 52, 53
Todorsky, Gen. A. I., 132, 183, 230
Tolmachev, Vladimir, 197
Triandafilov, V. K., 109
Trotsky, L. D., 1, 21, 27, 32, 33, 34, 38, 47, 48, 51, 60, 63, 64, 85, 90, 98, 99, 116, 119, 121, 124, 131, 133, 194, 236; Kronstadt ultimatum, 121-22; opposition in military, 147-48, 150, 151, 155, 158-59, 160, 168, 171; ouster from Communist Party, 171, 173
Trubochny factory, 114
Tsaritsyn, 35, 63
Tukhachevsky, Aleksandr, 231
Tukhachevsky, Igor, 23
Tukhachevsky, Marie, 11
Tukhachevsky, Marucia, 11, 66
Tukhachevsky, Mavra Petrovna, 11, 231
Tukhachevsky, M. N., 1-3, 5; friendship with Kirov, 4; a loner, 4; birth, 7; early education, 9; at Alexandrovsky Military Academy, 10; joins Semyenovsky Guards, 11; early war experiences, 12-13; captured by Germans, 14; first escape, 15-16; meets de Gaulle, 20; meets Msgr. Pacelli, 20; violinmaking, 21; final escape, 22-23; joins Red Army, 27; meets Lenin, 27; command on Eastern Front, 28; arrest by Muraviev, 30; in command of Fifth Red Army, 40; meets Frunze, 42-43; battle for Buzuluk, 44; telegram to Samoylo, 46; battle for Zlatoust, 49-50; quarrel with Ol'derroge, 52; awarded Order of Red Banner, 66; wife's suicide, 66; letter to Trotsky, 66-67; in command of Southern Front, 71, 73, 75; meets Budenny and Voroshilov, 76; field commander, 80; commands Western Front, 86, 89, 92, 93; "secret army," 97; on plan for attack on Warsaw, 101; faces Pilsudski counterattack, 105-07; orders retreat from Warsaw, 107; criticism of, 109: in command of Petrograd Military District, 122; at Petrograd, 123; interview about Kronstadt, 125; orders attack on

Tukhachevsky, M. N. *(continued)*
Kronstadt, 127–28; effects of Kronstadt on, 131; named to put down Tambov uprising, 132–33; on Tambov revolt, 140; on militia, 148–49; letter to Zinoviev on international Red Army, 150; head of Military Academy of the Soviet Union, 152; reported in Germany, 156; commands Western Military District, 159; marries for second time, 159; named deputy to Frunze, 160; *Maneuver and Artillery*, 161; friendship with Shostakovich, 166–67; comparison with Shaposhnikov, 171–72; urges new war with Poland, 172; "War as a Problem of Armed Struggle," 172; on Leningrad defenses, 176; treatment of subordinates, 179; experiments in Leningrad, 181–83; named deputy to Voroshilov, 184; 1932 visit to Germany, 187–88; scandalizes visiting Germans, 188; awarded Order of Lenin, 189; attitude to France, 191; at 1933 Revolution Day parade, 192; article in Pravda, March 31, 1935, 198; sent to London, 201–02; stopover in Berlin, 201; in London, 202; visit to Paris, 202–03; quarrel with Stalin, 204; consoles Shostakovich, 207–08; implicated by Putna, 209; German documents, 209–10; complains to Stalin, 212; mentioned at Radek trial, 213–14; at U.S. Embassy dinner, 218; at 1937 May Day parade, 218; on 1936 Field Service Regulations, 219; second visit to Britain canceled, 219; demoted, 221; farewell gathering, 222; leaves for Volga, 222; gets news of Feldman's arrest, 223–24; relieved of command, 225; trial, 226–30; appearance at trial, 228; final statement, 229–30; writing last book, 230; execution, 230; vengeance on relatives, 231; monuments to, 233; as Scarlet Pimpernel, 236; described as lover, 237; possible involvement in plot against Stalin, 238; ninetieth anniversary articles, 239
Tukhachevsky, Nadya, 11
Tukhachevsky, Nikolai, Sr., 8, 10; death, 11
Tukhachevsky, Nikolai, Jr., 13, 231
Tukhachevsky, Nina, 159, 165, 202, 231
Tukhachevsky, Olga, 8
Tukhachevsky, Sophia Alevtinovna, 8, 9
Tukhachevsky, Svetlana, 165, 231
Tupolev, A. N., 236

Uborevich, Yeronim P., 91, 111, 135, 137, 138, 158, 160, 168, 169, 188, 196, 201, 202, 217, 223, 224, 226, 227, 228, 238; recaptures Orel, 67; relieved of command, 225
Ufa Directory, 36
Uglanov, N. A., 124
Ulagai, Kuchuk, 68
Ulam, Adam, 194
Ulrikh, V. V., 225, 228, 229, 230
Unslikht, I. S., 159, 169
Uritsky, Moses S., 35

Vareikis, Josef M., 30–31, 195, 231
Vatsetis, Ioakhim I., 31, 39, 42, 45, 47, 51, 63, 64, 151, 152, 154, 160, 161; arrested, 66
Vekhlichev, 214
Verkhovsky, A. I., 152, 184
Versailles, Treaty of, 156
Vilna, 80
Vishinsky, Andrei, 213
Vishki (Soviet officer), 223
Volkov, I. M., 171
Volunteer Army, 26
Voroshilov, Marshal Klementi E., 4, 58, 67, 70, 72, 95, 96, 109, 125, 157, 159, 162, 168, 169, 170, 171, 172, 179, 184, 187, 188, 189–90, 192–96, 196, 199, 205, 216, 217, 218, 219, 224, 225, 226, 238; defense commissar, 164; conflict with Tukhachevsky, 168–69, 171
Voskanov, G. K., 104

Warsaw, battle for, 105–07
Wavell, Gen. Archibald, 204
Weygand, Gen. Maxime, 95, 97, 102, 103
Wilson, Woodrow, 25, 37

Witos, Vincent, 93, 95, 101
Witte, Count Sergei I., 60
Wrangel, Baron Peter, 35, 39, 62, 63, 74, 77, 83, 86, 92, 93, 96, 104, 111, 154

Yagoda, G. G., 194, 200, 209, 238
Yakir, Yona E., 91, 168, 196, 201, 209, 217, 221, 223, 224, 227, 238; arrest, 224; relieved of command, 225; at trial, 227–28, 230
Yegorov, Aleksandr I., 65, 69, 87, 89, 91, 92, 94, 96, 104, 187, 189, 196, 199, 205, 218, 221; on Polish campaign, 109
Yezhov, N. I., 194, 216, 221, 225, 227, 231
Yudenich, Gen. N. N., 26, 36, 45, 55, 63

Yurenev, K. K., 46
Yusupov, Prince Felix, 12

Zamora, Alcala, 204
Zhakovenko, 188
Zhilayev, Nikolai S., 9, 167, 332
Zhukov, Marshal Georgi K., 3, 68, 156, 177, 233, 234, 235; meets Tukhachevsky, 138
Zinoviev, Grigori E., 27, 114, 115, 116, 117, 118, 119, 120, 121, 123, 150, 152, 157, 162, 168, 178, 194, 199, 200–01, 206, 208; Kislovodsk conference, 157; expelled from party, 171, 173
Zlatoust, 49
Zorndorf (fortress), 18

3 1489 00183 8448

947.084 B   27.95
Butson, Thomas G.
The tsar's lieutenant

FREEPORT MEMORIAL LIBRARY
FREEPORT, NEW YORK
PHONE: FR 9-3274

**28 DAYS
NO RENEWAL** 200